THE SEXUAL CELIBATE

Donald Goergen

A Crossroad Book
THE SEABURY PRESS • NEW YORK

The Seabury Press
815 Second Avenue
New York, N.Y. 10017

Copyright © 1974 by Donald Goergen
Printed in the United States of America

Grateful acknowledgment is made to the following for permission to reprint sections from copyrighted material:

Doubleday and Company, Inc., for *The Jerusalem Bible*, copyright © 1966 by Darton, Longman & Todd, Ltd. and Doubleday and Company, Inc.
Farrar, Straus & Giroux, Inc., for Thomas Merton, *Disputed Questions*, copyright © 1953, 1959, 1960 by the Abbey of Our Lady of Gethsemane.
W. W. Norton & Company, Inc., for Harry Stack Sullivan, *The Interpersonal Theory of Psychiatry*, edited by Helen S. Perry and Mary L. Gawel, copyright 1953 by The William Alanson White Psychiatric Foundation.
W. W. Norton & Company, Inc., for Rollo May, *Love and Will*, copyright © 1969 by W. W. Norton & Company, Inc.

LIBRARY OF CONGRESS CATALOGING IN PUBLICATION DATA

Goergen, Donald.
    The sexual celibate.
    "A Crossroad book."
    1. Celibacy.   I. Title.
BV4390.G59 1975   253″.2   74–30103
ISBN 0–8164–0268–X

Contents

To Dan

Preface

IT IS NOT EASY to write, nor present to the public, a book which contains many of my own personal experiences, spiritual struggles, and theological convictions. Nevertheless, a book such as this is necessary.

The Sexual Celibate is based upon the growing conviction that friendship is not detrimental but central to celibate living, that celibate persons are also sexual persons, and that celibate life is a profound and rewarding way of living. The strength of this book is its attempt to bring together celibacy and sexuality; the weakness is that it leaves much unsaid about our life in Christ, the alpha and omega of celibate existence. One book on celibacy simply cannot say all that needs to be said about celibate life.

Among other strengths are the integration of psychological and theological data, a positive attitude towards both celibacy and sexuality, and the view that celibate men and women and married men and women are to be partners and equals rather than foes or strangers within the body of Christ. Another strength is the open and public discussion of issues which too easily and too often are detrimentally passed over.

I thank all whom I am not mentioning by name who have made this book possible. Special mention, however, goes to Gary Adams, Wanita Broessel, Marirose Donnellan, Janette Hewitt, Matt

Hynous, Bert Mahoney, Rita and Tom Garvey-O'Connor, Kathy Power, Pat Walter, and Cletus Wessels, because each has contributed in a special way. I especially thank Dan McGuire, who has allowed our Father to give me the grace of a very wonderful friendship.

Introduction

BOTH CELIBACY and marriage have been challenged at different times in Christian history. Both are challenged again today. The question is heard over and over, "Why would anyone choose celibacy today?" And the question is also here for those listening, "Why marry?" Neither alternative is without its critics.

Those questioning celibacy come from inside and outside the celibate community. Is celibacy compatible with human intimacy and sexual fulfillment? Is celibacy inevitably based on an anti-sexual asceticism and a chastity that is emotionally repressive? Is celibacy really a higher stage of Christian perfection?

Equally challenging arguments against marriage are often an attack against our society, which reflects the fact that marriage is seen by most people today more as a social than as a sacramental institution. A common argument is that marriage buys into the American social, economic, sexist system. Discussions are also found in books like *Eve's New Rib* and *Open Marriage*. Marriage can be repressive and restrictive, limiting one's relationships to only one other person.

Culture, religion, and sexuality all play their roles in the contemporary crises affecting traditional celibate and conjugal life styles. The crisis involves a critique of our culture, a critique of religion, and a more humanistic understanding of sexuality. A

re-thinking of the relation between religion and culture as well as a
re-thinking of the Christian understanding of sexuality are the tasks
confronting the Christian theologian in this crisis.

I am thus going to discuss celibacy in the context of the theology
and psychology of sexuality. I am not saying this is the best
approach; in fact, it is not the approach which leads to the deepest
insight into the nature of celibacy itself. A deeper appreciation of
celibacy can be gained by placing it in the context of the theology
of vows and the theology of spirituality. This, however, is not my
starting point. My starting point is sexuality itself.

Although celibacy discussed in the context of sexuality may not
be the best approach, it is one that is very much needed in our day.
How do we understand celibacy in the context of the theology of
the sexual life and in what does the sexual life of a celibate consist?

The first portion of the book, chapters one through five, is more
theoretical, and the final three chapters are more practical. I enter
into the world of the spiritual life of the celibate only after
discussion of the sexual life. This is not to say that the sexual life is
the most significant aspect of a celibate's life. It is simply an aspect
that needs intelligent and Spirit-filled discussion in our day.

My purpose is to show that the dichotomy between sexuality and
spirituality and between celibacy and marriage is destructive and
inappropriate. Integration lies in seeing how we can be both sexual
and spiritual simultaneously and in seeing that choosing one way of
life does not imply the inferiority of the other.

There are six questions that I pose in some form or other to
people who are seriously considering a celibate way of life. These
are:

1. What is it about celibacy that you find attractive? Why
   would you choose to be a celibate? What does celibacy mean
   to you? What does the notion of "call" mean to you?
2. What are the practical problems raised by a celibate life style?
   Are you willing to undertake these? What are your expectations of a celibate life? What are the expectations of other
   celibate people?
3. Are you personally capable of the commitment celibacy
   requires?

4. How do you come to grips with your sexuality? How do you feel about your sexuality? How do you express your sexual feelings? What does it mean for you to be a sexual man or a sexual woman?
5. Who is God for you? What does it mean to live your life in the context of a faith commitment? Do you trust in God? What does being a religious man or a religious woman mean? What is the role of prayer in celibate living?
6. How do you want to use your celibacy? How can you increasingly integrate it into the person you are coming to be?

I ask these questions so that men and women will look at the sexual and spiritual poles of their lives in such a way that they might make more mature choices, aware of the daily difficulties of any way of life. Celibacy as well as marriage can be seen from both the ideal as well as the concrete side.

It is important to emphasize that there are many issues which are not my concern here as well as many issues that I cannot treat with the thoroughness that one would like. In particular, I am not raising the question of optional celibacy within Roman Catholicism since I prefer to see celibacy as a larger issue. Celibacy is not only a Roman Catholic question. It is one of man's questions. It has entered into Eastern as well as Western religions. There always have been and there will continue to be people in the major religious traditions of the world who are single out of religious motivation.

Hinduism is the oldest of mankind's great religions.[1] It did not have a founder like most other religions but grew gradually in India over a period of some five thousand years. The ideal life in Hinduism consists in four stages. The first of these stages, *bramacarya*, is a life of celibacy, discipline, and education. The *brahmacarin*, or celibate student, somewhere between the eighth and twelfth years moves into the house of his *guru*, or teacher. The first stage lasts twelve years. It is a time of studying the sacred writings, a time of rigorous discipline, and a time of celibate living. The word used to describe this first stage, *bramacarya*, is the Sanskrit word for celibacy.

The second of the stages, *garhasthya*, is a life of activity, marriage, and family responsibilities. Those who complete the full twelve years of study are at least twenty. Those who do not finish the studies might be younger. There is no requirement of immediate marriage after the stage of study. The *garhasthin*, or householder, exemplifies the joy of physical love as a legitimate end of human life. A very few, specially dedicated to asceticism, do not become householders and remain celibate for life. Most, however, marry at this time. Hinduism has high regard for the stages of both celibacy and marriage. One can live each at different times in life.

Most people remain householders for life. A few, however, continue the path to perfection and follow the two final stages. The third stage, *vanaprastha*, is a retirement from active life to live as a hermit in the forest. This is a return to celibacy. Although the man's wife might accompany him, both are to live as celibates. The third stage is a time of asceticism, of separating from the previous life style, of loosening bonds. The final stage, *sannyasa*, involves complete renunciation including family and spouse. It is a time of total continence. From this point on, the *sannyasin* lives completely alone. His life is characterized by noninjury to any creature, unconcern for property, commitment to meditation, and silence. His life is a return to the celibate state of *brahmacarya*.

It should be kept in mind that this is the path of the ideal life. Not all by any means pursue the four stages. Hinduism has its caste system and, according to the formal structure, only members of the three upper castes are admitted to those stages of life; the fourth caste is excluded from all the stages except that of householder. Girls are also excluded from Vedic study. This ideal has never been followed by the majority, not even all those in the first caste. Celibacy is not tied to the priesthood in Hindu society. Not all celibates are Brahmins nor are all Brahmins celibate. Celibacy then plays a major role in three of the stages of the ideal life. Mohandas K. Gandhi, probably one of the best known Hindus in the western world[2], did not follow the four stages as outlined. Yet he did choose to become celibate later in his life after having married and raised a family.

In the sixth century B.C. there were many wandering ascetics in

India who chose a life of homelessness rather than householding. Gautama Siddhartha, who was to become the Buddha, was born into this evironment. He married at the age of sixteen or seventeen. At the age of twenty-nine he left his family for the homeless life which was already an ideal at the time Gautama began his ascetical activity. Six or seven years passed before he reached enlightenment while meditating in the lotus position under a large tree. The Buddha had remarkable success in gaining followers who entered the homeless state and became monks. The monastic orders were at first the only organized form of Buddhist life. Today there exist both monks and householders, the brotherhood of monks and hermits known as the *samgha* being a minority. In one sense, the monks are the only Buddhists in the proper sense of the term. Only the monk or *bodhisattva* can really pursue the life of perfection and ascetical discipline. Celibacy continues to be part of the ideal Buddhist life, the life of the *bodhisattva*, although Mahayana Buddhism grants that householders can also be *bodhisattvas*.

Poverty, celibacy, and inoffensiveness are the essentials of the Buddhist ideal. The monk has no private property, lives a homeless life, and relies on begging. Celibacy, or *brahmacarya*, is one of the cornerstones. Buddhism professes that the married man does not have the time to pursue contemplative life, that sexual abstinence promotes meditation, and that sexual relations lead to attachments destructive of essential monastic freedom. Later traditions (*Tantra*) held that a full sexual life was not incompatible with monasticism. *Brahmacarya* remains, however, at the center of Buddhist monasticism although there are married monks within Tibetan and Japanese Buddhism. In addition, vows are not for life so that someone can always return to the world. In some places, such as Thailand, it is normal for a large number of men to spend some months or more as a monk and then return to "secular" life.[3]

In Judaism young men were expected to marry although there were exceptions to this as well. The prophet Jeremiah was unmarried and there are also reports of three rabbis who practised abstinence from their wives in order to give themselves to the study of the Torah. Rabbi Akiba ben Joseph, *c.* 50–132 A.D., had the permission of his wife to separate from her for twelve years in order to devote himself to the study of the Torah. Rabbi Simeon ben Azzai, the husband of Rabbi Akiba's daughter, seems to have been separated from his wife to an even greater extent. Some sources suggest that he was a celibate and others that he was married but lived apart from his wife for the sake of study. He is reported to have said, "But what shall I do, seeing that my soul is in love with the Torah; the world can be carried on by others."[4] Rabbi Hananiah ben Hakinai also separated from his wife for about twelve years in order to study the Torah with Rabbi Akiba. In each of these cases permission from the rabbi's wife was sought.

In the two centuries before the coming of Jesus of Nazareth, there arose within Judaism the ascetical Essene sect and the Qumran community. The Qumran community was highly eschatological and believed in the early coming of a Messiah. The Teacher of Righteousness mentioned in the Qumran scrolls was not necessarily the founder but gave the group leadership. Although there were married Essenes and marriage at Qumran as well, the Teacher of Righteousness favored celibacy. The exact nature of the celibacy is difficult to determine. It seems that some vowed lifelong celibacy, others practiced temporary celibacy, and still others married. The Qumran community was a monastic form of life with a postulancy and two year novitiate. They practiced community of goods and valued poverty as well as celibacy.[5]

There is no need to go into detail on celibate life in the Roman Catholic tradition. Henry Charles Lea, a critic of Catholicism, has written an extensive history of celibacy in Christianity.[6] During the first three centuries there were few restraints placed upon the clergy with respect to marriage. The earliest legislation comes from the fourth century. The Spanish Council of Elvira in 305 decreed that all clergy were to abstain from their wives. The decree did not forbid marriage but simply required abstinence. The Ecumenical Council of Nicaea in 325 did not impose the practice of celibacy although it did forbid marriage after a person had received the diaconate. Those who married before ordination were allowed to continue as married. Celibacy existed in the Roman Church before the fourth century but there was no legislation making it obligatory. Emphasis on celibacy accompanied the rise of monasticism, which replaced martyrdom as the supreme form of witness to Jesus Christ. The virgin became the new martyr as Christianity became acceptable to the Roman Empire. It was also in the fourth century that Mary's virginity became universally accepted and in turn a foundation stone for the practice of celibacy.[7]

The history of the legislation concerning celibacy in the Roman Church is not our concern. The legislation finally formulated at the Council of Trent took a long time in coming to be. In the tenth century there were still married clergy, for the Council of Spalatro in 925 forbids clergy to contract second marriages but does not forbid a first marriage. The first ecumenical and universal council to require celibacy was the First Lateran Council in 1123. It forbade marriage for the clergy and required that if a marriage were contracted it should be broken.

The history of Christian celibacy includes much immorality just as the history of Buddhist celibacy does. Yet it also includes some of the highest points of Christian history. The commitment to apostolic life for men like Francis and Dominic, whose charismatic spirit brought new life to the Christian church, included celibacy and communal living. Celibacy still exists today within the many orders of religious men and women as well as for the clergy not vowed to religious life although there have been many efforts since the Second Vatican Council to have the legislation changed. In 1972 there were 205,786 religious men, 276,293 diocesan priests, and 1,031,356 religious women in the Roman Catholic Church.[8]

Celibacy has not been a prominent dimension of Protestant Christianity in general although it is not entirely absent either. Calvin himself recognized the possibility of a vocation to celibacy as well as a vocation to marriage. The nineteenth century gave rise to the Tractarians within the Anglican tradition and their re-discovery of both celibacy and monasticism. The twentieth century saw the emergence of the Darmstadt sisterhood and the Selbitz brotherhood as well as the more well-known community at Taizé.

The Taizé Communauté is an ecumenical community of celibate monks within Protestantism. It was primarily the work of one man, Roger Schutz, whose licentiate dissertation in theology was on *The Monastic Ideal Until Saint Benedict and Its Conformity*

With the Gospel. Schutz was influenced by his retreats with the Carthusians and the Trappists and the rising social consciousness surrounding World War II. The community began officially with seven people who took vows at the French village of Taizé in 1949. Today the community numbers about seventy brothers. They take the vows of celibacy, community of goods, and acceptance of an authority who is the prior. Their Rule gives special mention to the spiritual disciplines of joy, mercy, and simplicity. Max Thurian, theologian and writer, was one of the original seven. His book, *Marriage and Celibacy*, is one of the better discussions of those subjects available today.[9] The monks of Taizé represent about twenty different Protestant denominations. About one in six is ordained; the others are laymen.[10]

Celibacy then is not simply a Roman Catholic question; it is a larger religious question, cultural question, and human question—a question of life and alternatives for living one's life. It is in the context of this awareness that I have undertaken the task of looking at the meaning of celibacy within the context of sexuality as well as at the daily questions that face one who chooses a celibate way of life.

I would like to mention something about myself. In many ways the reflection and research in this book was motivated by my own personal search and struggle. In 1969 and 1970, I was working with emotionally disturbed and retarded children at the Kansas Neurological Institute, Topeka, Kansas, as well as being involved in a clinical program in conjunction with the Menninger Foundation. I was single, not in seminary, considering religious life as well as being close to marriage with a friend whom I had met in Topeka. Religion and psychology were major interests of mine academically at the same time that I was personally facing the question of where to go in my own life. In the fall of 1970, I joined the Dominican Order and completed what was left of my doctoral dissertation in theology on Teilhard de Chardin. I then began teaching at Aquinas Institute.

I chose to teach a course on celibacy as an issue in religion and psychology. I could soon see that what was coming forth from my own interest and struggle had meaning for many of my students and thus I decided to share what I had been thinking with a larger group through writing. I in no way consider this a final discussion of celibacy and sexuality. My own views will change through the years. My hope is that this book will contribute something simply by opening up intelligent discussion. We can no longer hide our heads in the sand. There is so much in our Christian tradition and in modern learning that needs to be integrated for the sake of Christian living today.

I am a theologian. My psychological training in Topeka was primarily Freudian. The following year I was opened up to Adlerian thought, and finally more and more I saw humanistic psychology as the arena where the dialogue between theology and psychology could take place.

I see both celibate and married people struggling with their sexual lives as well as spiritual lives. Too often I have found these lives dichotomized in people I have counseled. People felt that they had to choose between them—to be either sexual or spiritual. A fundamental presupposition of this book is that there is another alternative, that it is possible to be both sexual and spiritual whether celibate or married, and that this integration is for the greater glory of God. I am only thirty. My views, as I have said, will change. But as a Christian and as a secular man, I am dedicated to human growth—human growth through life in Christ.

PART ONE

1

Theology and Sexuality

THEOLOGY DOES NOT, of course, tell us all we need to know about sexuality. We need philosophy, psychology, sociology, and anthropology as well. The insights that do come from theology, however, are significant. There is no such thing, we soon discover, as only one theology—or Christian understanding—of sexuality. There are, and always have been, many of them. In the New Testament itself, the theologies of Mark, Matthew, Luke, John, and Paul are not always the same; they have different emphases and different perspectives.

I am not going to develop a theology of sexuality as such, but simply explore five different sources in order to see what understandings they provide. My purpose is not to give a history of the theology of sexuality but to show that there are various views in the Judaeo-Christian tradition. The five theologies which I will discuss are those of the Yahwist, the Song of Songs, Matthew, Paul, and Augustine. Two of these come to us from the Old Testament and two from the New. The Yahwist's theology is the oldest biblical theology we have. Augustine's is representative of the later development among the Fathers of the Church. Of the five I consider, Matthew's theology brings us as close as we will get to Jesus of Nazareth himself. While there are others, I consider these five representative. Understanding them will help us to appreciate sexuality in a positive way as Christian men and women.

THE YAHWIST

The Pentateuch, according to most biblical scholars, comprises four different sources: the Yahwist source, dated around 950 B.C.; the Elohist source, dated around 850 B.C.; the Deuteronomic source, dated around 700 B.C.; and the Priestly source, dated around 550 or 500 B.C. The Yahwist's theology is combined with the other three in the present form of the Pentateuch, but it is possible through historical critical methods to identify the theology of the Yahwist, which is the oldest theology in the Judaeo-Christian tradition.[1]

Genesis 1–11 is composed of both Yahwist and Priestly elements. Genesis 1–2:4a is the Priestly account of creation and Genesis 2:4b–2:25 is the Yahwist's account. All of Genesis 3 and 4 belong to the Yahwist; Genesis 5 returns to the Priestly source; Genesis 6 returns again to the Yahwist and so on. My main concern here will be with Genesis 2:18–25.

It has been held that the prophet Nathan is really the Yahwist; others have held that the Yahwist is Abiathar, the High Priest under David. We shall probably never know for sure. We do know that the Yahwist wrote during the reign of Solomon in the tenth century before Christ solidifying a tradition that had come down to him. The central figure in his theology is Yahweh and the central fact is Yahweh's love for his people. The enemy of the Yahwist is the religion of Canaan, which was polytheistic, directed toward fertility cults, and centered around Baal. It practiced infant sacrifice as well as sacred prostitution. The fertility cults of Canaan were the enemies of Israel and Israel's God. Yahweh is the true lord of fertility who creates for man a fertile garden in which to live. The Yahwist is not opposed to sexuality but only to sexuality as it is misused in Canaanite religion. His message is always Yahwism as opposed to Baalism. Yahweh and not Baal is the creator and lord of sexuality.

It is time to turn to the text of the Yahwist and let him speak for himself in Genesis 2:18–25.

Yahweh God said, 'It is not good that man should be alone. I will make him a helpmate.' So from the soil Yahweh God fashioned all the wild beasts and all the birds of heaven. These he brought to man to see what he would call them; each one was to bear the name the man would give it. The man gave names to all the cattle, all the birds of heaven and all the wild beasts. But no helpmate suitable for man was found for him. So Yahweh God made the man fall into a deep sleep. And while he slept, he took one of his ribs and enclosed it in flesh. Yahweh God built the rib he had taken from the man into a woman, and brought her to the man. The man exclaimed:

> 'This at last is bone from my bones,
> and flesh from my flesh!
> This is to be called woman,
> for this was taken from man.'

This is why a man leaves his father and mother and joins himself to his wife, and they become one body. Now both of them were naked, the man and his wife, but they felt no shame in front of each other.

In this first account of creation we see that God is concerned about man and aware that he struggles with loneliness. God said, "It is not good that man should be alone." He creates the beasts and the birds simply because He does not want man to be lonely. These, however, are not sufficient. So God creates woman, someone like man and yet different from him, a sexually different person. Now man will not be alone.[2] Man finds companionship in nature, but a more perfect companion comes when woman is created. Sexuality is not here associated primarily with propagation.[3] It is a gift for man so that man might live in fellowship and not be lonely.

Man leaves his father, his mother, and joins his wife and the two become one. Fellowship is finally achieved. Woman is the expression of God's creativity through whom loneliness is overcome.[4] There is a positive appreciation of sexual intercourse in the broadest sense of that phrase, by means of which a oneness is established in such a way that it resolves the problem of being alone. The man exclaims, "This at last is bone from my bones, and flesh from my flesh!" He rejoices, "I no longer have to be alone." This is something new in God's creation and a new experience for man. Being alone has come to an end. God says in verse 18, "It is not good for man to be alone." In verse 24 two have become one and loneliness ceases.

The passage with which we are concerned is not simply sensuous although sensuous activity is involved. The two are naked but are not ashamed. In no way is it indicated that the two should be ashamed. The undertone of the passage is not sensual however; it is one of fellowship and unity. The basic message is God's love; God so loves man that He does not want man to be alone.

This is the Yahwist's theology of sexuality. There should be no shame about it. It is a gift from God given to man as a part of God's creation. Sexuality was given to man in Paradise in order that man might be as God wanted him to be; it is a creation of God and must be understood in the context of the theology of creation, and not only the theology of the fall, which comes later.

The basic elements of the Yahwist's theology of sexuality are two: fellowship and goodness. Sexuality is basically good in that it enables man to be more complete, more as God wants him to be, not alone and isolated but in fellowship, a kind of fellowship which the birds and cattle do not provide. Sexuality, insofar as it enters into the theology of the Yahwist, comes from God.

THE SONG OF SONGS

The title of this work, Song of Songs, is simply a Hebrew superlative. One could translate the title as the best of songs or the best of all possible songs. This way of making a superlative is found in expressions such as the Holy of Holies or the Lord of Lords. Rabbi Akiba, in the first or second century after Christ, wrote, "The entire universe is not as worthy as the day on which the Song of Songs was given to Israel, for all the writings are holy, but the Song of Songs is the Holy of Holies." [5]

The Song of Songs is different from much of the other material in the Old Testament. It is celebrative literature—celebrating the relationship existing between two lovers.[6] Although the very first verse says that the Song is Solomon's, it is probably an anthology of lyric love poems that were compiled and put together. Our concern is simply the theology of its authors or editor.

There have been two primary ways of interpreting the Song of

Songs.[7] The first and more common is the allegorical interpretation in which the Song is not taken literally but symbolically. Among Jewish rabbis the Song symbolizes the relationship between Yahweh and Israel; among Christians it symbolizes the relationship between Christ and his Church. Later Christian interpretation, especially among Christian mystics, was that it represents the relationship between the individual and God, the union of the soul with God, the unitive way of mystical theology. Even interpreted allegorically, it tells us something about sexuality in that the relationship between the two lovers is used as an appropriate way to symbolize the mystical union. Erotic union is a symbol for spiritual union. Clement of Alexandria and Origen are well known for their allegorical interpretations. Bernard of Clairvaux, taking a mystical approach, wrote eighty-six sermons on just the first two chapters and three verses of the third chapter.

Today the literal interpretation is becoming more prominent. The literal interpretation goes back as far as Theodore of Mopsuestia in the fourth century and the school of Antioch. For Theodore these poems were simply a collection of love songs. More recently, H. H. Rowley writes, "There is nothing on all fours with the allegorical interpretation of the Song of Songs. For wherever the figure is used elsewhere, it is plainly symbolic, whereas here there is no hint whatever of allegory, and the whole Song can be read through without of itself suggesting any of the varied meanings the allegorists have read into it." [8]

The Song gives us an image of a very physical love and also recognizes the sacredness of such love. The Church has recognized this sacredness insofar as it has understood marriage as a sacrament. In the literal interpretation one sees a lover expressing feelings for the beloved. The theology of the Song of Songs goes further than the theology of the Yahwist. Not only is the sexual appreciated; it is celebrated. This is the back and forth movement within the poems—the beauty of the human relationship between two people who love each other, the expression of feelings, the celebration of erotic reality. The love is erotic, human, passionate, sensuous.

Let us look at the poems themselves:

> How delicious is your love, more delicious than wine!
> How fragrant your perfumes,

> more fragrant than all other spices!
> Your lips, my promised one,
> distil wild honey.
> Honey and milk
> are under your tongue;
> and the scent of your garments
> is like the scent of Lebanon. (4:10–11)

The poet is familiar with sexual experience and enjoys it. He is familiar with the beloved's mouth. "Honey and milk are under your tongue." We have erotic love, but not simply eros, because there is love underneath—love which bursts forth into sexual activity.

The Song's sexuality is in the context of a relationship, a relationship that breaks forth in a fundamentally good and positive way, an erotic way. There is the same positive appreciation of sexual love as we found with the Yahwist. The relationship here reminds us of the one the Yahwist speaks of later in Genesis—the relationship between Jacob and Rachel. "To win Rachel, therefore, Jacob worked seven years, and they seemed to him like a few days because he loved her so much" (Genesis 29:20). This is the same kind of exaggeration we find in the Song.

The Song's insights, however, go beyond those provided by the Yahwist. I will group these insights around four themes rather obvious to one who reads the dialogue between the two lovers: the intensity of the feelings, the particularity of the relationship, the pain of absence, and the ongoing strength of love.

The language itself is important.

> Let him kiss me with the kisses of his mouth.
> Your love is more delightful than wine. (1:2)

This is just the beginning. There is no end to the detail the language expresses.

> How beautiful are your feet in their sandals,
> O prince's daughter!
> The curve of your thighs is like the curve of a necklace,
> work of a master hand.
> Your navel is a bowl well rounded

> with no lack of wine,
> your belly a heap of wheat
> surrounded with lilies.
> Your two breasts are two fawns,
> twins of a gazelle.
> Your neck is an ivory tower.
> Your eyes, the pools of Heshbon,
> by the gate of Bath-rabbim.
> Your nose, the Tower of Lebanon,
> sentinel facing Damascus.
> Your head is held high like Carmel,
> and its plaits are as dark as purple;
> a king is held captive in your tresses.
> How beautiful you are, how charming,
> my love, my delight! (7:2–7)

Words are here expressing feelings; a language for love is being created. In all of this the lovers realize the inadequacy of words. He goes on and on—the feet, the thighs, the navel, the belly, the breasts, the neck, the eyes, the nose, the head, and yet in the end the words do not say it all. It is a verbose description and yet one does not tire. Both the insufficiency of language and its importance are revealed. Not only the language—but extravagant language. There is no end to superlatives. Verse seven of chapter four says, "You are wholly beautiful, my love, and without a blemish."

Chapter 5:10–16 is another outburst of this extravagant language needed to express the intensity of the feelings.

> My Beloved is fresh and ruddy,
> to be known among ten thousand.
> His head is golden, purest gold,
> his locks are palm fronds
> and black as the raven.
> His eyes are doves
> at a pool of water,
> bathed in milk,
> at rest on a pool.
> His cheeks are beds of spices,
> banks sweetly scented.
> His lips are lilies,

> distilling pure myrrh.
> His hands are golden, rounded,
> set with jewels of Tarshish.
> His belly a block of ivory
> covered with sapphires.
> His legs are alabaster columns
> set in sockets of pure gold.
> His appearance is that of Lebanon,
> unrivalled as the cedars.
> His conversation is sweetness itself,
> he is altogether lovable.
> Such is my Beloved, such is my friend.

Another reality that hits us is the particularity of the relationship. The poems are certainly about two particular people wrapped up in each other. See how they express it: "My Beloved is mine and I am his" (2:16). "I am my Beloved's, and my Beloved is mine" (6:3). "I am my Beloved's and his desire is for me" (7:10). Sexual love as it is experienced in the concrete involves an exclusiveness or particularity between the two.

The poems open up more than the intensity and the particularity within this relationship; they also point towards a sickness—lovesickness: "Feed me with raisin cakes, restore me with apples, for I am sick with love" (2:5). Lovesick people experience two sides to erotic love—a joyful aspect and a painful aspect. When they are not together, they feel the pain of absence.

> On my bed, at night, I sought him
> whom my heart loves.
> I sought him but did not find him.
> So I will rise and go through the City;
> in the streets and the squares
> I will seek him whom my heart loves.
> . . . I sought but did not find him.
>
> The watchmen came upon me
> on their rounds in the City:
> 'Have you seen him whom my heart loves?'
>
> Scarcely had I passed them
> than I found whom my heart loves.

> I held him fast, nor would I let him go
> till I had brought him
> into my mother's house,
> into the room of her who conceived me. (3:1–4)

She experiences the two sides of love: the intense joy of being together and the intense agony of being apart—the desire for union and the pain of separation. Erotic love is not only playful; it is also painful.

There is one more fact about the relationship that exists between these two people and the love that they share. The relationship is not simply erotic and sensual; it is ongoing and strong. The text does not reveal that they are married, although some so interpret it. It is stunningly clear, however, that they are in love. And the love is as strong as death. The last chapter reveals that:

> Love is strong as Death,
> jealousy relentless as Sheol.
> The flash of it is a flash of fire,
> a flame of Yahweh himself.
> Love no flood can quench,
> no torrents drown. (8:6–7)

This reminds us of the love of which Paul will later speak in his Song of Songs of the New Testament–I Corinthians 13, where he writes that "Love lasts forever." These poems are not about promiscuity. There is no sense of the lover running off and enjoying a relationship of this sort elsewhere. There is rather an endurance and permanence to the kind of love which the Song celebrates. The sensuality in all its beauty is playfully and painfully lived out in the context of a relationship and in the context of permanence.

We can bring our reading of the Song of Songs to these conclusions:

1. The attitude toward sexuality expressed by this poet of poets is appreciative of sexuality. He has a positive outlook with regard to the sensual sphere which was also the attitude of the Yahwist.

2. The erotic dimension is developed in the context of a

particular relationship, inseparable from the love that exists between these two. It is part and parcel of their love. The Yahwist saw sexuality in the context of fellowship; so too the Singer of the Song.

3. The Song moves further than the Yahwist in revealing the nature of sexual love. Sexual love involves an intensity of feelings, the need for verbal as well as physical expression, the importance and inadequacy of language, the particularity of an erotic relationship, the pain of absence or separation, and the permanence and strength of love.

4. A certain sense of fidelity emerges in the kind of love these two celebrate. This comes through in the way they express their belonging to one another as well as in the final affirmation that no flood could quench or destroy the relationship.

MATTHEW

The two theologies of sexuality explored thus far antedate Jesus of Nazareth. Our next, Matthew's theology, brings us close to Jesus himself. Yet I will speak of Matthew's theology of sexuality rather than Jesus of Nazareth's. The texts to which I will refer are Matthew 19:3–9 and 19:10–12. A parallel account of this discussion can be found in Mark 10:1–12.

Some Pharisees approached him, and to test him they said, 'Is it against the Law for a man to divorce his wife on any pretext whatever?' He answered, 'Have you not read that the creator from the beginning made them male and female and that he said: This is why a man must leave father and mother, and cling to his wife, and the two become one body? They are no longer two, therefore, but one body. So then, what God has united, man must not divide.' They said to him, 'Then why did Moses command that a writ of dismissal should be given in case of divorce?' 'It was because you were so unteachable' he said 'that Moses allowed you to divorce your wives, but it was not like this from the beginning. Now I say this to you: the man who divorces his wife—I am not speaking of fornication—and marries another, is guilty of adultery.' (19:3–9)

In response to the question raised, Jesus refers to the fact of sexual differentiation. We are male and female: a reference to the Priestly account in the first chapter of Genesis. This is not a new understanding, simply a reference to an earlier theology of sexuality upon which Jesus bases his own understanding. Then Jesus refers to the Yahwist's theology of Genesis, chapter two. A man leaves father and mother and clings to his wife and the two become one. Again Jesus uses Hebrew theology, reinforcing it with his own words. He emphasizes that they are no longer two but one, and indicates that this union comes from God. It is upon this ground that Jesus opposes divorce. Matthew's exception is not our concern here. Jesus bases his understanding on the Yahwist's theology and concludes that one should not divorce and marry again.

There is not much discussion about sexuality itself in the Gospels because they are not primarily concerned with the sexual life. They are concerned about the good news of the coming Kingdom, the life and death of Jesus, and proclaiming the Word of God. An emphasis on fidelity, however, comes through strongly. Divorce is frowned upon because it is a lax attitude towards fidelity. This notion was also in the Song of Songs; love is as strong as death. Matthew makes this even clearer. The two people are no longer two but one as a result of God's activity. Hence, there is a sacredness to this union. Once such a human relationship is created, it cannot be undone. Fidelity is the hallmark of true union and the value in the context of which the discussion takes place.

The disciples said to him, 'If that is how things are between husband and wife, it is not advisable to marry.' But he replied, 'It is not everyone who can accept what I have said, but only those to whom it is granted. There are eunuchs born that way from their mother's womb, there are eunuchs made so by men and there are eunuchs who have made themselves that way for the sake of the kingdom of heaven. Let anyone accept this who can.' (19:10–12)

After the question of divorce which came from the Pharisees, Jesus gets into a question which comes from the disciples. Jesus has just upheld a rather strict interpretation of marriage. The disciples reply, "If marriage is that strictly understood, and that's the way it is, would it then be better not to marry at all?" Jesus' interpretation of marriage is not something everyone can accept. The statement, "Not everyone can accept what I have said," refers to his previous discussion of marriage. Only those can live that way to whom it is granted by God.[9]

Jesus then faces the question of not marrying. He acknowledges that there are eunuchs and that some of these have chosen this way of life for the sake of the kingdom of heaven. He leaves the same impression here as he had with respect to his teaching on marriage. Let those live this way who can. The implications are that remaining unmarried is not easy either, that this too is something that cannot be done by everyone, that this too is granted by God as His gift. Both, marrying and not marrying, are difficult. Neither is given priority. Both are acceptable ways of life for one choosing to follow Jesus, and each will be difficult.

This is the first mention of the possibility of being a eunuch— whatever that meant concretely. Sexual unions can be beautiful human relationships. Yet such human relationships are not the only way to live out one's response to Jesus. There are those who have chosen not to marry for the sake of the kingdom of God and this too is acceptable. There is an appreciation of marriage, sexual relations, and the Yahwist's positive theology of sexuality. Yet this does not mean that one has to marry. There are different options, all of which are valid, and none of which is easy. This is the first theology of sexuality to open up this possibility.

Judaism looked upon celibacy as an abnormal state and expected men to marry. Eunuchs were forbidden to act as priests (Lev. 21:20). Yet celibacy did exist in the time of Jesus in the Essene community at Qumran to which I referred in the introduction. Pierre Benoit points out that the "eunuchs by choice" in Matthew 19 are probably the Essenes.[10] Nowhere else in Palestine at that time would there have been the ideal of celibacy. Jesus would have been familiar with the Essenes since he was the cousin of John the Baptist, who was probably a member of the Essene community for a time. Some of the Essenes may have accepted Jesus as the Messiah for whom they had been waiting.

Mention must be made of a new interpretation that is becoming more acceptable but is still a minority opinion, that of Dupont,

Fleming, Quesnell, and Harrington.[11] It is their contention that the word "eunuch" in this text does not refer to the unmarried at all. It is to be seen completely in the context of the previous discussion on divorce. A eunuch is not one who chooses not to marry but a married man whose spouse has been unfaithful and who must live in continence since remarriage is not a possibility according to Jesus' teaching. A man who puts his wife away and cannot remarry is in fact as much of a eunuch as those born unable to have sexual relations. He is a eunuch, however, for the sake of the kingdom of God since he chooses to witness to the reality of fidelity which is still demanded even if the other partner has been unfaithful. Infidelity on the part of one spouse does not permit infidelity for the other. The only choice open is to live as if one did not have a spouse. As Jesus says, this is difficult and only for those who can live it. So the entire eunuch text refers not to celibacy but to marriage itself.

My own interpretation is that the statement in verse 11 refers to the previous discussion on remarriage. "It is not everyone who can accept what I have said, but only those to whom it is granted." This helps to make sense of the previous discussion, provides a transition, and gives an answer to the objection of the disciples. Matthew then continues with the passage about the eunuchs which is broader than the previous discussion. There is no need to add any further comment if he is simply saying the same thing. The final "Let anyone accept this who can" of verse 12 is not simply a repetition of verse 11. The word *eunuch* includes both celibate men and women as well as those upon whom celibacy has now been enforced due to the infidelity of their spouse. Jesus would have been familiar with the celibate practice at Qumran and there is no reason why he would exclude reference to such a practice since he speaks of two other kinds of eunuchs—those born that way and those made so by men. In fact, this helps to elucidate the passage even more. If there are those born as eunuchs and if there are those made eunuchs by men and if there are those who voluntarily choose to be eunuchs, then is it asking too much to expect one whose spouse was unfaithful to live as a eunuch as well? My interpretation is that verse 11 refers to those who are called upon not to remarry but verse 12 refers not only to those but to other eunuchs as well. The disciples themselves have raised the possibility of not marrying at all and Jesus does not respond by saying they should marry in accord with the Judaism of his day.

The argument of Dupont, Fleming, Quesnell, and Harrington is not to be dismissed. If their opinion prevails, we simply do not have any Gospel text about celibacy. As of now, however, my own interpretation would incorporate both Jesus' awareness of the celibate practice of the Essenes and the further strength of his own argument if he includes these voluntary eunuchs in his list.

JESUS' SEXUALITY

We recognize today that the kingdom of God was a central concept in Jesus' own self-understanding as well as in his preaching. Everything is seen from this eschatological perspective. Jesus is not concerned about our sexuality as such; his concern is the kingdom of God. Yet we realize today that Jesus himself was a sexual being. If we are to accept the completeness of Jesus' humanity, we must accept the fact of his sexuality. He was like unto us in every way except for sin. Sexuality is not sinful and is a dimension of complete humanity. It is not possible to accept Jesus' humanity without accepting his sexuality.

This problem is posed because the Gospels tell us so little about Jesus' sexuality. Blenkinsopp, Driver, and Phipps have faced this question.[12] Yet the impression should not be given that Jesus' sexuality is nowhere to be found in the Gospels. It is there, but not in the way we expect to find it. It depends upon what we are looking for and what we mean by sexuality. I anticipate a distinction here which I will make clear in the next chapter—the distinction between sexuality, genitality, and affectivity.

Sexuality has both a genital and an affective dimension. Affectivity and all that it implies is a vital part of sexuality. The affective dimension of humanity consists in all those qualities of gentleness and tenderness which make sexuality truly human. Gentleness and tenderness are rooted in human sexuality. Compassion is a supreme sign of a well integrated sexual life. The Gospels portray Jesus as a compassionate, gentle, loving, tender, and warm person. He touches people—physically, psychologically, and spiritually. He has friends—male and female. One cannot underestimate the impor-tance of John, Lazarus, Martha, and Mary in his life. It is in this sense that his sexuality comes through.

Jesus says explicitly that he wants to be gentle (Mt. 11:28–30). He is in love with people in an affectionate and warm way. He values compassion (Luke 6:36). He spent much of his time involved with people and their concerns as well as with his mission of preaching the coming kingdom. He loved little children coming to him. The text of Matthew immediately after the discussion on divorce and celibacy continues with Jesus' welcoming the children (19:13–15).

In Matthew's theology of sexuality there is little explicitly said about sexuality but there is a framework in which it can be discussed, a framework of compassion, fidelity, and eschatology. There is no denial of sensuality although it is not the concern of the Gospel as such. Matthew has much of what was already in the Old Testament. Sexuality is good and exists in the context of relationships. Fidelity is given increased emphasis over what was there before.

The new value is that of the kingdom. It is this value which affects Matthew's theology of sexuality and changes it. For the first time we hear that not only is marriage good, celibacy is too. Celibacy is not preferred to marriage, nor vice-versa. Both celibacy and marriage are gifts granted by God. The important thing is not whether I am celibate or married; it is whether I am living in expectation of God's coming kingdom.

PAUL

The second New Testament theology of sexuality I will consider is that of Paul, who has a positive but cautious attitude. Although the major text is I Corinthians 7, there are others I want to mention first.

A man never hates his own body, but he feeds it and looks after it; and that is the way Christ treats the Church, because it is his body—and we are its living parts. For this reason, a man must leave his father and mother and be joined to his wife, and the two will become one body. This mystery has many implications; but I am saying it applies to Christ and the Church. (Ephesians 5:29–32)

Edgar J. Goodspeed proposes that this letter to the Ephesians was written by a collector of the Pauline epistles who undertook to introduce them to the Christian world, prefacing them with a letter cast in Pauline forms and bearing the name of Paul. Paul had written his letters to local churches to be read upon arrival but then frequently set aside and almost forgotten. One Christian, heavily influenced by Colossians, sought out the other letters and introduced the series as a whole to the Christian community.[13] Whether or not we accept Goodspeed's hypothesis, there is a close relationship between Ephesians and the other epistles. I will not concern myself with authorship here. Just as Goodspeed proposes that Ephesians may have been an introduction to the Pauline letters, so it can be an introduction to our discussion of Paul and sexuality.

The author uses the way a person treats his or her body as an analogy for the way Christ loves the Church. Then the author, as does Matthew, quotes the Yahwist's theology. The Yahwist theology occurs again and again in the New Testament as the starting point for understanding sexuality. This mystery of two becoming one has many implications. There is one in particular, however, that the author points out. The sexual union is analogous to the relationship between Christ and the Church.

This is very important. The sexual relationship is apparently the most appropriate analogy Paul can use to describe Christ's closeness to us. He would not have used an analogy that would have been degrading. He is concerned with articulating his understanding of Jesus, the Lord. He uses the analogy of a body with head and members to describe this intense oneness with diversity. Here he uses the sexual analogy of two becoming one to describe this relationship of love between Christ and his Church. This reflects a positive attitude towards the sexual union no matter how degraded the sexual union may become at times, as it did in fact among the Corinthians.

This is very important for Paul's theology of sexuality. A human relationship becomes a symbol of the divine relationship. The interpersonal union exemplifies the union between Christ and his people. For Christians, human love becomes symbolic of Christ's love. It is not that promiscuity is or is not bad; it is simply unacceptable to Christian people whose relationships are to give testimony to the kind of love Christ has. His love is committed, and ongoing. As followers of Christ, our relationships assume a new significance. Sexual union for the Christian is sacramental—a sign of Christ's love.

Love is always patient and kind; it is never jealous; love is never boastful or conceited; it is never rude or selfish; it does not take offence, and is not resentful. Love takes no pleasure in other people's sins but delights in the truth; it is always ready to excuse, to trust, to hope, and to endure whatever comes. Love does not come to an end. (I Cor. 13:4–9)

I quote this song of songs from the New Testament because it is at the heart of Paul's theology of sexuality. Love is the context for understanding sexuality and we need insight into the New Testament concept of love before we can have insight into its concept of sexuality. The ideal of love it proposes is high. Yet sexuality is related to this kind of love. All the theologies we have looked at see sexuality in the context of love. The Yahwist envisions two coming together, becoming one, overcoming loneliness. The Song of Songs, in all its appreciation and celebration, places sensuousness and sexuality in the context of a relationship between two who long for each other even in absence. Matthew not only places sexual union in the context of a relationship but quite explicitly claims that this relationship comes from God and should endure. Paul not only places the sexual relationship in a similar context but uses it as a sign of Christ's faithful and ongoing love. In all our theologies, sexuality is not separated from love. This is why Paul's celebration of love is at the heart of his theology of sexuality. This is the kind of love that sexual union brings about and expresses. This is the kind of love that is symbolic of divine love. This is the kind of love that gives sexuality its real greatness. This kind of love does not come to an end.

Paul would never use human love as a symbol of Christ's love if all human love were changing and fickle and transitory. The sexual is meant to be an expression of a divine gift and an expression of that which does not end. Such relationships, for Paul, are sacraments of another less tangible reality. They are expressions of God's relationship to us. If sexuality is placed in the context of love and love is the kind of love which lasts, then sexuality is placed once and for all in the context of permanence. The Song's love "as strong as death" becomes Paul's love which does not come to an end. Sexuality in any other context is not Christian.

We are now ready to explore the main passage from Paul on marriage and virginity in chapter seven of his first letter to the Corinthians.

Now for the questions about which you wrote. Yes, it is a good thing for a man not to touch a woman; but since sex is always a danger, let each man have his own wife and each woman her own husband. The husband must give his wife what she has the right to expect, and so too the wife to the husband. The wife has no rights over her own body; it is the husband who has them. In the same way the husband has no rights over his body; the wife has them. Do not refuse each other except by mutual consent, and then only for an agreed time, to leave yourselves free for prayer; then come together again in case Satan should take advantage of your weakness to tempt you. (7:1–6)

The Corinthian Christians had posed some questions for Paul. He is setting out to answer them in a pastoral way. Many of the questions facing the Corinthians concerned the sexual promiscuity rampant in the city of Corinth. Corinth had a reputation for sexual license. The Greek verb, *korinthiazein*, to live like a Corinthian, came to mean living a promiscuous life. Paul is thus hesitant to say anything that might lead the Christian community at Corinth to give in to the debauchery existing there. He recognizes that sex will always be a problem. He advises people to marry so that there is a proper place for sexual expression without their becoming promiscuous themselves. Paul is being cautious. He speaks of sex as a danger. Yet he is speaking of realities confronting his Christian community at Corinth. It is not surprising to hear him advocate each man having a wife and each woman a husband. Such marriages should permit a full sexual life as well as prevent a licentious life. It is not surprising that the marriage would be monogamous in the light of our earlier discussion on Paul's understanding of sexuality. Sex is to be found in the context of an ongoing and permanent commitment because it reflects Christ's love for his Church.

The husband is to give his wife what she has the right to expect and vice-versa. Marriage is a situation of real reciprocity including the right to sexual intercourse. It would be improper for one to refuse the other. The situation is mutual; each has the same right. The next verse strikes us as strong. The wife has no rights over her own body. The same applies equally to the husband. He has no rights over his body either. They belong to his wife. Perhaps we feel Paul is overstating the point because of our own individualism. We do not like to admit to anyone having rights over us, especially over our body, even in marriage. Paul is simply aware of the real mutuality that should exist in marriage, though he may be stating his case too strongly. The point is that sex should not be a weapon within marriage. Decisions about matters as important as the sexual should not be unilateral within a real relationship.

Not only should the two not refuse each other except by mutual consent; they should do so for only an agreed time. Paul is not opting for sexual abstinence in marriage. The reason why the two agree not to have sex is in order to pray. Paul, whose attitude is cautious, is really "going to town" at this point: one gets the feeling that for Paul there is nothing more for a couple to do than to have sex and pray. His main concern is that their sexual life not get in the way of their prayer life. Do not refuse except by mutual consent, then only for an agreed time, in order to pray, and then come together again.

This is a suggestion, not a rule: I should like everyone to be like me, but everybody has his own particular gifts from God, one with a gift for one thing and another with a gift for the opposite. (7:7)

Paul then makes a statement that he will make twice more in this chapter. In verse 12 he writes, "The rest is from me and not from the Lord." In verse 25 he writes, "About remaining celibate, I have no directions from the Lord but give my own opinion." In three different places he is careful to point out that he is giving his own opinion and that this is not something taught by Jesus, and so he inserts a personal suggestion. "You Corinthians don't have to accept it. Nevertheless I cannot help but mention it. It would be nice if all of you were unmarried as I am." Paul in his own pastoral way is trying to deal with the issues of the day. Yet he recognizes he cannot have his way because all people are different. Everyone has his own particular gift and it might not be the same as Paul's. One may well be given the gift of celibate life and another the gift of married life.

There is something I want to add for the sake of widows and those who are not married: it is a good thing for them to stay as they are, like me, but if they cannot control the sexual urges, they should get married, since it is better to be married than to be tortured. (7:8–9)

Paul intends to push his point a little. He has already expressed his own personal preference for the unmarried life. It would be good to remain unmarried if you are unmarried now. This is, of course, simply his own opinion. If, on the other hand, remaining unmarried means being tortured by one's sexual needs, by all means marry. Paul reluctantly accepts the reality that not all will choose as he has chosen.

For the married I have something to say, and this is not from me but from the Lord: a wife must not leave her husband—or if she does leave him, she must either remain unmarried or else make it up with her husband—nor must a husband send his wife away. (7:10–11)

Paul is careful here to say that this is *not* his own opinion, but something which comes from Jesus. He repeats what Mark and Matthew said about divorce. We can reflect once again on how Matthew handled the question Paul is now facing. Both point out that Jesus opposes divorce. Matthew points out that both marriage and celibacy are plausible options. Paul moves beyond this. He does not simply accept the possibility of celibacy; he endorses a preference for it. But both Matthew and Paul make it clear that Jesus himself did not prefer one to the other.

About remaining celibate, I have no directions from the Lord but give my own opinion as one who, by the Lord's mercy, has stayed faithful. Well then, I believe that in these present times of stress this is right: that it is good for a man to stay as he is. If you are tied to a wife, do not look for freedom; if you are free of a wife, then do not look for one. But if you marry, it is no sin, and it is not a sin for a young girl to get married. They will have their troubles, though, in their married life, and I should like to spare you that. (7:25–28)

This is the third time he has made the same point. By now we know how Paul feels; yet again he elaborates why he sees it the way he does. Paul is referring to the eschatological times in which the early Christians lived. They were all awaiting the coming of the Lord. This was not something in the distant future. Paul actually expected to see that day in his own lifetime. These were not times to get caught up in temporary situations. It would not be long before the end would be here.

His advice thus makes sense. It might only be a few years, if that, before Jesus will have established once and for all the kingdom of the Father. This is not the time to worry about being married or being celibate. If you are married, stay married; if you are not married, stay that way. If you decide to marry, however, that is acceptable too. That is not the issue. The issue is the proclamation of the good news and preparing the way of the Lord.

We must place Paul's advice not only in the context of his eschatology but also in the context of the fact that he may have been married himself at one time. It is possible that he was a widower and that his own experience with marriage was not the happiest.

Brother, this is what I mean: our time is growing short. Those who have wives should live as though they had none, and those who mourn should live as though they had nothing to mourn for; those who are enjoying life should live as though there were nothing to laugh about; those whose life is buying things should live as though they had nothing of their own; and those who have to deal with the world should not become engrossed in it. I say this because the world as we know it is passing away. (7:29–31)

Again Paul's eschatological emphasis comes through. Soon the world as we know it will be no more. One should not even be concerned about sorrow and joy. One should not become engrossed in anything right now except the work of the Lord—like Paul. Paul was in fact mistaken and wrong in his own eschatological expectation.

I would like to see you free from all worry. An unmarried man can devote himself to the Lord's affairs, all he need worry about is pleasing the Lord; but a married man has to bother about the world's affairs and devote himself to pleasing his wife: he is torn two ways. In the same way an unmarried woman, like a young girl, can devote herself to the Lord's affairs: all she need worry about is being holy in body and spirit. The married woman, on the other hand, has to worry about the world's affairs and devote herself to pleasing her husband. I say this only to help you, not to put a halter around your necks, but simply to make sure that everything is as it should be, and that you give your undivided attention to the Lord. (7:32–35)

Paul is not opposed to marriage; it is a good thing and in fact is a sign of Christ's love for his Church. Yet he personally prefers the celibate life because it frees him to give his complete attention to the Lord's work. Paul does not want his personal advice to be burdensome in any way. He is not out to put a halter around the necks of the people. In the very next verse (36) he goes on to say that if anyone feels it would be unfair to his daughter not to let her marry, he should feel free to let her do so. Yet, for Paul, in the context of the coming kingdom, remaining unmarried is better. Paul is simply being very practical in giving advice as he sees it. (The important thing is that one should feel free in this regard.)

Still, if there is anyone who feels that it would not be fair to his daughter to let her grow too old for marriage, and that he should do something about it, he is free to do as he likes: he is not sinning if there is a marriage. On the other hand, if someone has firmly made up his mind, without any compulsion and in complete freedom of choice, to keep his daughter as she is, he will be doing a good thing. In other words, the man who sees that his daughter is married has done a good thing but the man who keeps his daughter unmarried has done something even better. (7:36–38)

To bring our discussion to some conclusions, I would articulate Paul's attitude towards sexuality as positive but cautious. Between two spouses sexual relations are quite acceptable, to be encouraged as a solidification of their union, as long as they don't get in the way of prayer. Marriage itself is good. It is a symbol of Christ's love as well as an example of love which lasts forever. Even in these times of eschatological crisis, marriage is acceptable and one should feel quite free to marry. In fact it would be better to marry if not marrying is going to be too difficult. But Paul's cautious attitude is far from the celebrative attitude of the Song of Songs. Sex can also be dangerous if it becomes promiscuous as it did among the Corinthians. With Matthew, Paul affirms that celibacy is also an option. Then we see him going beyond any of the previous theologies. Celibacy is not only an option but Paul's personal preference, considering that the time is growing short. This preference must be seen in the light of his mistaken eschatology.

Sexual abstinence is not necessarily a value as such. It is simply that it would be foolish to marry if one is not already married, considering that the world is shortly to pass away, and it would be better to give undivided attention to Christ.

AUGUSTINE

Augustine gives a clear example of another approach to sexuality that has been influential in the history of Christian thought. Augustine has parallels among the other Fathers, but I am limiting my discussion to him for the sake of clarity. It is important to remember, however, that he is not the only nor the first to reflect these views.

Augustine was born in 354 in North Africa. His mother was a devout Christian; his father was a convert shortly before his death. Augustine himself had an interesting life which included early debauchery, an illegitimate son, and a turning to Manicheism, which taught that the body and matter were evil. His thinking was influenced by Neo-Platonism and Stoicism. He remains one of the greatest of the Christian writers. One of the many problems Augustine faced in his exposition of the Christian faith was the attack of Jovinian on virginity. Jovinian claimed that those who advocate virginity are actually condemning marriage. Augustine set out to defend both the good of marriage (*On the Good of Marriage*) and the practice of virginity (*On Holy Virginity*).

Augustine does defend the good of marriage but is unable to disclose the real goodness of sexuality. Among the theologies we are considering, Augustine's is a more negative theology of sexuality. In none of the theologies thus far was there any condemnation of sexual pleasure as such, even in Paul's cautious approach to the whole question. With Augustine, physical pleasure becomes an enemy of a man. Louis Bouyer writes of Augustine, "It seems that, in his own case at least, he never saw anything but the physical in the union of the sexes. Later on, as Bishop, he made loyal efforts to give a higher view of it to his Christians. But it must be admitted that the result was never to be very convincing." [14]

Two elements enter into his theology that we have not found previously. The first is that physical pleasure is bad; the second is that sexual union must be procreative. Neither the Yahwist, nor the Song of Songs, nor Matthew, nor Paul made sexuality exclusively procreative activity. Nor did any of them frown upon sensual pleasure itself. Some of them in fact celebrated it.

Augustine sets up a hierarchy with respect to the sexual life in terms of that which is better and that which is worst or most sinful. Beginning with the best first and the most sinful last, sexual expression can be classified as: 1) sexual abstinence or celibate chastity; 2) procreative sexual intercourse in marriage or conjugal chastity; 3) sexual intercourse in marriage for other than procreative reasons, which is venially sinful; 4) sexual intercourse outside of marriage, which is mortally sinful.

This is a rather clear hierarchy. Sexuality is not really good because it is concupiscent. Augustine's doctrine of concupiscence colors his doctrine of man. Man is basically a concupiscent being since the fall, unable to control himself, desiring pleasure. Bouyer also points out that although Augustine abandoned Manicheism for Christianity, he was still influenced by its dualism. Sensuality and spirituality were irreconcilable.[15] Sexual pleasure in itself was an enemy to spiritual man. Let us look briefly at some texts from Augustine.

Sexual abstinence, for Augustine, is preferable to sexual intercourse. In *The City of God* he speaks of "the shame which attends all sexual intercourse." [16] He also speaks of the "disease of concupiscence" and the "disease of lust" in his essay against Julian.[17] Even legitimate sexual intercourse does not escape shame:

Lust requires for its consummation darkness and secrecy; and this not only when unlawful intercourse is desired, but even such fornication as the earthly city has legalized. Where there is no fear of punishment, these permitted pleasures still shrink from the public eye. Even where provision is made for this lust, secrecy also is provided; and while lust found it easy to remove the prohibitions of law, shamelessness found it impossible to lay aside the veil of retirement. For even shameless men call this shameful; and though they love the pleasure, dare not display it. What! does not even conjugal intercourse, sanctioned as it is by law for the propagation of children, legitimate and honorable though it be, does it not seek retirement from every eye? [18]

In his essay on the good of marriage, he writes:

They are better in proportion as they begin the earlier to refrain by mutual consent from sexual intercourse, not that it would afterwards happen of necessity that they would not be able to do what they wished, but that it would be a matter of praise that they had refused beforehand what they were able to do.[19]

This does not sound at all like the teaching of Jesus nor even that of Paul. Paul did not even indicate that in marriage it would be good to begin to refrain from sexual relations. He encouraged them to refrain simply in order to have time for prayer. There are two remedies, according to Augustine, for the disease of lust which is basically what sexuality is.

Why do you praise the disease of lust, when you see a man will die of it unless the restraint of celibacy or the conjugal remedy resists it? [20]

Of the two remedies for sexuality, however, celibacy is the better. "Conjugal chastity also has its victory, although lesser, from the subjugation of this evil." [21] Conjugal chastity, which is a positive good although a lesser one, consists in limiting sexual intercourse to marriage and within marriage for the sake of procreation. Sensuality is no longer something we celebrate as in the Song of Songs; it is now lust and something we fight against. Augustine speaks of the "war which the chaste" wage.[22] Chastity can be celibate or conjugal, and conjugal chastity is still true chastity. Conjugal chastity limits sexual intercourse quite explicitly to procreation; this is not a biblical element but an influence of Stoicism.

He who exceeds the limits which this rule prescribes for the fulfillment of this end of marriage, acts contrary to the very contract by which he took his wife. The contract is read, read in the presence of all the attesting witnesses; and an express clause is there that they marry 'for the procreation of children;' and this is called the marriage contract.[23]

Conjugal chastity does not permit sexual relations at a time when they will be unproductive.

Such chastity abstains during menstruation and pregnancy, nor has it union with one no longer able to conceive on account of age. And the desire for union does not prevail, but ceases when there is no prospect of generation.[24]

In fact, these chaste people would prefer to have children in a way other than through sexual intercourse if that indeed were possible.

Those famous men who marry wives only for the procreation of children, such as we read the Patriarchs to have been, and know it, by many proofs, by the clear and unequivocal testimony of the sacred books; whoever, I say, they who marry wives for this purpose only, if the means could be given them of having children without intercourse with their wives, would they not with joy unspeakable embrace so great a blessing? Would they not with great delight accept it?[25]

While Augustine's attitude towards sexual intercourse is much more cautious than Paul's, he does have a positive attitude towards marriage. Marriage is not only good because of procreation but also because of the mutual companionship it provides.

This is what we now say, that according to the present condition of birth and death, which we know and in which we were created, the marriage of male and female is something good. . . . This does not seem to me to be good solely because of the procreation of children, but also because of the natural companionship between the two sexes.[26]

It is the goodness of marriage which in fact saves the act of sexual intercourse, which in this life is an act of lust. Sexual intercourse in marriage for procreation is not sinful. Intercourse that exceeds this limit, however, is.

The intercourse necessary for generation is without fault and it alone belongs to marriage. The intercourse that goes beyond this necessity no longer obeys reason but passion.[27]

Sexual intercourse within marriage for other than procreative reasons is "indulgence beyond what suffices for generating off-spring." [28] This includes those "men incontinent to such a degree that they do not spare their wives even when pregnant." [29] To seek intercourse beyond the need for procreation is a venial sin. Augustine is aware of Paul's words that a husband has rights over his wife's body and vice-versa. Thus it is permissible to have sexual relations for a reason other than procreation if your spouse demands them. To demand them of your spouse, however, would not be chaste.

While continence is of greater merit, it is no sin to render the conjugal debt, but to exact it beyond the need for generation is a venial sin.[30]

And in another place:

Is it not a sin in married persons to exact from one another more than this design of the 'procreation of children' renders necessary? It is doubtless a sin, though a venial one.[31]

So there are two times when sexual intercourse is permissible: procreation and the conjugal debt. If the spouse demands sexual relations, one must accede. The one rendering the debt is without blame. The one making the demand sins. "The crown of marriage, then, is the chastity of procreation and faithfulness in rendering the carnal debt." [32] The fact that venial sin can be associated with non-procreative intercourse in marriage is not a reflection against marriage however. Marriage is still good because it does not necessitate sinful intercourse.

Marriage does not force this type of intercourse to come about, but asks that it be pardoned, provided it is not so great as to encroach on the times that ought to be set aside for prayer.[33]

All sexual relations with someone other than a spouse are totally out of the question. This is adultery or fornication and more seriously sinful.

> In that other duty of marriage, sensual men seek for wives only to satisfy their sensuality, and therefore at length are scarce contented even with their wives. And oh! I would that if they cannot or will not cure their sensuality, they would not suffer to go beyond that limit which conjugal duty prescribes, I mean even that which is granted to infirmity.[34]

"To commit fornication or adultery is a crime that must be punished." [35] One quotation will suffice to summarize Augustine's hierarchy of permissible sexual expression.

> In marriage, intercourse for the purpose of generation has no fault attached to it, but for the purpose of satisfying concupiscence, provided with a spouse, because of the marriage fidelity, it is a venial sin; adultery or fornication, however, is a mortal sin. And so, continence from all intercourse is certainly better than marital intercourse itself which takes place for the sake of begetting children.[36]

Augustine is influenced here not simply by the New Testament alone. There is the influence of Stoicism as well.[37] For the Stoics pleasure for its own sake was taboo. This is an element that has entered into Augustine's theology of man and theology of sexuality from a nonbiblical source. Pleasure was the enemy of the Stoics. It is not the enemy of the Christian; sin is. But due to Stoic and Augustinian influence, pleasure came to be aligned with sinfulness.

In defense of Augustine, it must be said that there is a sense in which his defense of marriage was also a defense of sexuality, considering the times in which he lived. One can never isolate a theology from the culture in which it is formulated. In the first centuries of Christianity, the Encratites felt that marriage itself was sinful. The Manicheans were also skeptical of marriage and the sexual life. In defending marriage, Augustine helped to save sexuality from total rejection. This does not mean that Augustine's own attitude was positive. It means that it was less negative than other attitudes prevalent in his day.

Sex, in itself, was not evil for Augustine. It is concupiscence, the loss of control, that is evil. According to Augustine, there would have been sexual intercourse in the Garden of Eden even if man had not sinned; but it would have been directed by free will and not by lust. Sexual desire would have resulted from freely willing it for the sake of propagation. In spite of this, however, one can hardly label Augustine's view as positive. He is unable to separate sexuality as we experience it from lust. It is lust and not love that is his basic framework. As Peter Brown writes, "Of all the appetites, the only one that seemed to Augustine to clash inevitably and permanently with reason, was sexual desire." [38]

To summarize then, concupiscence and lust—not love—provide the context for Augustine's discussion. This is not to deny the centrality of love in the theology of Augustine but to say that love is not the background for his discussion of sexuality. His attitude towards sexuality as well as his attitude towards sensual pleasure is negative. Rather than a celebrative and playful approach as one finds in the Song of Songs, one finds himself at war with sexuality in Augustine's view. A basic principle, therefore, is that sexual abstinence is a higher goal than sexual intercourse. Celibate chastity is a higher goal than conjugal chastity because it is a more perfect victory over concupiscence. Marriage itself, however, is good although not as high a good as celibacy. Marriage is good both because of the value of procreation and also because of the companionship it provides. Sexual intercourse seen as an act of love is seldom recognized since generally speaking it is in fact an act of lust. The only reasons justifying sexual involvement are procreation and paying the marriage debt.

This is not the same theology of sexuality we have seen in the other theologies where sexuality is a created good and related to interpersonal love. It is even far from Paul whose caution did not lead him to limit sexual intercourse to procreation nor associate sexual pleasure with shame. It is definitely not the theology of Matthew and as far as we can tell of Jesus himself, who did not speak of the celibate life as higher than the married one. Even Paul quite explicitly says that his preference for the celibate life is not the teaching of Jesus but his own personal opinion. Bailey writes, "Augustine must bear no small measure of responsibility for the insinuation into our culture of the idea, still widely current, that

Christianity regards sexuality as something peculiarly tainted with evil." [39] That Christianity has a negative attitude towards the sexual is simply not true. Augustine's theology (and others of his day) is negative; the biblical theologies are not.

CONCLUSION

My main purpose in this chapter was to explore theological perspectives on human sexuality and to stress that there has been and is pluralism in this area. I find it more appropriate to talk about the theology of sexuality than the morality of sexuality since the notion of its morality so often implies questions of right and wrong. This is not my concern. A theology of sexuality, an understanding of sexuality itself, the role of sexuality in the life of a person, needs to be articulated first. The following are some general conclusions based upon the previous discussion:

1. Negativity in the face of sensual pleasure is not Judaeo-Christian. Too many theologies of sexuality in the past were based on a mistrust of pleasure which comes from a Stoic influence upon early Christianity. In the theologies examined, the Song of Songs shows the most celebrative attitude towards sensual pleasure and Augustine manifests the most negative. There is no New Testament condemnation of sensual pleasure as such—only its abuse in the lives of the Corinthians. Our attitude towards sensual pleasure needs to be appreciative, celebrative, and positive if our attitude towards sexuality is going to be affirmative. To say that something is wrong because it connotes pleasure is foolish. To say that it never needs restraint is equally foolish. Pleasure is not a Christian value nor is it a Christian enemy. Sin, not pleasure, is the enemy. The goal of the Christian life is living in the Spirit and the enemy of that goal is walking in darkness. The New Testament confirms the theology of the Yahwist, for whom sexuality was a creation of God and His gift to man.

2. The procreative potential of sexuality is not the only context for understanding sexuality. Sexuality is linked to fellowship and love in both the Old and New Testaments. Only Augustine gives it a totally procreative context. Sexual union is not simply a means to a procreative end. It is the Priestly theology of the Pentateuch

which contains the statement: "Be fruitful, multiply, fill the earth." This can be found in Genesis 1:28, 8:17, and 9:1. All of these references are from the theology of the Priest. This particular text is never quoted when the New Testament is discussing sexuality. New Testament references are most frequently to the Yahwist's theology—Mk. 10:7, Mt. 19:5, I Cor. 6:16, and Eph. 5:31. When the New Testament quotes the Priestly account, it quotes Genesis 1:27—"Male and female he created them." The Yahwist, the Song, Matthew, and Paul do not limit sexuality to procreation and there is no reason to believe Jesus did so. Cautious Paul himself, who places sexuality in the context of marriage, does not place it in the context of procreation. Sexuality is not primarily procreative as much as it is celebrative, expressive, eschatological, and unitive.

3. If pleasure and procreation are not the setting for the New Testament discussions of sexuality, fidelity and the kingdom are. The Yahwist places the sexual in the context of loneliness and fellowship. The Song places it in the context of two people totally wrapped up in their love for each other. Matthew places it in the context of two becoming one in such a way that an unbreakable bond exists. The Song says that the love underneath the sensuality it is portraying is as strong as death. Paul says that his conception of love is that it never ends. Sexuality is linked then to love and this love is ongoing. In this context, human sexual love is sacramental. It requires genuine fidelity, the kind of fidelity Yahweh exhibited towards his Chosen People and Christ exhibits towards his People.

4. Not only is fidelity important, so is eschatology, which is central to the New Testament. Our theology of sexuality must be thought through in the light of an eschatological perspective. The New Testament is open to celibacy as it relates to the kingdom. Paul exhorts married people to give undivided attention to the Lord. One does not remain unmarried in the New Testament because there is anything inferior about sexuality; one remains unmarried because of the kingdom. We make our life choice, to be married or to be single, in the light of that particular reality. Sexuality, eschatologically understood, is a realization of the presence of the kingdom, realized eschatology.

5. A mention must be made of sexual abstinence. The highest form of love, the norm for love, is not that which does not

culminate in sexual intercourse. The highest form of love is that which lasts, that which is strong, that which torrents could not drown. Sexual abstinence is not more perfect, so to speak, than sexual intercourse. Neither is it less perfect. Both sexual intercourse and sexual abstinence are New Testament values. Neither is the supreme Christian value. What is important is life in Christ.

6. We cannot ignore the creation of two sexes and its Christian significance. The two sexes exist for each other. Bailey likes to make the following point which certainly Christian discussion must consider.

Against all one sex institutions and orders, therefore, as against all vows of celibacy (compulsory and even voluntary), there is set an insistent question mark; save as urgent, emergency expedients framed to meet a temporary crisis, they are only justified if they do not hinder free and healthy partnership between the sexes.[40]

We must continue to theologize about the significance of the sexes. Partnership between the sexes may be cooperation, friendship, or teamwork. It is not necessarily marriage. Bailey continues, "Too often the obligation of partnership is misinterpreted as the obligation to marry, with the result that all Christian liberty in the sexual realm is denied." [41] Yet Bailey concludes:

Upon married and single alike God lays the same ineluctable obligation to live in belongingness, one sex with the other—and from this there can be no dispensation. A man or a woman is free to adopt the celibate life, but not to refuse or evade the duty of partnership; and the celibate is likewise free to follow any particular rule or discipline, provided that it does not, by express direction or customary interpretation, inhibit or preclude free personal intercourse and creative encounter with the complementary sex.[42]

We may agree or disagree with Bailey or feel he states his opinion too strongly, or wonder what partnership in the concrete actually means. We must not neglect, however, the significance that we are male and female and created for each other's good.

Sexuality is an indication that we are not created self-subsistent beings. We are created incomplete by ourselves, relational beings, in need of others. God does not intend us to be alone. Independence is not our goal. Love is the Christian value and sex is a gift from God that exists for the sake of this love. God's intention is not only that two become one but that someday we will all be one as Jesus and his Father are one. Sexuality is a part of the totality of the divine plan. It is not that sexuality is good only in view of reproduction. It is not that the sexual union should be reduced to a minimum in the Christian life. Christians must continue to reflect upon what being sexual means and further reflection upon its meaning is the purpose of the next chapter.

2

Psychology and Sexuality

JUST AS there is pluralism in theology, so there is pluralism in psychology. There is no one psychological theory of personality nor one theory of sexuality. The spectrum ranges from behavioristic to humanistic to psychoanalytic approaches. I want to exemplify this by looking at three theorists: Freud, Adler, and Frankl.

FREUD'S WILL TO PLEASURE

For Sigmund Freud, a person's conscious and unconscious activity centers around three basic structures: the id, the ego, and the super ego containing the ego ideal. The super ego and ego ideal give rise to the striving for perfection and are given less emphasis than the other structures. Early psychoanalysis was an id psychology and then moved in the direction of ego psychology. It never developed as fully a psychology of the super ego.

The ego has the task of integrating the demands of the id, super ego, ego ideal, and external world. It is the realistic component of the person and operates in accord with the reality principle. This is a counterpart of the principle in accord with which the id functions, the pleasure principle, a principle of tension reduction. It is the fundamental concept in the early writings of Freud. The id strives for pleasure rather than perfection, and pleasure is basically tension reduction.

The id contains the instincts which are a very important part of Freud's person. Freud writes, "We thus arrive at the essential nature of instincts in the first place by considering their main characteristics—their origin in sources of stimulation within the organism and their appearance as a constant force—and from this we deduce one of their further features, namely, that no actions of flight avail against them." [1] There are two general classifications of the instincts—the life instincts and the death instincts. The life instincts are hunger, thirst, and sex. The death instincts are aggression and the will to die. Libido refers to the energy by which life instincts work. Sex is the most important of the life instincts although hunger is the paradigm for understanding them. Freud writes, "On the exact analogy of 'hunger,' we use 'libido' as the name of the force (in this case that of the sexual instinct, in the case of hunger that of the nutritive instinct) by which the instinct manifests itself." [2] Hunger is the model in terms of which the other life instincts are understood. When I am hungry I seek satisfaction, which is tension reduction, which is pleasure. Sex is like hunger in Freudian psychology. It is the instinct to which Freud gave most of his attention. His libido theory is really a theory of sexuality and libido most often refers to sexual energy.[3]

Freud extensively discusses sexual development and the stages of psychosexual growth: the oral, anal, phallic, latent, and genital stages. The oral, anal, and phallic stages are infantile sexuality. The latent stage is a period of inhibited sexuality. Sexuality blossoms during the genital stage at the time of puberty. Freud also deals with the whole defense system in terms of which the ego operates—the mechanisms of fixation, projection, repression and others.

ADLER'S UPWARD STRIVING

Alfred Adler was a colleague of Freud from 1902 until 1908, and then he moved out in his own direction.[4] His psychology begins with the feeling of inferiority or sense of incompleteness within each person. This feeling is not abnormal. It is the driving force within personality. The person is pushed (or pulled) by the need to overcome it. Compensation gives rise to a striving for perfection in order to overcome the feeling of incompleteness, or a striving for superiority in order to overcome the feeling of inferiority. The early Adler spoke of inferiority and the will to power; later Adler spoke of incompleteness and the upward striving. Neither the will to power, the striving for superiority, nor the upward striving are individualistic notions. They are simply ways of postulating an urge to overcome imperfection. The individual, in fact, overcomes his feelings of inadequacy, incompleteness, helplessness, inferiority by developing social interest. The feeling of inferiority must be balanced by the feeling of community. This is why Adler's theory of personality is a *social* conception of the person and the beginning of social psychology. Freud's model of man is biological.

Style of life, another theme in Adlerian psychology, is the unifying and individualizing element. No two people have the same lifestyle. The transformation from an old lifestyle to a new one not yet formed is one of the most difficult of struggles. The lifestyle arises out of a person's creative power. Adler's emphasis on the creative dimension accounts for his emphasis on the ego and finality. For Adler, man makes himself as much as he is made. "It matters little what we bring into the world. Everything depends upon what we do with it." [5] The person advances from a minus to a plus situation, compensating for imperfection by striving for perfection. This striving for perfection or upward movement within the person is central and takes the form of a goal. Adler writes, "Movement, the basic law of all life, and consequently of all psychological life, cannot be thought of without goal and direction." [6] In this regard he differed with Freud. Adler maintained, "One cannot understand the psychological structure of a person through the drive life because the drive is without direction." [7]

Social interest was first perceived as a direction of growth for the individual and later for mankind as a whole. The future of man, individually and collectively, is not completely controlled by his past.

Adler writes of this social striving:

It means striving for a form of community which must be thought of as everlasting, as it could be thought of if mankind had reached the goal of perfection. It is never a present day community or society nor a political or religious form. Rather the goal which is best suited for perfection would have to be a goal which signifies the ideal community of all mankind, the ultimate fulfillment of evolution.[8]

This goal of ultimate perfection opens Adler to religious and spiritual realities. He writes, "It is not quite correct to say with regard to the intelligible viewpoint that the view of theological anthropology is completely different from that of psychological anthropology." [9]

FRANKL'S WILL TO MEANING

Viktor Frankl developed what he called the Third Viennese School of Psychotherapy.[10] His approach centers around "the will to meaning" as the primary motivational force in man. This is in contrast to the will to pleasure in Freud (the first Viennese school) and the upward striving (will to power) in Adler (the second Viennese school).

Frankl refers to his approach as *logotherapy*, a focus on man's search for meaning. The striving for pleasure, the striving for perfection, and the striving for meaning are the different fundamental motivational forces operative within the human person according to Freud, Adler, and Frankl respectively. These need not be seen as mutually exclusive. Nevertheless each theorist singles out one as primary. Frankl was a psychiatrist who spent three years of his life at Auschwitz and other Nazi concentration camps. The struggle for meaning was his own personal struggle.

Meaning, for Frankl, comes in three possible ways: by man's actualizing creative values, experiential values, or attitudinal values. The first is by doing something, the way of achievement or accomplishment. This is related to the significance that competence and self-esteem play in contemporary psychology. The second is by way of experiencing something or someone, whether truth or goodness or beauty or love. The third is through suffering, realizing value by the very attitude with which we face our destiny. Only that suffering is meaningful, of course, which is inevitable, unavoidable, absolutely necessary. It is masochism rather than heroism to accept as fate a cancer that can be cured. Frankl writes, "If there is any meaning in life at all, then there is meaning in suffering, since suffering is an ineradicable part of life." [11] The blows of fate not only give shape to our personality but one's acceptance of them symbolizes the intrinsic meaningfulness of life itself. Suffering contributes to personality growth. Yet it remains only one of the ways in which a person discovers his or her meaning in living.

Frankl was a student of Adler. They reflect similar attitudes towards sexuality in that they see it primarily as a social rather than as a biological phenomenon. Adler speaks of two phases of sexual development. The first phase is autoerotic because sexuality has not yet become social. It is a biological phase. Sexuality develops into a social phase in accord with Adler's basic social conception of man. Sexuality becomes mature when it becomes a task for two rather than one, when it becomes social and not simply biological. For Freud, sexuality also becomes mature when it becomes social in a heterosexual relationship and yet Freud still sees it as basically biological. Adler writes, "Love, as a task of two equal persons of different sexes, calls for bodily and mental attraction, exclusiveness, and a total and final surrender. The right solution of this task of two persons is the blessing of socially adjusted persons who have proved their right attitude in having friends, being prepared for a useful job, and showing mutual devotion." [12] Frankl writes in a very similar way, "Love is as primary a phenomenon as sex. Normally, sex is a mode of expression for love. Sex is justified, even sanctified, as soon as, but only as long as, it is a vehicle of love. Thus love is not understood as a mere side effect of sex but sex as a way of expressing the experience of that ultimate togetherness that is called love." [13]

There never has been only one psychology of sexuality or only one psychology of personality. There is no one concept nor one method in terms of which man can always and everywhere be understood. One psychology helps us to understand one dimension and another helps us to understand another dimension. There is that within the person which strives for a reduction of tension, which strives for a sense of completion, and which strives for meaningfulness. All of these are operative, at different times in different ways, in different individuals to different degrees. Any theory must have proper respect for individuality and not see a theory of personality development as a paradigm to which the individual must conform.

Freud makes us aware once and for all of the fundamental importance of sexuality in the life of a person. Yet sexuality is not *the* but *a* fundamental dimension. Sexuality must be understood within the total context of personality and not vice-versa. Sexuality is a dimension of personality and personality is the more basic concept. A *sexual* person is primarily a sexual *person*.

Being sexual therefore means many things, and this is what we want to explore in this chapter. Among other things, it means sexual differentiation, being female and male. It also means being relational—structured for the other—incomplete by oneself—inescapably social. Sexual existence is social existence. In my social life I encounter other sexual beings of my own sex and other sexual beings of the other sex. Being sexual also means being bodily and physical. My body is a sexual reality and is involved in what I do and how I act.

One further point needs to be made. Human sexuality is distinct from other forms of sexuality. It cannot be reduced to animal sexuality.[14] It is that and much more. Sexuality in men and women is human and not an expression of a lower nature. Human sexuality is filled with possibilities other than simply the potential for reproduction. There is more to human sexuality than this biological function; there are also the social functions. To explain sexuality in terms of its procreative function alone is to reduce it to pre-human sexuality.

AFFECTIVE AND GENITAL SEXUALITY

Sexuality has two dimensions—the affective and the genital. Although some equate sexuality and genitality, I see sexuality as a broader term that cannot be reduced to genitality alone. Genitality is only one dimension of the sexual life. Sexuality has to do with the sexes, with our attractions for other people, with our relational rootedness. In this complexity of sexual realities lies the genital dimension, which is primarily biological or physiological. Sexuality, however, has a social dimension as well. Yet genitality often emerges as the core of what we think of when we think of sexuality. We usually think of sexual intercourse as genital activity and the term has come to mean that in our own culture.

Freud himself introduced this distinction in his discussion of infantile sexuality. He emphasized a sexual history prior to the emergence of the genital potentialities that accompany puberty. These dimensions he spoke of as being oral, anal, phallic, and latent sexuality. Sexuality was not exclusively genital. There are many places in his essays and lectures where Freud refers to these two dimensions. He writes, "Whereas other people declare that 'sexual' and 'connected with reproduction' (or, if you prefer to put it more shortly, 'genital') are identical, we cannot avoid postulating something 'sexual' that is not 'genital'—has nothing to do with reproduction." [15]

Freud distinguished between the "affectionate" current of our sexual lives and the "sensual" current.[16] The affectionate current begins to be operative during the period of latency, the period when genital development remains more or less hidden. The sensual current emerges again at the time of puberty when the sexual aim becomes genital. The affectionate current, the non-genital aspect of sexuality, consists in by-passing the biological (genital) aim and in assuming a social one. Freud in fact uses the word "social" to describe the non-genital current in our sexual lives. He speaks of sublimation as the process through which or by means of which the social aim is brought forth.[17]

We can speak then of the affectionate-social side of our sexuality as well as the genital-physiological side. Yet the primary aim of our sexual lives for Freud is the genital. In fact, he speaks of the affectionate current as "aim-inhibited sexuality." The social dimension is not a direct sexual aim but only comes about because we inhibit or repress the genital aim which then gives rise to the affectionate current. Freud writes:

The social instincts belong to a class of instinctual impulses which need not be described as sublimated, though they are closely related to these. They have not abandoned their directly sexual aims, but they are held back by internal resistances from attaining them; they rest content with certain approximations to satisfaction and for that very reason lead to especially firm and permanent attachments between human beings. To this class in particular belong the affectionate relations between parents and children, which were originally fully sexual, feelings of friendship, and the emotional ties in marriage which had their origin in sexual attraction.[18]

The genital current is really the primary one; the affectionate current is aim-inhibited. This affective, aim-inhibited, social dimension of our sexuality consists in the tender relationships we experience. It is the affectionate, compassionate, and tender side of sexuality. Affection, compassion, tenderness, warmth are rooted in sexuality and expressive of sexuality although not specifically genital. In this class Freud places the relationships between parents and children, friendship, as well as the emotional ties within marriage. The affective dimension is an emotional bond as opposed to a specifically genital bond.

Most of us today do not limit our understanding of sexuality to a physical-physiological dimension. Sexuality includes the whole area of our emotional warmth as human beings. Related, however, to Freud's understanding was not only his distinction between sexuality and genitality but also the notion of genital supremacy. In many places Freud speaks about the primacy of the genital zone.

For the present you should keep firmly in mind that sexual life (or, as we put it, the libidinal function) does not emerge as something ready-made and does not even develop further in its own likeness, but passes through a series of successive phases which do not resemble one another; its development is thus several times repeated—like that of a caterpillar into a butterfly. The turning point of this development is the subordination of all the component sexual instincts under the primacy of the genitals and along with this the subjection of sexuality to the reproductive function.[19]

I reject Freud's genital supremacy but not his distinction between sexuality and genitality. Abraham Maslow, about whom I will say more later, and many others, question this doctrine as well. Maslow writes:

On the whole, however, the most widely accepted of the various theories put forth by Freud is that tenderness is aim-inhibited sexuality. That is, to put it very bluntly, it is, for Freud, deflected and disguised sexuality. When we are forbidden to fulfill the sexual aim of coupling, and when we keep on wanting to and do not dare admit to ourselves that we are, the compromise product is tenderness and affection. Contrariwise, when we meet with tenderness and affection we have no Freudian recourse but to regard this as aim-inhibited sexuality. Another deduction from this premise that seems unavoidable is that if sex were never inhibited, and if everyone could couple with anyone else, then there would be no tender love. Incest taboos and repression—these are what breed love, according to Freud.[20]

Herbert Marcuse in *Eros and Civilization* also calls the supremacy of genitality into serious question.[21] Erik Erikson, a neo-Freudian, sees the psycho-sexual life of which Freud speaks as psycho-social as well.[22] What we are talking about is the relative weight Freud attaches to the physical-biological as opposed to the affective-social side of sexuality.

For Erikson, the ultimate goal of the person is ego-integrity, which is accomplished with maturity and not puberty. The goal of sexuality and personality is not complete with the reproductive powers. The life tasks of which Erikson speaks in his eight stages are social tasks: trust, autonomy, initiative, industry, identity, intimacy, generativity, and integrity.

In fact, for Erikson, the task of intimacy, which is very much a sexual task, really comes after the time of puberty. At the time of puberty we are struggling with the question of sexual identity as well as other forms of identity such as vocational identity. It is only after this task is in some ways resolved that one can come to grips with his or her own intimacy needs. This implies socialization as a dimension of psycho-sexual growth. In spite of this framework, Erikson still speaks of the utopia of genitality. He does not completely abandon Freud's framework. Nevertheless, the utopia of genitality includes not only orgasm but also a loved partner, mutual trust, and in fact, work, procreation, and recreation. For Erikson the social is as fundamental as is the genital in one's personality growth. Once we make the distinction between the social and the biological aspects of our sexuality, the affective and genital aspects of our sexuality, we are still faced with the question of their relationship and relative importance.

It is significant that Freud speaks of that period between the end of the sixth to eighth year onwards until puberty as a period of latency. This implies that nothing significant is happening as far as our sexual life is concerned.[23] Even the word "latency" represents Freud's bias. Freud himself would say that what is happening at this time is the development of the affective-social current of our sexual lives. What is latent at this time is the so-called genital dimension which does not come to completion until after latency and during puberty. Freud calls this period latency when it is only genital latency. He sees it as a period of suppression or retrogression as far as our sexual lives are concerned.[24] I do not think we can any longer think of this period as latency nor can we speak of it as suppression or regression unless we have already established that the genital aim is the most specifically human and the most desired aim for sexuality. If that is not the case, this so-called latent period is significant as a period of socialization. This stage is a significant element in sexual-social development, especially as we begin thinking in terms of human sexuality and not only procreative sexuality. Although the procreative function has not come to full growth at this time, we have the emergence of the sexual-social goal. Harry Stack Sullivan attaches importance to this period of pre-adolescent growth as the "chum" period in sexual socialization. Rollo May also accepts the importance Sullivan gives to this period. He writes:

Harry Stack Sullivan emphasized the 'chum' period in human development. This period includes the several years, from about eight to twelve, before the heterosexual functioning of the boy or girl begins to mature. It is the time of genuine liking of the same sex, the time when boys walk to school with arms around each other's shoulders and when girls are inseparable. It is the beginning of the capacity to care for someone else as much as for yourself.[25]

This so-called latency period is the emergence of the ability to care and love and is of no small significance in the sexual development of the person.

Sexual development for Freud is di-phasic.[26] The first phase is from the age of two until the age of five and stops with latency.

The second phase begins with puberty. When Freud speaks of di-phasic sexual development, he is not only neglecting but is completely disregarding the period of latency as a real phase of sexual growth. Within the Freudian framework, if we are to give significance to the social dimension of our sexual lives, we have to see it as tri-phasic: the initial phase, the social phase, and then the genital-pubertal phase. Sexuality really involves four phases. After the emergence of genitality at the time of puberty, there is still further growth ahead. Puberty is not the be-all and the end-all of our sexual growth. There is a rhythm in our sexual lives as we see emphasis on the biological dimension in early life, with a shift to the social dimension around the sixth or eighth year, with a shift back to the biological dimension at the time of adolescence and puberty, with another shift back to the social dimension as men and women move toward maturity and mature interpersonal relationships. Puberty itself is not the culmination of our sexual lives but simply the emergence of full genital potentiality. The process of socialization as far as sexuality is concerned has not yet come to completion.

Socialization and not tension reduction is the primary goal of our sexual lives. Within the Freudian framework it is too easy to feel that there is nothing left for man's sexual life after puberty except repeated orgasms. The entire task of socialization remains and man cannot be seen simply in terms of the biological model but has to be seen as a social being, a fact which Jung, Adler, Frankl, Maslow and many others began to realize. The biological model of personality is inadequate for understanding human sexuality. Only if pleasure is the sole sexual aim and not sociality itself can we justify the use of the word latency as a label for that period in our sexual lives when new sexual aims appear, affective and social aims.

Although I agree with the value of distinguishing sexuality and genitality, I call genital supremacy into question. It seems to me that Freud misinterprets the value and significance of the affection-ate and social side of our sexual lives. Freud also errs in using basically a biological model for understanding personality. This is not to say that the biological dimension of personality is not extremely significant. It is simply to say that it is not adequate by itself. Rather than being aim-inhibited sexuality, latency is socially oriented sexuality. This undercurrent, this affective current, this social current is not aim-inhibited as much as it is aim-oriented and other-oriented.

We have looked at two dimensions of our sexual lives: Freud's distinction between the affectionate and genital currents. Sexuality has not only a biological aim; it has a social aim as well. Freud, however, underestimated the social aim. The relative importance of these two depends upon our basic understanding of the person. Do we basically understand a person as only a biological creature or do we see the person as a social creature? Is there a goal that transcends the biological functions?

The affective dimension is the totality of affection, friendship, and tenderness in life. This is the area exhibited in compassionate people who are not only able to socialize their sexuality but in rare cases universalize it. In these humanitarian people the task of socialization is brought to completion and perfection in universalization. Not only socialization but universalization is an aim of sexual life. The tender and compassionate person is a person who has reached sexual maturity.

It is only the person who has confronted the depths of sexuality, not only socially but physically as well, a person who has confronted biological and physiological drives in such a way that he can feel comfortable with genitality, who is able to really socialize himself. As long as we do not feel comfortable with our biology and physiology, we are not going to be able to socialize our sexuality. In other words, placing an emphasis on the affective current of our sexual lives in no way makes insignificant the genital side of sexuality. If the genital side of sexuality is repressed, it is going to lead to an affectively inhibited person. Our goal is not to be affectively inhibited but to become affectively universal. This can only be accomplished through comfort with genitality as well as affectivity. This does not mean, however, that comfort with one's genitality means we have accomplished all that we can with respect to sexual living. Sexual socialization remains. Teilhard de Chardin speaks of this socialization as affectionization, sensitization, and universalization.[27]

From now on, when I talk about sexuality, I will distinguish between the affective-social current and the genital-physiological current. Too often people make this distinction and still lapse back into equating the sexual and genital in discussion. For instance, we speak of sexual intercourse when we actually mean genital intercourse. Hugging, kissing, and personal conversation are also sexual intercourse. This lack of distinction causes the mistaken notion that the height of sexual intercourse is orgasm.

Not all by any means use the word "sexual" in the same way as I do to include both affective and genital dimensions. Harry Stack Sullivan uses the word to mean "genital." "A great many people in early adolescence suffer a lot of anxiety in connection with their new found motivation to sexual or genital activity—and I use those words interchangeably." [28] Yet he clearly distinguishes between what he calls "the intimacy need" and "the lust need." [29] The intimacy need arises in pre-adolescence out of the experience of loneliness and during the chum phase of development whereas the lust need arises during puberty. I see both man's intimacy need (affective sexuality) as well as his lust need (genital sexuality) arising out of his sexuality and thus being two dimensions of one sexual life. This does not mean they are not distinct. Man's striving after intimacy is not the same as his striving after genital satisfaction and the two should not be confused. Neither can they, however, be completely separated. Sullivan himself points out that a sharp distinction between relationships based upon lust and those based on intimacy is destructive. A total separation leads, among other things, to not being able to love those we have sex with and not being able to have sex with those we love. I do not see my own position that far removed from that of Sullivan. Although he tends to use the word "sexual" to mean "genital," he clearly distinguishes between the two dimensions and yet sees their interrelatedness. He writes, "One cannot, except for purposes of clarity of thinking, separate the manifestation of these two very powerful motivating systems of human life. But though these systems are intricately interwoven, at the same time they are never identical." [30] Affective and genital sexuality are distinguishable but not separable, different and yet related.

MASLOW, SEXUALITY, AND
SELF-ACTUALIZATION

The Freudian and neo-Freudian psychoanalytic movement as well as the behaviorist movement known in the work of B. F. Skinner are both significant today. Another movement, referred to as "the third force" in contrast to these two, is humanistic psychology, of which Abraham Maslow is a major representative.[31] One of his contributions was to approach research not through a study of neurotic and psychotic behavior, but through a study of those people whom most of us consider to be outstanding examples of human life. He refers to these as self-actualizing people.

A self-actualizing person exhibits self-acceptance and a lack of defensiveness, is not burdened by crippling shame or overriding guilt, and is simple and spontaneous. A healthy self-actualizing person is focused outside of himself and has a sense of mission. He enjoys privacy and solitude to a greater degree than the average person; he is not as dependent upon the culture in which he finds himself for his own identity. He enjoys a greater degree of freedom from the environment and is motivated interiorly.

This person has a feeling for mankind. Maslow uses the word Adler coined, *Gemeinschaftsgefühl*, a sense of community. Within the interpersonal life of self-actualizing people, there are deeper relationships than in the lives of many other adults. The self-actualizing person is more capable of fusion and love, demonstrates a democratic character, and learns from anyone who has something to teach. Although the self-actualizing person exhibits independence of the culture, he is strongly ethical, having definite moral standards and a strong sense of right and wrong, which is often not conventional.

This person exhibits a sense of humor, but one different from the average. It is not hostile humor, nor sensual humor, nor punning humor. His humor is exhibited more often in smiling than in laughing. Creativity was the most universal characteristic in all the people Maslow studied. There was no exception.

Due to their firm value system, self-actualizing people are frequently able to dissolve what are dichotomies for many people: the dichotomy between intelligence and emotion, between self-centered and other-oriented behavior, between the sensual and the spiritual. Although these are the main characteristics Maslow found, he also found imperfections. The self-actualizing person is imperfect and is able to accept and incorporate weaknesses.[32]

Another basic concept of Maslow is that of the hierarchy of human needs.[33] In *Motivation and Personality* he describes five of these. The first area of need is physiological: hunger, thirst, and sex. Until these needs are satisfied, a person will be unconcerned about other needs. If a person is starving, he is going to be concerned about food. After physiological needs, we seek safety and security. If hunger is not satisfied and we are starving, we will be willing to risk security in order to satisfy hunger.

Third come the belonging needs. These are related to Adler's social interest and are the needs for affection and love. Maslow discovered that the cause of much neurosis is actually the unsatisfied need for relationships with others. The belonging needs are essential to minimal psychological health. A sick person is one who has never learned to achieve good relationships. After these affective needs are met, the esteem needs appear. Self-esteem is a basic concept for much of the third force. The esteem needs include a sense of achievement, competence, and recognition. These are related to the motivating elements found in Viktor Frankl's psychology, where one of the values which contributes to our meaning is the sense of accomplishment.

But the highest need is for self-actualizing. After our physiological and safety needs are met, after we feel affection and competence, there emerges the striving to fulfill our human potential. Maslow writes that a greater value is usually placed upon a higher need than upon a lower by those who have been gratified in both.[34] Although the physiological and safety needs are more basic, self-actualizing people place greater emphasis and value upon the higher needs. The satisfaction of a higher need leads one more and more towards self-actualizing than does the satisfaction of a lower need. These two concepts of self-actualization and hierarchy of needs are basic elements in Maslow's understanding of personality. The next question is what role sexuality plays.

In discussing sexuality, it is important to introduce what Maslow calls "multiple motivation." A conscious desire on our part is not necessarily one desire but may contain a multiplicity of elements or motivations. The conscious desire may be a channel through which other goals are being sought. He elucidates this by looking at sexual desire.[35] It is a mistake to think that sexual desire means the need for genital sex; sexual desire may represent many things, such as the need to impress someone or the need to be accepted. For many adolescent boys, the size of the penis is extremely significant. It gives a sense of self-worth. Here sex is wrapped up with other needs. The sexual desire may be the need for reassured masculinity. The need for a boy to become a man with all that masculinity means in our culture is a tremendous burden. His sexual desire is frequently tied to his need to prove his masculinity. The sexual need may be and often is the need for closeness, intimacy, or love. The feeling of needing sex may be a combination of these. Sexual desire, then, is not simply the need for genital relations. It may be consciously experienced in that way, but what is actually needed in each individual case may be something different. It is easy to confuse the need for genital sex with the need for sexual identity, the need for self-acceptance, or the need for closeness.

Maslow found in self-actualizing people that genital abstinence is not harmful.[36] A self-actualizing person is able to accept genital deprivation and still be at ease with himself and his sexual life. Deprivation becomes pathogenic only when a pathogenic undercurrent surfaces—deprivation felt as rejection by the opposite sex, as inferiority, as lack of worth, or as isolation. It is not genital abstinence in itself but one's attitude towards it and how one experiences it that is significant.

Self-actualizing men and women tend not to seek genital sex simply for its own sake. The absence of sexual experience is more easily tolerated. Although these people are able to live comfortably with sexual deprivation, they do enjoy sexual pleasure intensely. Sexual pleasure is found to be very intense and frequently ecstatic. When they enjoy genital sex, they enjoy it wholeheartedly. They do not need genital experience but enjoy it when it comes and enjoy it more intensely than the average adult, yet it remains less important for the self-actualizing person within his total frame of reference. The self-actualizing person is less driven to love affairs, yet free to admit of and talk about his or her sexual attractions for other people. It would be good to have Maslow speak for himself:

It is certainly fair to say that self-actualizing men and women tend on the whole not to seek sex for its own sake, or to be satisfied with it alone when it comes. I am not sure my data permits me to say that they would rather not have sex at all if it came without affection, but I am quite sure that I have a fair number of instances in which for the time being at least sex was given up or rejected because it came without love or affection. . . . The sexual pleasures are found in their most intense and ecstatic perfection in self-actualizing people. If love is a yearning for the perfect and for complete fusion, then the orgasm as sometimes reported by self-actualizing people becomes the attainment of it. . . . In self-actualizing people the orgasm is simultaneously more important and less important than in average people. It is often a profound and almost mystical experience, and yet the absence of sexuality is more easily tolerated by these people. This is not a paradox or a contradiction. It follows from dynamic motivation theory. Loving at a higher need level makes the lower needs and their frustrations and satisfactions less important, less central, more easily neglected. But it also makes them more wholeheartedly enjoyed when gratified. . . . These people do not *need* sensuality; they simply enjoy it when it occurs.[37]

Another aspect of the self-actualizing person is that he or she makes no sharp differentiation between the roles and personalities of the two sexes. He or she is genuinely certain of his maleness or her femaleness and in that sense does not mind having some of the aspects of the opposite sex role.[38] Sexuality plays a role within Maslow's theory different from that which it plays in Freud's. Sexuality is not the basis for neurosis. It is really better to consider neurosis as related to spiritual disorders, to loss of meaning, to doubts about goals, to grief and anger over loss.[39]

Something needs to be said about sexuality and the striving after intimacy. Frequently we confuse these two. We experience sexual desire and think it is genital satisfaction that we need when actually the sexual desire represents the need for intimacy. For Maslow, the higher need in man is the need for intimacy. If this need is met and satisfied, the need for physiological genital experience is lessened.

Man is very much an intimacy-seeking animal and one can have intimacy without genital sex.

In the previous section, I noted Sullivan's distinction between the intimacy and genital needs. Rollo May also points out this same fact: "For human beings, the more powerful need is not for sex per se but for relationships, intimacy, acceptance, and affirmation." [40] Irene Josselyn notes the same fact in her study of adolescence: "The sexual behavior of many young adolescents is not typically an experience of a basic sexual need as much as an attempt, through sexuality, to meet a more all encompassing need. Young people with a strong wish to be loved, unable to find gratification for it in a framework that appears to them to be crippling, may turn to sexual relationships as a way of attaining closeness to another person." [41]

The self-actualizing person is not uncomfortable with the opposite sex. He finds it easy to enjoy friendships with the opposite sex without fear because friendship or even sexual attraction does not necessarily imply the need for genital interaction. It is intimacy and not genitality that man needs. It is possible to experience genitality, physiological sexuality, without intimacy; it is also possible to experience intimacy without genitality.

Genital intercourse in a self-actualizing person is frequently a peak experience. Nevertheless, such a person does not feel the necessity of genital intercourse because it is not necessary for fulfillment. It becomes a problem only when very much related to our self-worth or similar issues. Yet self-worth can never be proved through repeated genital experiences. Maslow writes, "It is now well known that many cases are found in which celibacy has no psychopathological effects. In many other cases, however, it has many bad effects." [42] What the sexual deprivation represents is what determines the effect.

For the self-actualizing person genital intercourse is not the initial step in forming a relationship. Rather, it is the deepening of intimacy and the culmination of one's striving after it. Sexual and genital expression are very much related to one's love for another person; therefore, sex is not the way a self-actualizing person initiates a relationship. Genital intercourse is a paradox, not needed while also intensely enjoyed, frequently enjoyed as an ecstatic, mystical, or peak experience. For Maslow, the goal of one's life is not to strive after pleasure or tension reduction, but to become fully human and actualize one's human potential.

FEMININITY AND MASCULINITY

We have explored two dimensions of sexuality—an affective and a genital dimension. There are also two others—a feminine and a masculine dimension.

I raise two questions in regard to femininity and masculinity. The first question is: What does it mean for me as a man to have a feminine dimension to my personality? The second question is: What does it mean for me to be a man? I am not asking the questions of what it means to be a woman nor what it means for a woman to have a masculine dimension because I am unable to answer them, not having had the experience of being a woman. A woman can reflect upon both of these questions in a vein similar to the way in which I approach the question of my manhood and my femininity.

The first question is the question of psychological bisexuality, the fact that none of us is purely feminine or purely masculine. My goal as person is to incorporate and integrate both into my personality. Not only am I man; as man I have a definitely feminine dimension. I distinguish between the concepts "man" and "woman" and the concepts "masculinity" and "femininity." Robert Stoller in his study of sex and gender distinguishes the "sense of maleness" and the "sense of masculinity." [43] The sense of maleness is related to one's biology, refers to a person's certainty that he belongs to only one of two sexes, and is fixed early in life by psychological as well as by biological determinants. But the awareness, "I am male," differs from the awareness, "I am masculine." Masculinity refers to a cultural stereotype.

Those qualities which the culture ascribes to a man or to a woman are not inherent in sexual differentiation itself. The so-called masculine qualities are not the exclusive prerogative of men, nor are the positive qualities which the culture ascribes to women the exclusive property of women. As man I want to be loving, tender, and warm. Women should be free to take initiative and be assertive. There is the need to de-sexualize the status of strength and weakness so that men and women can show both strength and weakness. Each of us should be capable of assertiveness, but each of us should also be capable of generosity. There are times when I need to be gentle and times when I need to be aggressive—whether man or woman.

As a sexual person, I am both affectionate and genital. As a sexual person, I am also both feminine and masculine. Maslow mentions the fact that the self-actualizing person is more comfortable than others with characteristics of the other sex. Following are a series of quotations from one of his later works:[44]

The close relationship between intra- and inter-personal communication is seen with especial clarity in relations between masculinity and femininity. Notice that I do not say 'between the sexes,' because my point is that the relations between the sexes are very largely determined by the relation between masculinity and femininity *within* each person, male and female.

The antagonism between the sexes is largely a projection of the unconscious struggle *within* the person, between his or her masculine and feminine components. To make peace between the sexes, make peace within the person.

The man who thinks you can be *either* a man, *all* man, or a woman, and *nothing but* a woman, is doomed to struggle with himself, and to eternal estrangement from women. To the extent that he learns the facts of psychological 'bisexuality,' and becomes aware of the arbitrariness of either/or definitions and the pathogenic nature of the process of dichotomizing, to the degree that he discovers that differences can fuse and be structured with each other, and need not be exclusive and mutually antagonistic, to that extent will he be a more integrated person, able to accept and enjoy the 'feminine' within himself (the 'Anima' as Jung calls it). If he can make peace with his female inside, he can make peace with the females outside, understand them better, be less ambivalent about them, and even admire them more as he realizes how superior their femaleness is to his own much weaker version. You can certainly communicate better with a friend who is appreciated and understood than you can with a feared, resented, and mysterious enemy. To make friends with some portion of the outside world, it is well to make friends with that part of it which is within yourself.

*   *   *

Not only has Maslow pointed to this notion; Carl Jung did the same. Jung is known for his classic distinction between the *anima* and the *animus;* the *anima* is the feminine dimension in the man and the *animus* the masculine dimension in the woman. Each of us has both dimensions. Robert Stoller also maintains, "The evidence for biologic or psychologic bisexuality does not contradict this division (the division between two sexes and two genders), but only demonstrates that within the sexes there are degrees of maleness and femaleness (sex) and of masculinity and femininity (gender)." [45]

Jeanne Humphrey Block, of the Institute of Human Development at the University of California in Berkeley, has done cross-cultural and longitudinal studies with respect to the sex role. She writes, "I am assuming, with a growing number of others, that the ultimate goal in development of sexual identity is not the achievement of masculinity or femininity as popularly conceived." [46] Her empirical study corroborated the hypothesis that personal maturity is associated with greater integration of femininity and masculinity within the personality. She refers to this integration of feminine and masculine traits and values as "androgynous," rather than bisexual.

Feminine and masculine sex roles are influenced by child rearing practices and socialization: boys are encouraged to control affect while girls are encouraged to control aggression.

The leitmotiv of socialization practices for boys across the several age levels studied reflects an emphasis on the virtues of the Protestant Ethic: an emphasis on achievement and competition, the insistence on control of feelings and expressions of affect, and a concern for rule conformity.

For girls, on the other hand, emphasis is placed, particularly by their fathers, on developing and maintaining close interpersonal relationships: they are encouraged to talk about their troubles and to reflect upon life, are shown affection physically, and are given comfort and reassurance. [47]

Block makes use of two fundamental *modalities*, or general patterns, "agency" and "communion," agency being masculine and communion feminine. The notion of agency is linked to adjectives such as adventurous, ambitious, assertive, competitive, critical, dominating, rational, responsible, and practical. The notion of communion goes with the adjectives artistic, considerate, curious, generous, idealistic, impulsive, loving, perceptive, sensitive, and sympathetic. Optimum functioning depends upon a balance between agency and communion, masculinity and femininity.

Cross-culturally, differences were also noted. Few sex differences and less emphasis on agency characterized those countries with a long and well established commitment to social welfare, Sweden and Denmark.

Explicit cross-cultural comparisons among the countries reveal that American males are distinguished, at or beyond the .05 level of significance, from the males of other countries by placing greater emphasis on the following adjectives: *adventurous, self-confident, assertive, restless, ambitious, self-centered, shrewd,* and *competitive* in their conceptualizations of the masculine ideal—adjectives reflecting greater agency. Interestingly, American women also described their ideal in more agentic terms than did women in the other countries studied.[48]

Three primary dimensions were found to distinguish American child-rearing values from the other five societies studied: Norway, Sweden, Denmark, Finland, and England. In America there was significantly more emphasis placed upon competitive achievement, significantly less importance attached to the control of aggression in American males, and significantly greater emphasis placed on early and clear sex typing. Taking into consideration American child rearing and socialization practices as well as the previously established fact that higher levels of maturity reflect an androgynous integration of agency and communion, the American cultural emphasis impedes personality growth. Block's studies show that the socialization process socializes males and females in the direction of being masculine or feminine rather than in the direction of being both. James McCary writes:

When men and women recognize that free expression of affection is certainly nothing to fear, nor a barometer of weakness or effeminacy, all their human relationships, including the sexual one, will be much fuller and happier.[49]

* * *

Cultural stereotypes are not the context in which we should define personality growth. When we talk about men and women we are talking about sexual differentiation; when we talk about femininity and masculinity we are talking about cultural stereotypes and socialized roles. The notion of bisexuality does not affirm the validity of these roles and stereotypes but simply says that in the process of coming to sexual identity these cultural stereotypes and social roles have to be dealt with. Bisexuality arises from these conceptions which I face as a growing person. In this sense I am both feminine and masculine. I am not both man and woman. I am a man with a feminine dimension.

For Teilhard, the process of personalization is a process by which each of us becomes a person.[50] The personalization process is always the personalization of a man or of a woman. Yet this is not simply the personalization of a *man* or of a *woman;* it is the *personalization* of a man or of a woman. In other words, the goal of my growth is to be a person. The more fundamental concept is person not man. I am to understand sexuality in the context of personality and not vice-versa; to be a man is to be a person. This does not deny the fact that this particular person is a man. But the man-woman encounter is always an interpersonal one. Teilhard, although he speaks of the eternal feminine, is not speaking of a stereotype as such but of a dimension of personality. For Teilhard, this dimension of personality is not limited to the human person alone but is actually a dimension of the entire evolutionary process.

The feminine cannot be identified with woman nor the masculine with man. Each of us is both. My task is not to become a masculine person; it is to become a person, who is in fact a man. Nor is it the nature of a woman to be exclusively feminine; it is the goal of a woman to be a person, a person who is comfortable with her femininity as well as her masculinity. A woman is not a feminine person but a human person. Man-woman and masculine-feminine are different categories. I am a man. This is a biological fact with psychological and spiritual implications. Masculinity is a cultural category and social role. It is a concept external to me, to which I relate. In order to feel comfortable with the fact that I am a man, I not only have to be comfortable with my masculinity, but comfortable with my femininity.

Now I will raise the second question: given the value of bisexuality, what does it mean to say I am a man? First of all, manhood ("maleness" as Stoller would say) is not something I know *a priori*. Although manhood frequently enters into my frame of reference or into my way of speaking, it is not something I can with any kind of precision pin down. Being a man is something I discover and not something I know. I can only tell you what it has meant to be male for the past thirty years, but I cannot say what it means to be male as if there is some essence I can pin down. The sense of maleness is a continuing process of discovery as I experience life.

Being man is not only something I discover; it is something I discover vis-a-vis the other sex, in relationship to woman. I discover many aspects of sexuality with other men. First sexual experiences are often with one's own sex. The first phases of sexual exploration can be with one's own sex. What it means to be a man, however, is not something I discover only in relationships with my own sex. Abel Jeanniere writes, "Woman becomes a woman under the gaze of a man, but one must assert with equal emphasis that man does not truly become man save under the gaze of a woman." [51] Maleness is something about myself that I discover in relationships. I need others to help me find out who I am, and I especially need the other sex in this task of self-discovery.

The process of becoming a man is not a simple one. It is a way of experiencing life in an environment and culture which calls upon me to achieve as a man. I often experience manhood as a striving for masculinity although being male is not this cultural stereotype nor the mystique of masculinity. Being a man does not mean being a masculine person. Yet manhood as I experience it is very much wrapped up with that concept.

A boy will measure his self-worth in terms of how masculine he is. The experience of manhood involves relating oneself to a cultural definition of masculinity and being comfortable with who I am vis-a-vis this cultural stereotype.

Being a man also means experiencing something that a woman will never experience. She will never experience the anxiety that accompanies a boy's first erection, the experience of walking down a street and having a noticeable erection in public, the experience of being a young adolescent boy. As a man, I will never experience the anxiety that comes from the first menstruation. I will never experience the monthly period, childbearing, breastfeeding, and motherhood. A woman will have to differentiate her real self from a culturally stereotyped femininity which is frowned upon and degraded. Each of us has to learn to be comfortable with who we are and to separate our own self-worth from cultural definitions. Ignace Lepp wrote:

If men were one hundred percent masculine and women one hundred percent feminine, they would constitute, psychologically at least, two heterogeneous species. They would not be complementary to each other.[52]

In growing then, I as a boy and as an adolescent and as a man have to come to grips with the fact that I am man in a culture which sets certain expectations for me. I must differentiate my personal growth from these cultural expectations if I am to become the person I freely choose to be. In this process, however, I have to become comfortable with my own sexuality. I have to have a certain sense of pride in saying I am a man. I have to be able to *feel* that I am a man. A healthy sexual identity is a function of self-esteem as well. Nathaniel Branden, in his psychology of self-esteem, points out:

The single most pertinent factor in determining a person's sexual attitudes is the general level of his self-esteem: the higher the level of self-esteem, the stronger the likelihood that his responses to his own sexuality will be appropriate, i.e., that he will exhibit a healthy sex psychology. A healthy masculinity or femininity is the consequence and expression of a rationally affirmative response to one's own sexual nature. This entails: a strong, affirmative awareness of one's own sexuality; a positive (fearless and guiltless) response to the phenomenon of sex; a perspective on sex that sees it as integrated to one's mind and values (*not* as a dissociated, mindless and meaningless physical indulgence); a positive and self-valuing response to one's own body; a strong, positive response to the body of the opposite sex; a confident understanding, acceptance and enjoyment of one's own sexual role.[53]

Robert Stoller, in his research into gender identity, maintains that gender is primarily culturally determined. Although he does not dismiss biological forces, his research points to postnatal psychological forces and the primary role of parental attitudes as being more powerful in creating gender identity.[54] Although his research moves in the direction of cultural and psychological determinants without excluding biological determinants, Judith Bardwick clearly points to biological data as significant.

Endocrine data from animal studies, observations of infants, the longitudinal studies of human beings, and the implications of the endocrine related effects in adult women all lend support to the idea that there are differences between the sexes that have, as one origin, differences in the endocrine systems and possible differences in the central nervous system. The existence of these differences implies that there are modal differences in response potentials between the sexes and it further implies that there are likely to be other differences of which we are not yet aware." [55]

It is too soon to decide the weight that must be assigned to the biological as opposed to the cultural and the psychological factors that distinguish the sexes. The direction of the evidence, however, is more in the direction of the cultural and psychological factors. Even Bardwick, after pointing to the biological differences, writes, "The overwhelming majority of cultures have *socialized* their children in such a way that original differences between the sexes are maximized." [56] And she agrees that "traditional role divisions have been far too restrictive." [57]

Sexual differentiation involves both the concepts of manhood and womanhood (maleness and femaleness) as well as those of masculinity and femininity. Both of these are distinct but interrelated tasks of sexual identity. It is important for sexual identity that the woman have a sense of femaleness and that the man have a sense of maleness, to be able to say and feel that I am a man or I am a woman. It is also important in sexual identity and for the sake of self-actualization for the man to be aware of and accept his own femininity and for a woman to be aware of and accept her own masculinity, to be able to accept that I as male am also feminine or I as woman am also masculine. My maleness or femaleness is biologically and psychologically determined. My femininity and masculinity are culturally and socially defined. Sexual identity is that task which enables me to say and accept positively that I am both man and feminine or both woman and masculine. It is important that I become androgynous or bisexual in order to be complete.

SEXUAL ATTRACTION AND MOTIVATION THEORY

In addition to the motivational concepts of men like Freud, Adler, Frankl, and Maslow, there has been much empirical research into the psychology of motivation during the past two decades. This reasearch covers a broad field and has been brought together by men like C. N. Cofer and M. H. Appley. Although both of these would admit that a definitive psychology of motivation does not yet exist, there is one thing that most of these psychologists have in common—a rejection of the drive theory for explaining motivation.

The drive theory is based on instinctual energy and internal stimulation. Cofer and Appley write, "Instinctual or drive energy was seen to accumulate, as would water flowing into a closed container, and if undischarged, the accumulation would ultimately burst the vessel. Behavior again was seen as regulative so far as this energy accumulation, or tension condition, is concerned. There is an implication of an inexorable accumulation of energy which stirs the organism into regulatory activity." [58]

Robert White writes, "Drives arise from lacks and deficits. They are powerful and persistent internal stimuli which arouse the organism from homeostatic bliss and promote activities that ultimately eliminate the deficit, thus reducing the drive. Reduction of drive supplies the selective principle whereby patterns of behavior are retained or discarded." [59]

The new psychology of motivation lays stress on external and situational factors rather than on internal, enduring states. Deprivation, an operative concept in classical drive theories, is not sufficient to explain motives such as achievement, affiliation, curiosity, esteem, exploration, and love. The declining emphasis on drives and instincts accompanies incentive theories which maintain that external events, either innately or through learning, can motivate organisms or induce states of arousal.[60] Incentives refer to external stimuli such as rewards, situations, knowledge of results, praise, and competition. Some examples are: grades, wages, prizes, social recognition, diplomas. These are positive incentives. There can also be negative incentives such as threats.

Recent motivation theory also involves the importance of discrepancy, e.g., Festinger's theory of cognitive dissonance. Festinger holds that cognitive dissonance motivates behavior. "In general, one might say that a dissonant relation exists between two things which occur together, if, in some way, they do not belong together or fit together. Cognitive dissonance refers to this kind of relation between cognitions which exist simultaneously for a person. If a person knows two things, for example, something about himself and something about the world in which he lives, which somehow do not fit together, we will speak of this as cognitive dissonance. Thus, for example, a person might know that he is a very intelligent, highly capable person. At the same time, let us imagine, he knows that he meets repeated failure. These two cognitions would be dissonant—they do not fit together." [61] Dissonance motivates someone to behave in such a way that he or she might reduce the state of tension to which the dissonance gives rise. "Just as hunger is motivating, cognitive dissonance is motivating. Cognitive dissonance will give rise to activity oriented toward reducing or eliminating the dissonance. Successful reduction of dissonance is rewarding in the same sense that eating when one is hungry is rewarding." [62] A state of dissonance is a stimulus which arouses or activates behavior.

In addition to incentive and discrepancy, much study has been done relating anticipation to arousal states. Cofer and Appley point out that anticipation can arouse or excite an organism and enhance its responsiveness to stimuli.[63] Behavior with anticipation is more vigorous than it is in the same stimulus situation without anticipation. Cofer and Appley speak of an anticipation-invigoration mechanism (*AIM*) to account for the role of anticipation in motivation. They also speak of a second mechanism, the sensitization-invigoration mechanism (*SIM*), to account for those factors, such as the hormonal state in sexual arousal, which sensitize one selectively with respect to certain stimuli. *AIM* depends upon learning and *SIM* does not depend upon learning. There are thus two factors in sexual motivation. "The hormonally ready male rat is more likely to respond to and be aroused by the receptive female than he would be if not hormonally ready or than he would be if the stimuli were nonsexual." [64] Sexual arousal is an interplay of hormonal readiness (*SIM*) and external stimuli or receptive partners (*AIM*).

When drive and instinct theories were dominant, sexuality was seen as similar to hunger and thirst—internal stimulation which sexual activity reduced. Frank Beach, among others, points to the inadequacy of drive theory and the importance of external stimuli in understanding sexual behavior as well as other forms of behavior. He writes:

To a much greater extent than is true of hunger or thirst, the sexual tendencies depend for their arousal upon external stimuli. The quasi-romantic concept of the rutting stag actively seeking a mate is quite misleading. When he encounters a receptive female, the male animal may or may not become sexually excited, but it is most unlikely that in the absence of erotic stimuli he exists in a constant state of undischarged sexual tensions. This would be equally true for the human male, were it not for the potent effects of symbolic stimuli which he tends to carry with him wherever he goes.[65]

The principal difference between man and the lower mammals lies in the extent to which the sexual arousal is affected by symbolic factors.

Sexual behavior today is seen to be a result of two factors: a hormonal condition and external stimulation.[66] Neither of these two is sufficient by itself. Hormonal readiness is not a sufficient condition for sexual behavior to occur, although it is a necessary condition. The degree of hormonal control in sexual behavior varies across species and seems to play less of a role in human sexual behavior. The important factor in human sexual arousal is that of an external stimulus, especially that arising from another person or partner. Sexual behavior seems not to occur in the absence of such stimuli although in human beings these stimuli can be symbolic. There is little value in continuing to think of sexual behavior as a consequence of a 'sex drive.'

Experience also plays a role in human sexual behavior. The variety of forms, positions, as well as attitudes among human societies point to a role for learning in sexual behavior. If sexual satisfaction repeatedly occurs under certain conditions or in a certain place, these conditions or that place are capable of inducing arousal on later occasions. All sorts of stimuli can thus induce arousal on the basis of learning.

I also want to say something about sexual attraction and its relation to love. Sexual attraction is not so much a question of drives and instincts as it is hormonal readiness and external and symbolic stimuli which lead to sexual arousal. Sexual arousal, however, is not the same as love and the two need to be clearly distinguished. Sexual arousal, attractions, and desires do not imply love for another person by whom we are aroused or to whom we are attracted. Too often or too frequently we confuse the two. Sexuality is to be integrated increasingly into our loving relationships. Nevertheless, frequently, there is sexual attraction and sexual desire for others than those whom we love. Love here implies both a deep commitment to and compatibility with the other person.

Love may remain when sexual attraction diminishes. Love may exist in a very deep and real way when sexuality in its deepest physicality does not enter in. Love may exist without the presence of felt sexual forces. Likewise sexual attraction can be experienced apart from affection and love. Too often, due to a misunderstanding of romantic love, we identify sexual attraction with love. This is one of the most serious inadequacies in our cultural misunderstanding of sexual love. This does not mean we should mistrust romantic love but simply that we need to reject that conception of romantic love which says where sexual attraction exists there love is present. Sexual *attraction* is not sexual *love*. A cause of instability within relationships stems from this misunderstanding. Two people who have mistaken sexual feelings for a loving relationship will eventually be frustrated.

Eric Berne talks about the Santa Claus fantasy or the magical orb.[67] Many of us grow up believing in Santa Claus. Although early in life we set aside the belief that Santa Claus exists, we do not completely set aside the fantasy. Much of our lives can be spent waiting for that moment of supreme happiness, waiting for that peak of enjoyment, waiting for that time of complete adjustment which we *expect* to find in this life. It may be finishing a degree, getting married, finding the right job. We are looking to a magical future time. We are waiting for Santa Claus.

Eric Berne tells us that healthy people must learn to resign this particular quest in favor of what the real world has to offer. This does not mean that one has to set aside his striving after perfection nor Adlerians their notion of upward striving. But the striving has to be seen in the context of the world in which we live. In this world there is not and will not be a Santa Claus. When we first come to this realization, we experience some of the despair that comes from setting aside a fantasy that has been important.

For Eric Berne, the closest one gets to such an experience is intimacy. I see another possibility for approaching this and in a later chapter will talk about spiritual joy. Nevertheless, intimacy is certainly one of the ways and a very deeply fulfilling way in which we do find that kind of fulfillment for which we search. The counterpart of the intimacy, as we saw in the Song of Songs, is separation. We are never continually or totally present with the person we love. Even in intimacy human beings do not find a time of total human satisfaction. Even in the climactic experience of a loving genital orgasm, the two people discover after the experience that the two who have been one are still two. The intense moment no longer remains.

Sexuality is not a panacea for human problems. People do look to the sexual world for salvation. Many of the problems that confront us in celibate or married living are not problems that confront us because we are celibate or married but simply because we are living. Many of the crucial and most painful experiences are simply aspects of any way of life. A part of us always continues to cling to the fairy tale that somehow someday I will be happy forever and ever. The adult and decision-making portion of our personality, however, must be ready to accept what the world has to offer.

The adult can differentiate between sexual desire and genuine love. This is not to say that genuine love is not sexual. It is simply to say that not all that is sexual is love. We must continue to distinguish between sexuality and love with the hope that we might integrate our sexuality increasingly into our love life, but realizing at the same time that all of our sexual feelings and sexual attractions are not a sign of deep interpersonal commitment.

HETEROSEXUAL AND HOMOSEXUAL RELATIONSHIPS

I have spoken of two dimensions of sexuality: affectivity and genitality. I have also spoken of two other sets of distinctions: femaleness and maleness, and femininity and masculinity. Now I would like to discuss still another twofold way of looking at our sexual lives, what I refer to as two kinds of sexual relationships: a relationship with a member of the other sex or a relationship with a member of my own sex.

In discussing these two kinds of interpersonal relationships, there are three points I will make: 1) heterosexual and homosexual relationships are two kinds of interpersonal relationships; 2) heterosexuality and homosexuality in pure form both represent extremes on a continuum; 3) the task of sexual identity is not the same as but not unrelated to the task of integrating homosexuality which exists in all of us.

Heterosexual and homosexual relationships are two kinds of interpersonal relationships. I am using the word homosexual here in a positive way and in a way different from its ordinary usage. I distinguish between healthy and unhealthy homosexual relationships, but I do not consider the word *homosexual* to necessarily imply that which in itself is unhealthy. Because we misunderstand homosexuality in our culture, it may be to our benefit to use a different word. To use a different word, however, would be to dodge the issue that healthy relationships can be homosexual. It is important to realize not only that femininity and masculinity are culturally misunderstood, but also that heterosexuality and homosexuality are often culturally misunderstood.

All our human relationships are sexual in the broadest sense of the word. This does not mean that all our relationships include the fullness of genitality. It does not necessarily imply that all our relationships fully involve the affective dimension of sexuality. Yet, I approach every relationship with my own personality, which in fact is a sexual personality. This does not mean that it is only sexual, but it does mean that my sexuality is involved. I approach life as a man as differentiated from a woman or as a woman as distinguished from a man. In no way can I escape the sexual dimensions of my person when I approach another person in a relationship. Sexuality in some way is influencing my way of relating.

This, then, means that at least every affective relationship is either heterosexual or homosexual. If I relate to an employee or a friend, I am relating heterosexually if this person is of the other sex. When I relate to a friend or colleague of my own sex, homosexuality is present. This does not mean that the most significant thing about these relationships or the best way to describe them is in sexual terms. The sexual dimension is not necessarily the most obvious nor most significant aspect. If we do describe the sexual component in the relationship, however, we are talking about heterosexuality or homosexuality.

Different words are used to discuss these two ways of relating. People have spoken about heteroerotic and homoerotic relations. We can talk about heterogenital and homogenital sexuality. A homosexual relationship is not necessarily a homogenital relationship. People have used words like "ambisexual" or "bisexual" to show that every person is not so much monosexual, oriented toward one sex, but oriented toward both sexes. Another word people use is "plurisexual" to indicate that our sexuality is not uni-directional but multi-directional. There is no one innate direction in our sexual lives. Sexuality moves us out of ourselves towards others, towards many others, and towards many different kinds of others.

Every affective relationship involves some sexuality. Although friendships are not best described in sexual terms, they involve the totality of our person. There is more to friendship than our sexuality, but we cannot deny that sexuality enters into friendship. The sexual aspect in such a relationship can perhaps better be described as affectionate, romantic, or somatic. The problem is one of terminology as to how best to describe these two kinds of relationships with members of our own sex and with members of the other sex. Whatever words we use, there are two kinds of interpersonal relationships; both are sexual.

Heterosexuality and homosexuality in pure forms both represent extremes on a continuum. All of our affective relationships are either heterosexual or homosexual. This means that there is a heterosexual dimension as well as a homosexual dimension to our personality. Usually we misunderstand heterosexuality and homosexuality in terms of cultural stereotypes as if we are totally one or the other. Healthy people integrate both, just as healthy people integrate both femininity and masculinity.

A person who is exclusively caught up in heterosexuality so that he is unable to relate affectively with members of his own sex has certainly moved in the direction of pathological heterosexuality (A).* His heterosexuality manifests an inability to face his own homosexual dimension. His masculinity may be so insecure that he cannot incorporate homosexuality into his own personal growth. He identifies masculinity with heterosexuality. Many times this person, seen as the epitome of heterosexual masculinity, is unable to be warm and tender even in his heterosexual relationships because he is blocking much of his sexual life. Heterosexual relationships can be pathological just as homosexual relationships can. Health is not a category I attach to heterosexuality and pathology a category I attach to homosexuality. There is not only healthy heterosexuality but also pathological heterosexuality. It is not homosexuality but *mono*sexuality that is pathological.

Not all homosexuality is pathological; not all homosexuality is an exclusive preoccupation with one's own sex or a total inability to relate to the other sex. A man who is not able to relate tenderly to his own sex is pathologically heterosexual; a man who is not able to relate tenderly to the other sex is pathologically homosexual (B). Pathology enters when exclusiveness with one sex predominates and impairs our ability to relate to both sexes. People need to feel comfortable with and express affection in homosexual relationships as well as in heterosexual relationships.

* See chart on page 80.

Sexuality
within
Relationships

Heterosexuality — healthy — in a heterosexual person (C)
                           — in a homosexual person (E)
                — pathological (A)

Homosexuality — healthy — in a heterosexual person (D)
                          — in a homosexual person (F)
               — pathological (B)

An interpersonal relationship, insofar as it is discussed in terms of its sexual dimension, is either a heterosexual relationship or a homosexual relationship. There is no such thing as an asexual affective interpersonal relationship. It is possible, however, to clarify further healthy heterosexual and homosexual relationships. Healthy heterosexuality exists within a predominantly heterosexually oriented person (C) as well as within a predominantly homosexually oriented person (E). Even in those people whose basic orientation may be homosexual in the sense that they are more comfortable with their own sex or actually prefer sexual experience with their own sex, there can be a heterosexual dimension (E). They may relate well on an affective basis and in terms of deep friendship with members of the other sex although their more basic choice is for their own sex.

Homosexuality can be pathological (B) but it can also be healthy (D and F). When we talk about healthy homosexuality, we are talking about two kinds. On the one hand, it may be the healthy homosexuality that exists in a heterosexual person (D). Even though a person is basically heterosexually oriented in that he or she prefers genital experience with the other sex, he or she may still manifest genital interest in his or her own sex. There is a degree of homosexuality in a heterosexually oriented person.

On the other hand, we can also speak of healthy homosexuality that exists in a basically homosexually oriented person (F). A person who is homosexually oriented does not have to look upon his homosexuality as the unhealthy dimension of his personality and the heterosexual relations as the healthy dimension of his personality. A person whose basic orientation is homosexual still has two dimensions to his sexuality, a heterosexual dimension and a homosexual dimension. Heterosexually oriented people also have two dimensions to their personalities, a heterosexual dimension and a homosexual dimension. These two need not be extremes. They become pathological only to the degree that they exclude the ability to relate to one sex or the other. Generally there is a continuum.

THE HETEROSEXUAL—HOMOSEXUAL CONTINUUM

healthy
bisexuality

pathological   pathological
heterosexuality   homosexuality

Del Martin and Phyllis Lyon write, "The lines of division between previously conceived polarities of heterosexuality and homosexuality are not so clearly delineated." [68] Abraham Maslow writes, "We have learned from Evelyn Hooker to speak of the many kinds of homosexualities." [69] Martin Hoffman in his study of the homosexual also refers to the classic work of Evelyn Hooker:

UCLA psychologist Evelyn Hooker made the classic study that refuted the disease concept of homosexuality. She found 30 homosexuals, not in treatment, whom she felt to be reasonably well adjusted. She then matched 30 heterosexual men with the homosexuals for age, education and I.Q. Hooker then gave these 60 men a battery of psychological tests and obtained considerable information on their life histories. Several of her most skilled clinical colleagues then analyzed the material. They did not know which of the tests had been given to the homosexual men and which to the heterosexuals; they analyzed the tests blind. Hooker concluded from their analyses that there is no inherent connection between homosexual orientation and clinical symptoms of mental illness. She stated: 'Homosexuality as a clinical entity does not exist. Its forms are as varied as those of heterosexuality. Homosexuality may be a deviation in sexual pattern that is in the normal range, psychologically.' This conclusion is based on the fact that the clinicians were unable to distinguish between the two groups. Nor was there any evidence that the homosexual group had a higher degree of pathology than the heterosexual group.[70]

Albert Ellis writes, "Instead of being innately born either a heterosexual or a homosexual animal, man is essentially a plurisexual creature, who easily can be conditioned to copulate with males, females, lower animals, and even inanimate objects. If anything, as many sex authorities have indicated, man is biologically inclined to be bisexual rather than monosexual; so that, theoretically, anyone who is fixated exclusively on heterosexual *or* homosexual relations is fetishistically deviated." [71] Kinsey's research also illustrates the impossibility of categorizing people as simply heterosexual or homosexual. He devised a seven-point scale to indicate the heterosexual-homosexual continuum.[72] Evelyn Hooker, referring to the Kinsey research, writes:

One finds a continuum from those who are interested exclusively in members of their own sex to those who are interested exclusively in the opposite sex, with a large percentage of persons who have been or are currently erotically aroused by both sexes in varying degree. In the strict sense of the word, therefore, the term "homosexual" may be applied only to those who have an interest *exclusively* in members of their own sex; for all others it is necessary to specify the degree of homosexuality and/or heterosexuality.[73]

The conclusions of researchers vary. Kinsey's statistics are being replaced by the research of Morton Hunt.[74] His critique of Kinsey's research on homosexuality as well as the honest appraisal of his own research are invaluable to future research in this area.

Harry Stack Sullivan makes the point that it is simplistic to speak in terms of homosexuality as a category. Saying "I am homosexual," or "I am gay," does not describe one's sexuality.

Since I have set up three classifications of intimacy, four classifications of the general interpersonal objective of the integration of lust, and six classifications of genital relationship, this results in seventy two theoretical patterns of sexual behavior in situations involving two real partners.[75] As a matter of fact, there are only forty five patterns of sexual behavior that are reasonably probable; six are very highly improbable, and the rest just aren't possible. From this statement, I would like you to realize, if you realize nothing else, how fatuous it is to toss out the adjectives 'heterosexual,' 'homosexual,' or 'narcissistic' to classify a person as to his sexual and friendly integrations with others. Such classifications are not anywhere near refined enough for intelligent thought; they are much too gross to do anything except mislead both the observer and the victim. For example, to talk about homosexuality's being a problem really means about as much as to talk about humanity's being a problem.[76]

I agree with Sullivan that it is seldom beneficial simply to describe someone as homosexual. In that sense, to be homosexual would mean to be affectively exclusive and hence pathologically homosexual. In my framework, homosexuality is not necessarily pathological and it is usually simplistic to label someone as "homosexual." In this sense, my earlier diagram is inadequate in that it does speak of "heterosexual" and "homosexual" persons, which is a simplification. I should have spoken there of bisexual persons since I was talking about health. At that point, however, I felt it necessary to speak in that way in order to make the point that heterosexuality exists in those people whom we generally label as homosexual and that homosexuality exists in those we generally label as heterosexual.

Martin Hoffman in his study of homosexuality points quite clearly to the inadequacy of the concept of homosexuality as a disease.[77] Homosexuality may be a deviation of the sexual pattern but is not necessarily psychologically unhealthy. Both heterosexual and homosexual people admit of health and both admit of pathology. Frequently the psychiatric world looks upon the homosexual relationship as being pathological because in fact so many of the people who come for help are indeed struggling with pathological dimensions of their homosexuality. It would also be true to say that the heterosexual people who come for psychiatric help frequently are struggling with pathological dimensions of their own sexuality and in that sense one could also conclude from psychiatric evidence that heterosexual relationships are pathological. Those people whose homosexuality has been well accepted and well integrated do not go to the psychiatrist.

Dr. George Weinberg in his work, *Society and the Healthy Homosexual*, makes a similar point.[78] A sick person is not one who is homosexual but one who fears the homosexual dimension. Weinberg prefers to use the word *homophobia* to describe the traditional attitude of many people. Homophobia is a fear of homosexuality whether it be the fear heterosexual people have of homosexual feelings within themselves or whether it be the fear, self-denial, and self-hatred that homosexuals themselves might manifest. Homophobia and not homosexuality is the disease. Weinberg does not consider a person healthy until he or she has overcome his or her prejudice against homosexuality.

We need not only a re-evaluation of the cultural concept of homosexuality, we need to look at it in terms of our own sexual growth. We need to see the homosexual dimension as a part of our personality. It is necessary to move towards a new definition of homosexuality, a positive definition rather than a negative one, without excluding pathological manifestations. We generally think of a homosexual person as one whose primary emotional and erotic interest is directed towards a member of the same sex. We have already pointed to the inadequacy of this simplification. A better definition, however, is one that comes from the *Gay Manifesto*, where homosexuality is defined as "the capacity to love someone of the same sex." [79] The homosexual dimension of our personality is the facility and the ability to love fully someone of the same sex. This dimension exists within all of us. It is found more in some people than in other people because some people's capacity to love someone of the same sex is damaged or hindered during development. Our goal as sexual beings, however, is to develop both the capacity to love someone of the same sex and also the capacity to love people of the other sex so that neither kind of sexual relationship is impaired by inhibited sexuality.

The task of sexual identity in itself is not the same as but not unrelated to the task of integrating homosexuality. Sexual identity is concerned with being a man or a woman (maleness and femaleness) and feeling comfortable with one's sex. Being homosexual does not mean being less a man or less a woman. Homosexuality will move in the direction of being unhealthy to the degree that it is perceived by a person as a loss of maleness or femaleness. The process of sexual identity is the process of becoming man or becoming woman. It is the process by which I become comfortable in saying that I am a man and the process by which I can identify with my own sex. Sexual identity does not mean becoming heterosexual. In fact, healthy sexual identity means accepting both the heterosexual and homosexual (bisexual) dimensions within my sexuality and being unthreatened by either dimension. It does not threaten my sense of self-acceptance nor my manhood or womanhood. Henri Nouwen writes, "When we are still struggling with finding out who we really are, homosexual feelings can be just as strong as heterosexual feelings. There is nothing abnormal about homosexual feelings at a time in which our life has not yet formed a definite pattern. Perhaps the absence of these feelings is more abnormal than their presence." [80]

Homosexual feelings and even strong homosexual feelings need not and should not get in the way of self-acceptance; they should not prevent confidence in ourselves as men or as women. They should not in themselves threaten sexual identity. If we healthily accept homosexuality, our homosexual feelings, and homosexual relationships, we are moving towards a healthy sexual life. The problem is in confusing homosexuality with a lack of masculinity for the man and vice-versa for the woman. Being a man does not necessarily imply being heterosexual rather than homosexual. Being a man implies being a person, which means incorporating feminine and masculine dimensions into who I am as well as incorporating heterosexual and homosexual dimensions into who I am. Homosexuality can threaten, but need not threaten, sexual identity. To the degree that it does threaten our sexual identity it is destructive. To the degree that it does not threaten us, it can be healthy. It is very possible to feel manly (maleness) and at the same time to feel homosexual feelings. One need not exclude the other. Sexual identity does not mean becoming exclusively heterosexual, crippling the ability to relate to one's own sex, nor does it mean that the person whose primary orientation is towards one's own sex need be looked upon as unhealthy rather than healthy.

There are masculine homosexual men, as Robert Stoller points out: "One can have the rather comfortable identity of being a homosexual (even in the many cases where this is the end product of a stormy, neurotic personality development), just as one can have the rather comfortable identity of being a heterosexual." [81] Homosexuality is not psychologically destructive if it does not destroy one's core gender identity—one's sense of maleness or sense of femaleness. A healthy homosexual person who has satisfactorily faced the task of sexual identity "considers himself to be a male and a man, though he clearly identifies himself as being a man of a particular class: homosexual." [82] Even this particular classification is not the best way for a homosexual person to see himself. As pointed out above, homosexuality is not simply one classification. The task of sexual identity means being able to feel one's femaleness or one's maleness and at the same time accept one's degree of heterosexuality and one's degree of homosexuality, which degree cannot be best described simply as "I am heterosexual," or "I am homosexual." Here again maturity is bisexuality.

The supposed, stable, sexual (either heterosexual or homosexual) identity at which most people arrive can also be a defense due to enculturation and social expectations. Not that this is in itself destructive, but the conflicting tension can be as growth producing as stability. In our culture such a bisexual identity will contain a certain amount of instability. Sexual identity in its most mature phase means being able to *feel* that one belongs to and identifies with his or her own sex, male or female, which identity should not exclude feminine or masculine, heterosexual or homosexual, poles of personal life. Sexual identity which is achieved at the expense of, or to the exclusion of, one of these poles is as detrimental to human growth as is identity confusion.

CONCLUSION

Books have been and will continue to be written on the topic of human sexuality. I began this chapter by raising the question of what it means to be a sexual person. It means being first a person; then it means being affective, genital, feminine, masculine, heterosexual, homosexual, attractive and relational. It also includes the capacity to be a father or mother. Human sexuality becomes more complex the more we discuss it. Many different dimensions of our personality enter into being sexual. Psychology, as does theology, assists the process of self-understanding. We are sexual beings and we continue to wonder and explore what that means. It does not mean simply one thing; a whole language emerges which helps us to convey the meaning and significance of sexual being. As we continue our discussion of sexuality as it is related to celibate life, I will affirm that being celibate does not mean being asexual. Being celibate involves deeply the core of our being where we are not only with and for God, but also with ourselves, our affectivity, genitality, femininity, masculinity, heterosexuality, homosexuality, attractiveness. It is not a question of uprooting sexuality but of becoming sexual in a different way. Sexuality, for the celibate as well, remains a wonderful gift of God, given because He loves us.

3

Chastity and Tactility

TOUCH IS ESSENTIAL to being human, involving the whole realm of non-verbal communication. Among many Christians, however, and within our own culture, there exist fears and taboos. Ashley Montagu in his lengthy study of touch writes, "Perhaps it would be more accurate to say that the taboos on interpersonal tactility grew out of a fear closely associated with the Christian tradition in its various denominations, the fear of bodily pleasures. One of the great negative achievements of Christianity has been to make a sin of tactual pleasures." [1] I do not say that the Christian churches are exclusively to blame. To whatever degree they are to blame, however, they need to do penance and change. Certainly the suspicious attitude towards eroticism and sensuality led to a non-touch and even anti-touch asceticism within the Christian tradition. Touch needs to be rescued from negativity and that is the very purpose of the virtue of chastity.

Chastity is the virtue concerned with touch. All too often, Christian moralists view the virtue as directed against the "dangers" of touch. I prefer to see the chaste person as one who understands, endorses, and integrates touching. We need a chastity which affirms the value of human tactility and the role it plays in our affective and emotional lives. We need to affirm the significance of touch for interpersonal growth. A person who is uncomfortable with the tactile world is not a chaste man or woman, as we will see. Since chastity can be understood only if touch is appreciated, I will first examine the human significance of touch and then the virtue of chastity itself.

THE SIGNIFICANCE OF TOUCH

The sense of touch occurs in our speech when we are not aware of it. We "rub people the wrong way" or someone "gets under our skin." We speak of something being only "skin-deep," of someone being very "touchy." An experience which we feel very deeply is described as "touching." Caressing, clapping, cuddling, eating, hugging, itching, kissing, licking, lifting, loving, petting, rocking, rubbing, scratching, stroking, sucking, all involve touch.

In the mammalian mother, the washing given to the young in the form of licking is much more than cleansing. The newborn mammal must be licked in order to survive. If he remains unlicked, especially in the perineal region (the region between the external genitals and the anus), he is likely to die from a malfunction of the genito-urinary system and/or the gastro-intestinal system. The frequency with which the mother cat licks the different parts of the kitten's body has been studied. The region receiving the most licking is the genital and perineal region, then the regions around the mouth, the underbelly, and the back and sides. The mother licks the kitten three to four times per second.[2]

The tactile stimulation found in the pre-human world continues in the human world as well. In human mothers, there is a long period of labor wherein the contractions provide stimulation of the skin. The contact with the warmth of the mother's body after birth plays a role in continued stimulation. Breastfeeding also continues contact with the mother's body.[3]

Anna Freud has pointed out that tactile stimulation facilitates the transition from the waking state to the sleeping state. Children need warm contact with another person's body before falling asleep. There is a relationship between closeness and warmth. Those whom we experience as being close are described as being warm. The child who is falling asleep needs this close and warm contact. In our western culture this biological fact is frequently disregarded and children are exposed to long hours of solitude. A substitute is often provided in the terms of a pet or toy or soft material. Sometimes thumb-sucking, rocking, and masturbation perform the same service of transition to sleep.[4]

Some forms of asthma are due in part to a lack of early tactile stimulation. Putting one's arms around an asthmatic when he is having an attack can help to alleviate the attack. We are also aware of the need for body contact during intensified periods of stress. Taking anyone's hand during stress or holding him or her tightly reduces anxiety. Strong repressed needs for love find their expression in forms of itching or scratching. Eczema is the unconscious striving for the attention denied to the skin which the skin needs. Body contact is important in establishing a healthy affective relationship. Relationships grow when there is an increasing experience of the warmth of the other's body.[5]

There is probably no experience of massive skin contact in the adult as great as in genital intercourse. Nevertheless tactile stimulation and genital stimulation are not the same and not to be identified, although tactile stimulation can lead to genital stimulation. Just as love and genital expressions have come to be identified in the western world, so have touch and genitality come to be associated. The preoccupation with genitality is often the need for bodily contact. We are tactually deprived and think we are sexually deprived, which means to many genitally deprived. It is important to recognize our need for tactile stimulation without confusing tactile needs with genital needs.[6]

The American culture is a "no-touch" culture. Yet we know that more growth takes place when there is affectionate contact. Margaret Mead, in her study of Balinese children, points out that in Bali the child spends most of its first two years within the arms or on the hip of another human being. Practically speaking, the only occasion when the child under five or six months is not in someone's arms is when it is bathed. The child is carried by all sorts of people, male and female, young and old. The child enjoys different skin surfaces, different odors, and different ways of being held. In our culture the practice of husband and wife occupying separate beds is growing. Separating the mother and baby, dressing the baby in clothes, limits the amount of tactile contact between mother and child. Instead of sleeping in another human being's arms, the child in the western world sleeps alone.[7]

Tactile contact is even more limited between males. I quote from Ashley Montagu:

Tactile demonstrations of affection between mother and daughter are not as inhibited as they are between father and son. The very thought of any such demonstration of affection between father and son is something that makes most American fathers squirm. A boy putting his arms around the shoulders of another boy is cause for real alarm. It is simply not done. Even women are reluctant to indulge in such open displays of affection towards members of their own sex. One touches others largely in a sexual context. To touch others out of such context is open to grave misinterpretation, since touching is to a large extent restricted to and associated with sex. When intercourse is completed the male ceases to touch his partner and usually retires to his twin bed to spend the rest of the time in pleasurable lack of contact all by himself.[8]

Two American anthropologists, Caudill and Plath, studied sleeping habits among Japanese families. Westerners often view Japanese sleeping patterns as a result of overcrowding; Caudill and Plath state that a more direct cause is the strength of family bonds. They argue further, "The frequency with which children co-sleep with parents expresses a strong cultural emphasis upon the nurturant aspects of family life and a correlative de-emphasis of its sexual aspects." [9] Co-sleeping does not necessarily imply sleeping in a Western-style bed; only 10% of the adults in the sample had Western-style beds. The others sleep in mat-floored rooms on a quilt (*futon*) which is spread out each evening and taken up during the day. Sleeping on one's own *futon* is being closer to others, however, than sleeping in one's own bed or crib. The Japanese quilts of several co-sleepers are laid out next to each other with the edges almost touching. One need only reach over to touch or care for another without getting up. I present here only the conclusions of Caudill and Plath's work.

In summary, then, an individual in urban Japan can expect to co-sleep in a two-generation group (a child and at least one of the parents or parents and at least one child), first as a child and then as a parent, over approximately half of his life. This starts at birth and continues until puberty; it resumes after the birth of the first child and continues until about the time of menopause for the mother; and it reoccurs for a few years in old age. In the interim years the individual can expect to co-sleep in a one-generation group with a sibling after puberty, with a spouse for a few years after marriage, and again with a spouse in late middle age. Sleeping alone appears to be an alternative most commonly found in the years between puberty and marriage, and to be a reluctantly accepted necessity for the widowed parent toward the end.

We wish to make one broad generalization, and one speculation. The generalization is that sleeping arrangements in Japanese families tend to blur the distinctions between generations and between the sexes, to emphasize the interdependence more than the separateness of individuals, and to underplay (or largely ignore) the potentiality for the growth of conjugal intimacy between husband and wife in sexual and other matters in favor of a more general familial cohesion.

The speculation concerns the coincidence of those age periods when sleeping alone is most likely to occur, with the age periods when suicide is most likely to occur in Japan. The rates for both types of behavior are highest in adolescence and young adulthood, and again in old age. It might be that sleeping alone in these two periods contributes to a sense of isolation and alienation for an individual who, throughout the rest of his life cycle, seems to derive a significant part of his sense of being a meaningful person from his sleeping physically close by other family members.[10]

There has been conditioning in non-tactility among many Englishmen of the upper classes where touching is culturally viewed as being vulgar. Public demonstration of affection is permitted only to those outside of "sophisticated" culture, the Latins and Russians. Even further in the direction of non-tactility than the English are the Germans. Austrian males are more demonstrative tactually and embrace close friends. Among Jews tactility is highly developed. Americans of Anglo-Saxon origin are not as non-tactile as the English or the Germans but are not far behind. American boys neither kiss nor embrace their fathers after ten years of age. Nor do American males embrace their friends. There are clearly contact-peoples and non-contact-peoples and Americans are among the latter.[11]

There are also noticeable differences in tactility between the sexes. The woman is more comfortable with touch than the man. There is inability in the male to relate tactually to another human being. Women complain generally of a man's lack of tenderness. The male is also more tactually deprived as a child. Girl babies receive more demonstrative acts of affection. This tactile deprivation contributes to the awkwardness of the deprived male even in genital love.[12]

The basic conclusion of Ashley Montagu is that body contact is a basic human need. Affectionate tactile stimulation is fundamental for human beings and is one of the elements in the genesis of the ability to love and the ability to have healthy emotional relationships.[13]

Not only anthropologists and psychologists but philosophers as well point to the human significance of touch. Ortega y Gasset writes:

It is clear that the decisive form of our intercourse with things is in fact touch. And if this is so, touch and contact are necessarily the most conclusive factor in determining the structure of our world.[14]

Martin Heidegger speaks of two kinds of touch when he speaks of two kinds of being. This is his basic distinction between things and persons. Water is in a glass or a bench is in a room. This is different, however, from the way a friend is inside of me. The first is the "being-in" of *things* and is more a relationship of location or place. The being-in that human beings experience is a different kind of being-in. Saying Dan is inside me is quite different from saying the chair is inside the room. When human beings touch each other, there is more than simply physical contact.

Heidegger writes:

Taken strictly, 'touching' is never what we are talking about in such cases (namely the case of a chair touching the wall), not because accurate re-examination will always eventually re-establish that there is a space between the chair and the wall, but because in principle the chair can never touch the wall even if the space between them should be equal to zero. If the chair could touch the wall, this would presuppose that the wall is the sort of thing for which the chair would be *encounterable*.[15]

*   *   *

For Heidegger, of course, *human* being is that kind of being for whom care is a possibility. Care can be communicated through touch. When human beings make contact, it is more than simply physical. Things experience alongsideness but not insideness in the way two human beings get inside each other. Human beings get inside each other in the sense that the other person can really matter.

Tactility in man has a specifically human dimension. One must be aware of the role touch plays in life as well as of what touch communicates. This leads us to be both more free to touch and also more careful of touch. He who touches everyone, *touches* no one. At its finest, touch is an affective sexual expression.

Before I discuss chastity, I want to emphasize the significance of both sexuality and tactility so that our discussion of chastity begins with a positive attitude towards both. The question is how does a positive appreciation of these two affect our understanding of chastity. Chastity is not intended to lead one into a "no-touch" style of life.

THE THEOLOGY OF CHASTITY

The first two chapters and the first part of this chapter move in the direction of a positive attitude towards sexuality. As we reflect on chastity, we cannot set aside this perspective. Chastity is not negative about touch, sexual feelings, and sexual experience. There are two attitudes which have affected the history of Christian spirituality. The first of these is that sexual relations are more or less suspect. A too common attitude among Christians is that the sexual is sinful. Despite recognition of the sanctity of marriage, Christian tradition has not conveyed positive attitudes towards sexuality. The other attitude with respect to sexuality in the history of Christianity is that the sexual is primarily procreative. It exists so that the species might continue. Neither of these presuppositions is the basis for my theology of chastity. Neither is biblical nor is either self-evident in the twentieth century.

Chastity is that virtue concerned with the integration of sexuality into our lives as Christians. It is important because sexuality is important. If sexuality were insignificant to our lives as human beings, we would not have to be so concerned about chastity. *Chastity is that virtue which helps us to utilize the totality of our sexuality and put it at the service of our becoming Christian.* It brings together the sexual and the spiritual. Chastity does not integrate the two by denying or negating one while affirming or positing the other. It affirms both.

We need to distinguish between celibacy, chastity, and virginity. A chaste person is not necessarily a celibate, nor necessarily a virgin. Nor is a celibate necessarily a virgin.

A person is a virgin who has never had genital intercourse and chooses to abstain genitally as a form of dedication to God. I am not speaking of the promiscuous kind of virginity among people who are willing to engage in genital activity but not go "all the way" in order that they might be "virgins" on the day of marriage.

Chastity is not virginity. If one is not a virgin, this does not mean one is not chaste. It does not mean that one cannot be celibate. Chastity and celibacy differ from virginity; neither in themselves demands virginity. I discuss virginity further in chapter five.

So what then is celibacy? It is found in the important distinction between chastity as a vow and chastity as a virtue. The vow of chastity, as it has come to be understood, is really celibacy. Although married people are also vowed to chastity, nevertheless, as the distinction has become part of our heritage, the vow of chastity is understood as a commitment to a celibate way of life.

Chastity as a vow need not be understood this way. The married person takes the vow of conjugal chastity. Nevertheless, when we think of vowed chastity, we usually think of celibacy. I discuss celibacy in the next chapter. I introduce it now to make the point that *chastity is not simply celibacy.* Chastity applies to married life as well. I prefer to approach chastity not as a vow but as a virtue which is important for all of us.

The virtue of chastity can refer to either celibate chastity or conjugal chastity depending on whether the virtue is being lived out in the celibate life or the married life. In either case, however, we are considering one virtue. In our day one can also consider questions of pre-conjugal chastity and pre-celibate chastity. Does chastity imply anything different in a pre-conjugal situation from what it implies in a conjugal situation? Likewise, one could ask a similar question of one who has not yet taken the vow of celibacy but is moving in that direction and is already in religious formation. I will not deal directly with these questions but pose the fact that the virtue of chastity ought to be understood with respect to the concrete circumstances in which one lives. In this sense, then, celibate chastity is different from conjugal chastity and both may differ from pre-conjugal chastity, pre-celibate chastity, or the chastity of the single state. Yet the basic notion of chastity is the same in all of these. Everyone is called to be chaste, since chastity is part of that perfection to which all have been called by Christ. "You must therefore be perfect just as your heavenly Father is perfect" (Mt. 5:48).

Chastity and sexuality are not enemies. Chastity and sexual fulfillment are not incompatible. Chastity is concerned with our sexual lives, but not with a denial or a repression of them. The goal of chastity is to integrate our sexual lives into our Christian lives so that we might be one person and not divided. In order that we be not split in our Christian lives between our sexual lives on one hand and our spiritual lives on the other, we need the virtue of chastity to integrate these two basic parts of our humanity into a unified whole. The purpose of chastity is to integrate sexuality into our total Christian personality.

Virtue is defined as an acquired disposition. Chastity then is acquired; it does not come to us all at once. It is acquired only by repeated action. It is renewed every day in our daily choices. We can in one act take the vow of chastity or commit ourselves to a life of celibacy, but we cannot in one act acquire virtue. As a virtue, chastity is not a state one enters but a lifelong task one chooses to live.

In addition to being acquired, however, a virtue is also a fundamental disposition of the person, a fundamental orientation of the person, a fundamental attitude as well as a way of behaving. The question raised by chastity is how are we disposed towards our sexuality? A chaste person has a healthy attitude towards his or her sexuality. A chaste person has a good feeling about his maleness or her femaleness and about his or her sexual responses. A chaste person has an ability to relate bodily on the sexual level. A chaste person exhibits kindness, understanding, openness, and imagination. A person who is uncomfortable being sexual is not chaste. Chastity begins with sexual acceptance. A chaste person is a sexual person and is in fact a supreme exemplification of what it means to be sexual. Chastity begins by recognizing the attraction, beauty, and pleasure in sexual love.[16]

Thomas Aquinas' understanding of chastity can be a point of departure. For Aquinas chastity is a part of the virtue of temperance, which is the virtue that regulates the pleasures of touch. Aquinas writes, "Temperance is properly about pleasures of meat and drink and sexual pleasures. Now these pleasures result from the sense of touch. Wherefore it follows that temperance is about pleasures of touch." [17] These pleasures are of three sorts: eating, drinking, and sexual or venereal pleasures. Hence there are three specifications of the virtue of temperance: abstinence, sobriety, and chastity. Aquinas writes, "Chastity, which is about venereal pleasures, is a distinct virtue from abstinence, which is about pleasures of the palate." [18] Abstinence is that virtue which gives order to our desire for food; sobriety gives order to our desire for drink; and chastity gives order to our desire for sexual pleasure.

The goal of a virtue is to bring moderation or order into our lives so that we might be more capable of life in Christ. The virtues are not repressive. Their goal is to humanize and christianize living. Albert Plé, in his discussion of Thomas on chastity, makes the point that "a man's control over his passions is imperfect when they suffer violence and are condemned to sterile inactivity." [19] The control of the emotions is not to be violent or repressive. Both Aristotle and Aquinas use an analogy at this point. They say that control of the passions (emotions) should not be modeled after the police methods of a tyrant. They should rather be governed democratically since they have rights of their own. Aquinas quotes Aristotle saying, "Reason rules the irascible and concupiscible powers by a political command." [20] He distinguishes political command and despotic command. Aquinas elaborates what Aristotle says by defining political command as "that by which free men are ruled who have in some respects a will of their own." [21] The language of Aquinas is unfamiliar to us. What he is basically saying, however, is that the virtues are necessary for living properly but should not function oppressively and repressively. Repression would be despotic, to use Aquinas' word. When Aquinas speaks of control, moderation, or order, he is not envisioning something despotic and oppressive. These desires are treated as having rights of their own. They are to be governed democratically.

Aquinas also does not consider pleasure in itself to be evil. He writes, "Some have maintained that all pleasure is evil. . . . But they were wrong in holding this opinion. . . . We must therefore say that some pleasures are good and that some are evil. . . . The pleasures of good actions are good and those of evil actions are evil." [22]

The pleasures of touch are a very important part of life. They therefore need to be integrated into our Christian life. This is the function of the Christian virtue of temperance, which does not act oppressively. It simply moderates one's drives so that a person is not governed by them but in turn governs them. One governs them democratically, however, respecting them. The pleasures attached to them are not evil unless a particular action is evil. In itself the pleasure accompanying them is good.

A final point which Aquinas makes shows his appreciation of these pleasures. Insensitivity to them is not only not virtuous but is a vice. He writes again, not in the language of our day but in the language of his: "Those are called insensitive who are deficient with regard to the pleasures of touch. . . . Now insensitivity is opposed to the virtue of temperance. . . . Therefore insensitivity is a vice." [23] The insensitive man is as intemperate and unchaste as is the carnal and promiscuous man. These are two different extremes both of which do violence to the Christian life. Chastity moderates or orders one's sexuality. It does not make sexuality the end of man nor the enemy of man. Either of these attitudes would be unchaste and unchristian according to Aquinas.

Aquinas' approach, as I see it, is fundamentally right in at least two ways. He recognizes the significance of tactility and sexuality to such a degree that special virtues are singled out to order our tactile and sexual lives and to christianize them. Aquinas is also right in realizing that Christians do not act only for the sake of pleasure. In no way is physical pleasure sinful in itself. This is an Augustinian attitude. Although physical pleasure is not sinful, nevertheless, Christians still do not live for the sake of pleasure.

They live for the sake of the kingdom. Christians moderate pleasure and integrate it into their lives as Christians. This does not mean they repress their desire for pleasure but rather that they order it in such a way that it serves the higher value of life in Christ. Aquinas sees the genital act as basically in order when it serves the purpose of procreation or prevents incontinency in one's spouse. This was still the classical understanding of sexuality as primarily procreative. I disagree with this concretization of the prescriptions of chastity although I affirm Aquinas' basic approach to the virtue, which I interpret in the light of our own understanding of sexuality today. Temperance was for Thomas that virtue concerned with integrating the striving for pleasure within the person into our lives as Christians. He recognizes man's striving for pleasure and sees the need to put it at the service of the Christian life.

Adrian Van Kaam makes an interesting observation in seeing the vows of poverty, chastity, and obedience as efforts to diminish the occasions for making power, pleasure, and possessions the basic meaning in life.[24] For Van Kaam the vows point to fundamental attitudes which help us to humanize and spiritualize these drives so that they do not become inordinate in such a way that our lives are based upon the striving for power, the striving for pleasure, or the striving for possessions. These basic elements within man are recognized by spiritual writers who see that if they are to help man rather than hinder him, they need to be properly directed. Rollo May makes an interesting point when he says that the demonic is any natural function which has the power to take over the whole person.[25]

It is not surprising then that spiritual writers have seen the striving after power, pleasure, and possessions as actually being associated with the demonic since these are really those personality ingredients that have the power to control the personality. It is important not only to recognize the basic dimensions of personality but also to integrate them, humanize them, and spiritualize them. This is the function of virtues. Chastity is not in any way opposed to sexuality. It simply asks the question: how do we christianize sexuality. Chastity accepts man's striving for pleasure, values man's striving for pleasure, and attempts to put that striving in the service of other human and Christian values. It attempts to integrate the striving for pleasure into the other strivings which form the spiritual part of man.

In genital action itself, the goal is not pleasure as much as expressing love by providing pleasurable experience for the other person. One places the intense pleasure associated with the genital interaction at the service of love. This is the most human and meaningful way to view sexual pleasure. Rollo May makes the point that sexual love involves an element of sheer play but at the same time cannot be completely casual.

Sexual love cannot only be play, but probably an element of sheer play should be regularly present. By this token, casual relationships in sex may have their gratification or meaning in the sharing of pleasure and tenderness. But if one's whole pattern and attitude towards sex is only casual, then sooner or later the playing itself becomes boring. The same is true of sensuality, obviously an element in any gratifying sexual love: if it has to carry the whole weight of the relationship, it becomes cloying.[26]

As I see the relationship between sexuality and procreation, it is not necessary to say that genital activity need be specifically procreative. There are other functions, specifically human functions, for genital activity other than procreative functions, such as expressing affection and love. Whether genital intercourse is appropriate only in marriage is another current question. This question is not my primary concern here. As far as this study has taken us, all I will say is that genital activity should be the expression of a permanent relationship which involves fidelity. For the Christian, genital activity is a sign of the relationship of God to his people. In other words, it is a sign of permanent fidelity. This is why genital activity should be an expression of a permanent and faithful relationship. This is not to solve the question, however, of whether there is the possibility of a permanent relationship of this sort which is not institutionalized through marriage but has the fidelity and permanence necessary to permit genital activity. For the Christian, fidelity and love give order to the activity. It is not procreation which gives order to the act but fidelity and love. Chastity is that virtue that moderates tactile and sexual pleasure in accord with the Christian values of fidelity and love so that every concrete genital expression is an exemplification and expression of this kind of interpersonal commitment. Chastity opposes casual and promiscuous genitality.

Much can be said about the living out of chastity and the difficulty it involves. It is not easy to be chaste. Nevertheless we are all called to sanctity, to holiness, to perfection. This is intrinsic to our Christian vocation. Only a disciplined person can live a chaste life. This means that there is a necessity for conjugal discipline as well as for celibate discipline.

Other virtues also help support a chaste life, for example modesty. To be modest does not mean to be prudish. Modesty is simply the most natural thing in the world if a person chooses to be chaste. He is going to have to order or moderate how he dresses as well as what he looks at if he is going to be concerned with a healthy integration of his sexuality. This does not mean that one should shy away from sexual feelings or be uncomfortable with sexual attractions. It is good, healthy, and Christian to find attraction in sexuality. A person who does not find attraction in sexuality is more likely to have an unhealthy attitude and thus more likely to not be chaste. A chaste person appreciates and enjoys the sexual and is capable of integrating it into the total framework of Christian life.

CONCLUSION

In this chapter I have made the effort to articulate a positive understanding of chastity. In the past we have often opposed chastity to sexuality. This dichotomy is unhealthy for us not only as Christians but as human persons as well. Chastity affirms sexuality and sexuality needs chastity in order to perfect itself. Chastity does not mean a negative attitude toward sexuality, nor does a positive attitude toward sexuality mean a negative attitude toward chastity. I see chastity as positive just as I see sexuality as positive. Christian chastity recognizes the human significance of touch. There is not one kind of chastity for married people and another kind for celibate people. There is but one virtue. Both celibate and married are called to be chaste; both are called to accept their sexuality; both are called to integrate their sexuality into their Christian lives. Neither seeks genital pleasure for itself alone. Genital pleasure is always in the context of genital love. Genital love is genitality expressed in the context of permanent love, love that lasts forever, an ongoing interpersonal commitment.

Only a chastity based on a negative understanding of sexuality affirms that celibate chastity is more beautiful or more Christian than conjugal chastity. Celibate chastity is not a higher degree of chastity but simply a different concretization of it. Chastity helps us to perfect ourselves as Christians no matter what the concrete state of life might be. Being chaste is being a sexual person and allowing one's sexuality to serve the Christian vocation. Chastity brings together and helps us integrate what it means to be both a sexual person and also a daughter or son of God.

I offer my own personal definition: chastity is that virtue which integrates the totality of sexuality into our lives as Christian men and women, which strives to unify the sexual and spiritual dimensions of a person whether single or married, which universalizes affectivity in the direction of compassion and sees genitality as a sign of God's love for man by limiting it to a faithful and sustained commitment.

I realize that I must still apply this understanding of chastity to the celibate life. Before doing so, however, I want to proceed with the further discussion of celibacy and virginity. The first three chapters have pointed to the fact that we are tactual and sexual beings; chastity does not direct us away from this fact but towards a complete acceptance and integration of it. After an attempt to understand the meaning of celibacy and the value of virginity, I shall return to a discussion of the sexual life of the celibate. One thing we already know, however, is that celibate chastity is not a no-touch chastity. A no-touch attitude is not chaste. Chastity does not deny the tactile interpersonal world. Aquinas points to insensitivity as a vice against the virtue of chastity; a no-touch attitude is an extreme like promiscuity, not a virtue.

4

Celibacy and Marriage

Too OFTEN we attempt to understand celibacy in cultural and psychological terms only, but I am convinced we cannot understand it only in that way. Celibacy is very much related to one's faith, one's response to Christ, the mystery of God Himself. The following reflections are very much my own. What I say makes sense to me; it may not make sense to others. It is how I see celibacy today; it may not be how I will see celibacy tomorrow.

There are many myths associated with celibacy and marriage. I point out some of these at the end of the chapter. Both marriage and celibacy need demythologizing. Both need to be put in the context necessary for understanding them—that of the Christian life. That is why I will begin the chapter with the Christian vocation in general and not the celibate life in particular. The major portion of the chapter, however, faces the question of the motivation for being celibate. The three topics I consider in this chapter are: the Christian vocation; the motivation for celibacy; and myths about celibacy and marriage.

THE CHRISTIAN VOCATION

In ordinary speech we speak of vocations rather than vocation. The word is most appropriate in the singular, however, and not in the plural. There is in reality one vocation and that is to follow Christ: the call to discipleship. All are invited by Jesus himself to follow him. The call is universal; it comes to both Jews and Gentiles, to slaves as well as free persons, to both men and women. There is no discrimination. This call, however, can be lived out in a variety of ways: as a single person or as a couple, with vows or without vows, by myself or in community. There are many variations of how one lives out his or her response to Jesus. Bonhoeffer makes the point that the call to discipleship is individualized.[1] We experience it differently; we are called differently. Yet we are all called to the one vocation of following Christ.

Roman Catholic tradition has given rise to three major ways in which we live out our call. These have traditionally been listed as celibate life, married life, and single life. These are not totally different responses. Married people seek community and celibate people seek intimacy. The single life is not without couples when we look at the reality of friendship.

I am mainly concerned with celibacy and marriage since these two are closely interrelated in discussions about celibate life. There are two points which I will make. The first is that celibacy and marriage do not necessarily have to be defined in terms of each other. Being celibate does not mean being unmarried. Nor would the best definition of marriage be to define it in terms of celibacy. Being married does not mean choosing not to be celibate. The second point is that although these two cannot be completely understood in terms of each other, they still need to be differentiated.

When I speak of celibacy, I can speak of its significance or of its distinctiveness. In discussing what celibacy means to me personally, I prefer to speak of its significance. Its most significant aspects, however, might not distinguish it from other ways of life. That which is most significant for celibate life might not be distinctive to celibate life but rather something which a celibate person shares in common with a married person.

Let me use an analogy. Two people choosing celibacy can distinguish between a Dominican and a Franciscan vocation. These are two possible ways of concretizing further the one vocation to follow Christ. Nevertheless, that which is most significant about each is not that which is distinctive but that which they share in common: love of God, service, living in Christ.

As a celibate, I can love God and others with my whole heart. This does not mean, however, that a married person does not feel the same. The fact that we share this in common, however, does not mean that I cannot include this in my understanding of celibacy. If I cannot include it, I am forced to leave out what is most significant in my own motivation. That which is most significant might not always distinguish various ways of life. This does not mean there is no need at all to differentiate the two. We do need to differentiate, but we also need to see that the differences may not in the end be the most significant things we have to say. This does not mean they are unimportant. Differences enable pluralism, individuality, and diversity to emerge. Paul uses the analogy of the body to speak about the Christian life. We are not all eye or all ear. The body would suffer if it were simply a nose. Each member serves a different purpose. The diversity of purposes contributes to the beauty and functioning of the body. Yet that which is most significant about each is that it is a member of the body. The fact that it is a member of the body, however, does not reduce it to being the same as every other member.

In our own day, we are witnessing a rise to even further differentiation within lifestyles. Celibacy and marriage seek new forms of expression. Some of these will undoubtedly survive; others will not. Adler's concept of style of life is that it is the individualizing ingredient in personality.[2] If lifestyle is individualizing, one's way of life brings together those whose lifestyles have enough commonality that they can be mutually supportive. Within Dominican life there is individualization and differentiation. There is enough commonality, however, for life in common. Dominican life differs from Franciscan life and Jesuit life but yet there is commonality among all these in their celibacy. All Christian ways of life, although different, share the most significant aspect of their lives in common, namely life in Christ.

Both marriage and celibacy are ways of concretizing the Christian vocation. Thus we cannot compare celibacy as a Christian vocation to marriage as a cultural institution. We can only compare celibacy to Christian marriage.

The opinion of Judaism was that everyone should marry. For Christians, however, marriage is not the only way of living out one's response to God. Celibacy and marriage are both valid. When celibacy is too little understood, as Max Thurian points out, marriage will be thought of as a reality in the purely natural order. It will lose its Christian dimension.[3] It will also lead to the impression that every person ought to marry. If the cultural imperative is that people ought to marry, marriage itself will suffer as a free choice. If there is no legitimized form of the single life, we are not free to do anything other than marry. Karl Barth also has reacted against the naturalistic conception of marriage.[4] Marriage as we understand it as Christians is not simply a natural institution but a Christian vocation. Both Karl Barth and Max Thurian point to the vocational character of marriage and consequently are able to emphasize the vocational character of celibacy as well.

It is important to reject the idea of the superiority of one over the other. One is not better than the other. One might be better for a particular individual, as for Paul, but not in itself. Celibacy is not a more perfect response to Christ than marriage, nor is marriage a more perfect response than celibacy. Both are valid responses to Christ. These are two ways; there are also other ways. If we talk about celibacy and compare it to marriage, we must realize that we are comparing it to Christian marriage. In this sense, then, much that can be said about celibate life can be said of Christian marriage as well. It is not that positive spiritual good falls on the side of celibate life and human realities and satisfactions fall on the side of married life.

There is always a tendency to justify the less common in relationship to the normal, although that may not be the best way of understanding the abnormal or atypical. For instance, the most important thing about a vegetarian is not that he does not eat meat. This is simply the most distinctive thing. We tend to identify a vegetarian as one who does not eat meat because most people love steak. We define the one in terms of a norm. There is no reason as far as I can see, however, why being normal in this sense is more growth-oriented or humanly fulfilling. There is no reason why being like half the population is what each of us should strive to become. Each of us strives to become himself or herself and to actualize his or her full potential in order to give a fuller response to Christ. A more important thing about a vegetarian is that he is trying to become sensitive to life or choosing to live an ascetical life. He may be choosing to carry a non-violent lifestyle beyond the confines of his human brothers and sisters into the world of nature as well. These motivations are seldom thought of because we define him in terms of a norm.

Although the tendency is to justify the abnormal in relationship to the normal, the abnormal seeks to express its own uniqueness. In that sense celibacy does not have to justify itself by continually distinguishing itself from marriage. At the same time we must realize that Christian marriage is as abnormal as celibacy is. Most people tend to marry, but most marriages are not Christian marriages in the sense of faithful commitments symbolic of God's love itself. The Christian life itself is abnormal in the sense that it is not the cultural standard. Celibacy resists this cultural imperialism which makes only one way of life (the American way of life, for example) normative. For the Christian, a cultural norm is never the standard. This is why it is important to have a faithful people or a people of God who give rise to a different environment within which we can understand ourselves. Otherwise the culture becomes the only context man has for self-understanding. Celibacy thus resists cultural imperialism for the sake of the kingdom of heaven and for the good of marriage itself. Celibacy and marriage, although different ways of life, share their most significant dimensions in common. Both are ways of living out that one vocation of discipleship to Christ.

MOTIVATION FOR CELIBACY

Celibacy comes from the Latin word "caelebs," which means "alone" or "single." A celibate person in some way stands alone. The celibate person does not face life "coupled." Every person, in some way, stands alone and every person is, in some way, "coupled." A single person needs friends; a married person needs solitude. Nevertheless, being single rather than partnered is at the heart of celibacy.

I define celibacy as *a positive choice of the single life for the sake of Christ in response to the call of God.* There are many reasons why one might choose to be single, e.g., in order to be a playboy. To choose celibate singleness, however, is to put one's life and one's freedom in the context of a particular response to God. There are two major dimensions to celibate life: a positive choice of all that is implied in the single life as well as putting this choice in the context of the Christian vocation. One does not choose the single life for itself alone; he or she chooses it for the sake of Christ.

Underlying the discussion of celibacy today is the crisis of motivation and the area of conscious and unconscious motivation. Before we can answer the question of why someone chooses celibacy, we must discover meaning in celibate life itself.

Celibacy is an ideal, not the only Christian ideal but still an ideal. Ideals always have been and always will be attractive. In this sense celibacy is attractive, not only to mature people but to naive people as well. When one is first attracted to celibacy, he or she may not have a deep understanding of himself or herself or of that which draws him or her forward. Eventually he or she must seek this understanding.

Celibacy, then, requires conscious motivation sufficient to make an intelligent choice. In a theological framework where the celibate life was a higher state of perfection than the conjugal life, it can be understood why one would choose the celibate life. This no longer seems to be the case, and the question, "why would someone choose such a way of life?" is articulated even more strongly today. It is also true that in the past some chose celibacy because it is attached to priestly ministry without questioning whether this attachment is intrinsically necessary. This too is no longer unquestioned. I might want to be a priest or minister but not necessarily celibate.

The New Testament presents celibacy in the context of eschatology and not as an ascetical practice. It is worthwhile to distinguish between ascetical and eschatological motivation. New Testament eschatology is corporate and social, the eschatology of the kingdom. In time, however, eschatology became individualistic, the eschatology of saving souls, of heaven and hell. Contemporary theological understanding, at the same time as it affirms the significance of eschatology, is moving away from individualism.

Death, heaven, hell, and purgatory are not the primary eschatological realities of the New Testament. We find a much more magnificent eschatology, the hope for a coming kingdom, which is related to our response to Christ in the world. We are charged with keeping his presence alive. We participate in his reign. It is in this context of God's reign that we must seek to understand celibacy, i.e., celibacy for the sake of the kingdom.

A primary motivational stimulus for all Christians is that of striving after holiness. Man's journey through life involves his journey to God. This movement towards God is a fundamental motivating force even though it is dormant or repressed in many people. A basic question for theology as well as psychology is what are the motivational factors in our lives. I spoke in chapter two of the personality theories which sought to articulate motivational concepts in terms of which man can be understood. These concepts seek to explain why man acts as he does.

For Freud this motivational force was the will to pleasure. That which clarifies man's behavior and choices centers around unconscious motivation, the theory of libido, and tension reduction. Adler postulated the upward striving. Frankl, after his own experience of suffering in the concentration camp, labeled the fundamental motivating factor in human life the will to meaning. Exploring elsewhere Teilhard de Chardin's understanding of personality, I hold that for Teilhard the fundamental element and motivating factor in terms of which the person can be understood is the will to union. For Teilhard the drive behind personality is to be united while remaining oneself. All of evolution for Teilhard moves in the direction of differentiating unification.

Spiritual writers throughout history have postulated another reality in terms of which man can be understood, what I would call the will to God, a striving towards God, a drive towards God, or a call from God. The history of spirituality sees man as being-to-towards-God. It is not pleasure; it is not social striving; it is not simply meaning; it is not human unity; it is God whom man ultimately seeks whether he recognizes this or not. The Christian theologian postulates along with the other motivating factors in human life a striving after holiness. I am not saying that Adler's, Frankl's, and Teilhard's concepts are separable from this will to God. All of these are interrelated. They are not mutually exclusive but simply different ways of seeing the tendency of a person to transcend life by some kind of forward and upward movement. This is basic to Christian anthropology. The upward quest or call forward[5] is that in terms of which the Christian lives his or her life and in terms of which Jesus himself understood his life.

Man cannot therefore be understood adequately apart from this fundamental religious dimension, this fundamental spiritual stimulus. This is the motivational factor which helps us to understand the life of Jesus of Nazareth, Augustine of Hippo, and Nikos Kazantzakis. This in no way indicates that man can be understood in terms of the spiritual dimension alone. Man is not only a spiritual being but is also a bodily, emotional, and intellectual being. Many disciplines must confer if man is to be understood: biology, psychology, anthropology, sociology, philosophy, theology, and others. My postulating a fundamental religious factor as motivational for man is not in any way new. It is new only in the sense that we have not integrated it with all the psychological data which we now have.

Religious living is a specific manifestation of man's search for meaning, an affirmation that meaning is ultimately related to God. The religious person is a person who believes in God. A celibate person is one exemplification of a religious person. A person in Christian marriage is another such exemplification. The celibate person chooses to give specific witness to this spiritual dimension. As long as there are celibate people, there will be people who say by their lives that a primary motivational force in man is the desire to be one with God. The same is true of Christian marriage although Christian marriage can easily be naturalized by the culture. Celibacy resists such enculturation. Christian marriage is as much a witness to man's spiritual dimension, but the society in which we live can easily dismiss Christian marriage as simply a natural institution. Celibacy can never be reduced to a cultural institution. Celibates witness to God as a source of motivation in a way that resists naturalization.

The celibate witness points to the fact that he or she believes in God. This is something that secular culture will reject. Even though we hold as American people that we are religious people, it is no longer true, except in the sense of civil religion. Secular culture will reject people who live their lives based upon a reality which is not a culturally endorsed one. Celibate people are called upon to raise the consciousness of people to an awareness of God's presence in the world as well as His future for man. A fundamental motivating force in celibate life is this striving to make God real in one's own life as well as in the world. *Celibacy means love of God.*

Celibacy also means freedom. This is a second fundamental motivation in celibate life. This is not something separate from one's striving toward union with God; it is the freedom to be with God, for God, and to do the work of God. At the end of a celibate formation process, a person should be more free. I speak here of interior freedom, the freedom of the sons and daughters of God, which comes from prayer as well as from a well-integrated personality.

If we choose celibacy, the evangelical counsels make sense. They help us to be free. Celibacy implies free people, freed people, people freed for Christ's work and structures which free these people for his work. Celibacy does not simply mean freedom from family, power, and possessions, but rather freedom for the work of the Father and for the sake of His kingdom. To choose to be celibate is not simply to choose to be single but to choose to be single in order to serve God. A celibate is a person who puts freedom in the context of a commitment. The celibate is freed from the responsibility of raising a family, but is not free of the anxieties and responsibilities that accompany interpersonal living. He or she is never freed from responsible interpersonal living.

A third motivational factor in celibate life is what has been called its sign value but what I would like to refer to as its protest value. Celibacy is protest.

One cannot understand celibacy unless he or she has a different value system from the culture. The church, or people of God, has always been in some form or to some degree countercultural. In some respects, it represents an "anti-environment," to use an expression from Marshall McLuhan.[6] The church is a people within a larger world who are attempting to live out a particular value system which is different from the value system of the culture or society.

The notion of a counterculture as an effort to resist an encroaching secular value system is familiar to us today. It is related to the generation gap, the social and political consciousness of our people, as well as the protest movement and struggle for liberation. Celibacy is lived in tension between God and the world or between Christ and the culture. Celibates are to be holy radicals, holy in the sense of striving to live the life of God, radical in the sense of living out a basically different lifestyle than that endorsed by society. Christian marriage is also a counterculture. Yet Christian marriage is not as able to resist enculturation. Since marriage is such a natural institution, it is easy for the culture to reduce Christian marriage to simply natural marriage. Many people in discussing marriage never think of Christian marriage but simply of marriage as it exists in our society.

Celibacy points toward another value system than the one society endorses; it has social and political implications as well as religious ones. Celibacy becomes an invitation to live out an alternative value system, not necessarily an invitation to live the celibate life but an invitation to understand life differently. Celibacy is an invitation to a society where love and not orgasm is the goal of sexuality and God not comfort is the goal of man. This is not to say that there is anything wrong with orgasm or that there is anything wrong with comfort; it is simply to say that there is more to life than these.

Celibacy is not something valuable in the same way a virtue is. Justice by definition is good simply because its opposite by definition is not. No one would want to live out his or her life on the basis of injustice. Celibacy is not a good in this same way since its alternative, Christian marriage, is equally good. This has to be emphasized since we do not give witness simply by being celibate. We give witness only by the way we live our celibate lives. We are the witnesses and not celibacy. Celibacy does present, however, the possibility of witnessing to a Christian value system in a specific way and being a sign by protesting and refusing to live the culturally institutionalized way of life. This may be one of the most significant dimensions of celibacy in our own times.

These three things, striving after God, striving for freedom, and striving to witness to Christian values are three of the elements in the motivational structure of celibate life. The discussion about celibacy, however, takes place on two levels. There is the level of the ideal and the level of concrete living. I have been talking about celibacy as an ideal. In the concrete, many celibate people do not discover God, do not achieve interior freedom, do not witness to a more human value system. Just as two people do not talk about marriage only theoretically, so I cannot talk about celibacy only theoretically. There are many subjective elements that enter into everyone's choice. No two people choose celibacy for exactly the same reason or same combination of reasons. Individual motivation as well as a mixture of motivations must be recognized in each person's choice. Not only are there subjective elements, there are unconscious elements as well. These unconscious factors, however, are involved in any choice and in all behavior. They are there to be discovered and do not necessarily invalidate a conscious decision. They will be with us for the rest of our lives. We will never be completely aware of all of the aspects of our personality which lead us in a certain direction. Conscious motivation is as significant as unconscious motivation.

The process of becoming celibate is a growing process in which motivation matures. The choice itself matures in living it. A man or a woman is never completely aware of all the motivations that have entered into his or her choosing a particular spouse. They will never be able to completely grasp why they either fell in love with or chose to marry each other. The living out of that life will bring to consciousness elements that entered into that particular decision. New discoveries, however, do not invalidate the previous choice. Celibacy must be placed in the context not only of radical discipleship but also of mystery. It is something that will never be totally understood although it is something which we seek to understand.

Karl Rahner makes the point that decision involves giving up some alternatives in favor of one limited good.[7] A time comes in a person's life after consultation and reflection when he or she must make a choice. One does not make this decision carelessly, without sufficient consideration of alternatives. The concrete decisions in a person's life spring from a tangle of motivations but eventually a decision is made. The time comes when I eventually decide if I want to live out my Christian vocation as a celibate person, as a married person, as a single person without vows, or in some other way. Rahner writes: "Everything beautiful and noble, everything that is or would be possible 'in itself', cannot be crammed simultaneously into one life." [8]

We cannot try all the alternatives. We cannot explore each and then start over in order to live a 'right' one. We can never be sure if the choice we make is the 'right' one. No decision is perfect. It is simply a fact that at a certain time in one's life a decision must be made and then life changes from moving towards that decision to living it out and to continually discovering implications which were never dreamed of ahead of time. When I choose to marry someone, I am not aware ahead of time what marriage to this particular person really will be. Marriage is a continual process of mutual discovery. Not all the factors can be sorted out and understood ahead of time.

Celibacy and marriage refer to two ways of loving as much as they do to two ways of living. They refer to universal love and particular love. Just as I incorporate the feminine and masculine into my personality, so also should I incorporate these two modes of love. They are not exclusive. The celibate way of love is a universalizing kind of love in which the person struggles to love all people. Conjugal love is a commitment to one other person in particular. In marriage, however, I not only want to develop this particular friendship to which I have vowed myself, I also want to universalize myself. Marriage today seeks community. Marriage seeks celibate and universal love as the counterpart of conjugal and particular love. In celibacy as well, I not only love others and God but love some in particular even though I have not vowed myself to them or to him or to her. The vows which I make as a celibate person are different from the vows which I make as a married person, but in both I still seek to love particularly as well as universally. The vows are different and the lives are different but not totally different. The two ways of loving are two ideals and each of us should choose in our lives to love in both ways.

Within celibate life, we seek to be free for whatever the kingdom of God asks. It is not that we do not seek particular friendship. We strive after friendship but also prepare to live without its constant presence. The celibate person consciously chooses a different kind of availability to God's people than married people. The celibate person sustains himself through non-genital relationships. The celibate person needs relationships but seeks these non-genitally. The celibate abstains from genitality but not from sexuality. Celibacy in this sense is not a negative thing; it is not sexual abstinence. It is choosing to forego the genital within interpersonal relationships in order to be free within them to do the work of God. The celibate person, to the degree that he or she is mature in his or her choice, sees celibacy as a positive non-involvement in genital relations in order to be free to love God and to work for His kingdom.

Celibacy is not negativity to sexuality nor to genitality. Nevertheless, our choice in life, although it is not bound up with a renunciation of sexuality nor a negativity towards it, will integrate sexuality into the way of life we choose. In that sense celibate chastity differs from conjugal chastity in the concrete. The choice of the single state is made as a celibate for varied and religious reasons, involving call, response, and faith. This single state requires integrated sexuality and interpersonal relationships which forego genital love. It is, nevertheless, a state which is committed both to love of God and to loving others.

MYTHS ABOUT CELIBACY AND MARRIAGE

Much mythological thinking goes on in our culture with respect to both marriage and sexuality. McCary, in *Sexual Myths and Fallacies* and earlier in *Human Sexuality*, points to myths about sexuality. Lederer and Jackson, in *The Mirages of Marriage*, point out false assumptions many have with respect to marriage. No similar investigation has been done in regard to celibacy. Nevertheless it is important for us to do the same in order that celibacy be better understood and less disappointing. Celibate people can look towards the day of profession or ordination with the naivete of two people entering marriage. They soon find out that life is different from what they had expected. Some of this disappointment can be avoided.

The first myth that I will point out is *the myth of perpetual happiness*. This is not far removed from the Santa Claus fantasy referred to earlier. The myth holds for the possibility of a frustration-free life. In reality such does not exist. Lederer and Jackson write, "Marriage today, by and large, is a disappointment. It is a relationship too frequently not relished but endured." [9] At least one person out of every three who gets married will be divorced in ten years. When we talk about marriage on the ideal level, it is beautiful; the way it is experienced in the concrete is often different. Lederer and Jackson classify marriages into four major groupings: the stable-satisfactory marriage, the unstable-satisfactory marriage, the unstable-unsatisfactory marriage, and the stable-unsatisfactory marriage.[10] Most marriages fall in the two middle categories. Only about five percent of the marriages actually move toward the stable-satisfactory category. If we take into consideration that one out of every three marriages ends in divorce and that only about five percent of all marriages fall within the best of the classifications, we realize that marriage is not an automatic key to happiness.

Not only must we recognize this myth about marriage, we have to recognize a similar myth about celibacy as well. Celibacy for many is a disappointment. If we were to classify the lives of celibates on a similar continuum, we would see that the ideal is seldom achieved. It is a myth to maintain that all celibates are happy just as it is a myth to maintain that most married people are happy. This does not mean that we give up the possibility of finding genuine happiness in life, but that we be realistic about what we expect of life. Disappointment enters into every lifestyle. People should not be disappointed if they are not in a constant state of love.

A second myth is *the myth of normality*. It is a cultural imposition as well as a psychological tendency to define that which is desirable in terms of that which is normal. By normal, I mean being like half the population. First of all, no one is normal. Lederer and Jackson point out that there is no such thing as a normal marriage.[11] The most creative people and the most creative lifestyles are not normal. A self-actualizing person is not normal.

Self-actualizing people are those who fulfill their human potential and the more actualizing they become the more they move away from normality.

Celibates need not feel defensive about their way of life. There is no need to be like everyone else. It is false to think that celibacy is the only abnormal way of life. Christian marriage is equally abnormal. So is radical discipleship. To choose to respond radically to Christ in our culture is not the normal thing to do. To choose to be Christian is to choose to be out of place within the culture in which we live. Jesus of Nazareth was not normal; neither were most of the saints; nor are the self-actualizing people of whom Maslow speaks. Each of us has to accept where we are and incorporate both strengths and weaknesses into our personal growth. To accept as a direction for one's growth a striving after normality is to strive for less than one can achieve.

A third myth is that *sex means happiness*. The question is often raised whether men and women can abstain from genital sexuality and be humanly fulfilled. This way of thinking is based upon the myth that genital sex is the key to happiness. Lederer and Jackson point out the mythological character of this way of thinking. Unsatisfactory sexual experience is not the cause of bad marriages.[12] Maslow states that sexual deprivation is not a detriment to self-actualization.[13] Genital sexuality is not the most important value in life. This is not to say that it is not a significant dimension of life, a central dimension of life, an important dimension of life. It is not, however, the key to happiness. This myth is related to the myth of perpetual happiness. Many of those who believe that they can find a frustration-free happiness in this life feel that it can be found through sexual experiences. If they are not completely happy, there must be something wrong with their sexual lives. Every sexual experience, according to the myth, should lead to intimacy. Related to this myth are the myth of instant intimacy and the myth that genital experience is the same as intimacy.

A fourth prevalent myth is that *marriage cures loneliness*.[14] This is another derivation of the myth of perpetual happiness and the myth that sex means happiness: an inability to live creatively the loneliness that is a part of every person. Loneliness is not the basis for a stable and satisfactory marriage; only love is. People who cannot be alone marry out of desperation and not out of love. Lederer and Jackson point out quite clearly that lonely people who do marry each other in order to correct this situation often discover that the most intense loneliness is that which is found in marriage.

People have to learn to relate, to love, to communicate. Marriage in itself is not a cure. It is important for celibate people to be aware of this since mythological thinking affects the celibate who feels that the loneliness he experiences in his own life can be solved by marriage. There is the tendency to compare something which exists on the real level to something else on the ideal level. We have to be aware that when we are talking about celibacy and Christian marriage we are talking about both as ideals. This is different from living in the concrete. When disappointment comes in the celibate life, the tendency is to compare my concrete living of the celibate life with the ideal of married life. The opposite can be equally true, a celibate trying to justify the celibate life by comparing the day by day problems of marriage with the ideal of celibacy. If we are to compare celibacy to marriage we must compare them both on the ideal level or both on the real level. On the ideal level both are attractive; on the real level both are difficult. This does not mean that both cannot be satisfying. Yet the possibilities for disappointment, frustration and pain in each are plentiful.

A fifth myth is that *the decision to marry is usually free.* Many celibate people think that their decision to be celibate was not free. As they mature in their decision, they come to an awareness of many levels of motivation which were involved in their original decision. We have already spoken of this fact. One has to realize that the same is true of a person who decides to marry. Most people do not make a decision to marry. Their decision is not to be celibate or to marry but simply whom to marry. There is tremendous anxiety for many as they move into the late twenties and realize they are not yet married. They feel pressure. The decision of whom to marry is also unfree in many situations. As two people who have become partners grow and mature, they come to the realization that many other motivations were involved in the fact that they fell in love. Whatever the destructive elements involved in that unconscious motivation, they must be dealt with.

The fact that there is a lack of freedom in every decision should not be alarming. Neither the decision to marry nor the decision not to is totally free.

A sixth myth is that *a person who has not experienced genital intercourse is a virgin*. I will be speaking about virginity in the next chapter. There are those who sleep together with various degrees of sexual expression but who do not have genital intercourse and say they are virgins. A person who has not experienced intercourse is not necessarily a virgin. Virginity implies much more than never having had a penis penetrate a vagina. Virginity is as much an attitude as it is a physical reality.

The above are cultural myths that affect both celibacy and marriage. Now I would like to consider some *myths about celibacy* in particular which exist in our society.

The myth that all celibates are virgins. Secular culture thinks of celibates as sexually inexperienced people. One cannot assume that a celibate man or woman has or has not had genital intercourse. Celibates are discovering what women have discovered, that society does not see them as having sexual needs. Men are permitted to have sexual needs; women are not. The same is true of celibates. They are seen as sexless people. Celibacy does not mean sexual naivete nor diminished sexual needs although this may be true in some cases. Many celibates have been sexually involved at some time in their life, though we have no statistics on how many or how few.

The myth that celibacy means no intimacy. Deep relationships that have been seen by spiritual writers as both praiseworthy and dangerous form between celibate people. Friendship is not absent from the life of a celibate person unless he or she so chooses. Neither celibacy nor marriage are sure paths to intimacy which we all seek.

The myth that intimacy means genitality. Where close friendship exists, genital expression does not necessarily enter. It is possible to have intimacy without full genitality and vice-versa. Orgasm is not the goal of sexuality nor the goal of intimacy. Although it is the most intense of the physical pleasures, it does not necessarily increase the psychological and spiritual intimacy which friendship seeks.

The myth that celibacy is total sacrifice. Discipleship in any form involves sacrifice. Christian marriage involves sacrifice as does celibacy. There is no value in maintaining that one is more of a sacrifice than another. Celibacy, even as an ideal, is not all giving up. There is so much that is gained. People ask celibates the question, "How can you give up so much?" This reflects a particular value system. Celibacy is a positive choice. It is not that I choose not to have some things; I choose to have other things which are to me more important. Celibacy should be a deep engagement in counterculture because the person sees that there is value there and not only sacrifice.

The myth that one chooses celibacy because he (she) has not considered other options. Most celibates look at options more seriously than most non-celibates do. A person does not choose celibacy from a lack of experience or a lack of options. Some do, and this gives rise to immature decisions. This is the myth that one who falls in love would never choose to be celibate because he or she would have really discovered the greater value. People do not choose celibacy because of unawareness or inexperience. Celibacy results from a combination of factors involving call, choice, response, circumstances, mystery, and God.

Next I want to mention some *myths among celibates* realizing that many celibates are affected by the above myths as well. The following are more exclusively celibate myths than the above societal myths:

The myth that physical virginity automatically promotes and symbolizes universal love and union with God. Abstaining from genital intercourse does not necessarily mean closeness to God or increased ability to love. The foolishness of this is found in the cold and unfriendly celibate who loves no one but says he loves God. Simply because he is celibate does not mean he is loving. Physical virginity does not automatically lead to love any more than physical sexuality leads to love. Neither genital involvement nor genital abstinence are automatic. They are simply different ways of loving. Chastity, celibacy and virginity are not primarily concerned with genital abstinence as a way of life. Abstinence in itself is not the heart of celibate life. We can have on the celibate side the same thinking we have on the cultural side, where people think that if they have not had intercourse they are virgins. Some celibate people think that because they have not had intercourse they are celibate. To have or not to have intercourse is not the question. Virginity and celibacy imply much more.

The myth that we can achieve union with God through our own efforts. This semi-Pelagian tendency lies behind some spiritualities although never having been endorsed in sound theology. Cassian wrote, "Excess of fasting and gluttony come to the same thing." [15] Although many would not claim this myth, they frequently live it. A regular schedule, increased fasting, increased spiritual exericses, and vows do not mean holiness. Union with God does not come through external practice. We can only dispose ourselves for that union which is always His gift.

Not only, so to say, does the habit not make the monk, neither does the rule, nor material obedience to a superior, nor any practices that may be laid down but only the interior life to which all practices are ordered, the life which no practice, however well ordered, can produce of itself. The true monk is not and never will be the man who has succeeded in conforming his conduct to a framework, however ideal; he is the 'spiritual man' above all, and the 'spiritual man' who is judge of everything and who cannot be judged by an exterior criterion.[16]

The myth that the main problems in celibate life are sexual. This is not to say that many problems in celibate life are not sexual. Sexual problems in celibate living have to be understood and handled constructively. Many problems of the celibate experience revolve around loneliness and intimacy. This is also true, however, of marriage. Many of the problems of celibate living are not a result of the fact that it is celibate but that it is simply living. Many of the problems are a part of life and any person who lives life deeply will experience them. Many problems in celibate life revolve around interpersonal relations and many revolve around our relationship to God. The main problems are not simply sexual. Sexual problems exist but frequently are symptomatic of other issues.

The myth that the main problems in celibate life can be solved spiritually. Prayer is not the solution to every problem. Spiritual direction and prayer are necessary, but not all problems can best be resolved in this way. Some problems are emotional and require psychological counseling or therapy. A good spiritual director is aware of this. The core of celibate living is the spiritual life and problems that exist on the spiritual level must be dealt with. This does not mean that every problem is best dealt with through strictly spiritual means.

The myth that celibate life can grow without the ardent desire to love God. I do not know how prevalent these myths are. I simply know that they exist. There are those who feel that human motivation is sufficient for living celibate life. To some degree this is true. There are people who choose the celibate life for human reasons. For a Christian celibate to grow, however, he or she needs the desire to love God more and more experientially.

CONCLUSION

The freedom of the sons and daughters of God accompanies acceptable diversity within the body of Christ. Just as the body is made up of many parts, so is the Christian community. Just as a body would be less if it were all eye or all leg, so would the Christian community if there were not men, women, Indonesians, Latin Americans, Mennonites, Anglicans, blacks, whites, celibates, single men and women, married men and women, and many, many more. Celibacy not only contributes to the diversity within the one body; it also exhibits diversity within itself. The celibacy of the secular priest, the celibacy of the hermit, the celibacy of the cloistered contemplative, and the celibacy of an apostolic religious community are all different.

It is impossible to delineate all the motivation involved in choosing celibacy. The reason a diocesan priest, a cloistered nun, or a religious brother choose celibacy are all different and very much related to the total choice of what they want to do with their lives. In the end the decision to be celibate is very existential. A person who has the charism to live one kind of celibacy might not have the charism to live a different kind. There are also individual differences. Each person's answer to the question will differ. In every case, however, Christian celibacy is related to the spiritual life of the person. One cannot grasp the celibate's choice apart from a clear understanding of his or her spirituality. Chastity as a virtue is concerned with our sexual lives. Celibacy, however, as a way of life, is not a decision about our sexuality as such. Once the decision to be celibate is made, celibate chastity will integrate the sexual dimension into that decision. The decision to be celibate is related to one's spiritual goal. If someone asks why a person chooses celibacy, the response must begin with a mutual exploration of their spiritual lives.

The decision to be celibate is not the most important decision the celibate makes about his life. The most significant thing about being a celibate is life in Christ, being a member of the body of Christ, preparing the way of the Lord. Celibacy must be seen in that context along with marriage and along with the other variations of the one fundamental call which Jesus of Nazareth issued. Our basic vocation is to follow Christ.

5

Virginity and Faith

THREE WORDS frequently used in discussions concerning celibate sexuality are "celibacy," "chastity," and "virginity." Christian celibacy, as defined earlier, is a vowed way of life in which a person chooses, through the single state, to consecrate himself to God.

Chastity is a virtue necessary for all Christians trying to live the life of Christ. It can be either celibate or conjugal and is concerned with putting sexuality at the service of Christian living.

Virginity, as I will be using it, has both a physical and a spiritual dimension. A person is physically virginal who has never had genital relations. Not having had genital relations is not sufficient, however, to maintain that one is a virgin; virginity also means living one's life as an act of faith. Both of these dimensions are essential to virginity as I use the word. Not every chaste person is a celibate person; not every chaste person is a virgin; not every celibate is a virgin. A virgin is one who has integrated the sexual and spiritual dimensions of life in such a way that genital abstinence is integral to his or her spiritual life. The two dimensions of virginity are its physicality and its spirituality. One cannot have the physical dimension without the spiritual, nor vice-versa, and still consider oneself to be a virgin in the Christian sense.

Mary has undoubtedly been a supreme exemplification of virginity. Before we explore the meaning of virginity in our day, it is important to consider the virginity of Mary. My own opinion is that Mary need not be seen as a virgin in the sense in which I use the word. Yet her witness to faith remains supremely significant. Just as we spoke of the sexuality of Jesus, so we can speak of the sexuality as well as the virginity of Mary. Mary was a person who integrated her own sexuality into her life of faith. In this sense, she is a supreme exemplification of the life of chastity. She was not celibate; she may not have been a virgin. The significance of her chastity still remains. After exploring the sexuality of Mary through the doctrine of her virginity, I will explore further the real question of the significance and value of virginity for us today.

THE SEXUALITY AND VIRGINITY OF MARY

There are three questions I want to address in discussing the virginity of Mary: 1) What can we say about Mary's virginity from the perspective of the teaching of the Roman Church? 2) What can we say from the perspective of the biblical material? 3) What is the meaning or significance of Mary's virginity?

The triple formula with respect to Mary's virginity: *ante partum, in partu, post partum* goes back as far as Augustine. In English, the teaching of the Roman Church has been that Mary was a virgin *before*, *during*, and *after* the birth of Jesus. Each of these is a question in itself. I am concerned only with her virginity *ante partum* (before Jesus' birth) since this is all the Scriptures refer to.

The physical virginity of Mary is not a defined doctrine in the sense of an explicit teaching on the part of the extraordinary magisterium. I am using technical theological terms at this point. Officially the doctrine has the status of what theologians call *de fide sed non definita*.[1] This means that it is a teaching of the ordinary magisterium. The extraordinary magisterium, sometimes called the solemn magisterium, is the Roman Church teaching officially but in an extraordinary or solemn way, namely by means of an ecumenical council or the pope, whose intention is to speak infallibly. The teaching concerning Mary's virginity is not of this sort—*non definita* (not defined).

Mary's physical virginity, however, still pertains to the faith, *de fide*, as theologians would say. This means that it is a teaching of the ordinary magisterium in its day-to-day work. The teaching of the ordinary magisterium is binding on Roman Catholics in varying degrees and yet is not as clearly understood. Teaching at one time considered to be true by the ordinary magisterium is no longer taught as true, e.g., creation in six days.

The teaching on Mary's virginity is challenged today by those who consider themselves orthodox as well as by those who reject the Christian faith. It is questioned by those who not only accept the divine sonship of Jesus but also feel that the virginity of his mother symbolically points to that divine presence. In other words, although the physical virginity of Mary is still officially taught as a part of the ordinary magisterium, it is questionable whether it will continue to be taught in that way. The Church has not solemnly defined it and the reflective Christian will continue to grow with the debate. Piet Schoonenberg is one in particular who objects to the argument from the ordinary magisterium.[2] I would agree. The doctrine and its meaning are being questioned and it will become increasingly difficult to uphold on the basis of an argument from the ordinary magisterium.

Matthew and Luke seem to have believed that Mary did not have intercourse with Joseph. Their accounts are what biblical scholars today refer to as "infancy narratives." These narratives are a different kind of material from the rest of the Gospel material, and their historicity is· questioned due to the kind of material we have in the scriptures. Scripture is not science. Nor is it primarily history in the sense that we understand history. It is salvation history but not history in the sense of an actual account of past events recorded for the sake of an accurate record. Historicity and salvation history are two different things. Historicity refers to the reliability of the documents with respect to past historical facts. Salvation history refers to an interpretation of the past and its influence on the present.

There is much material in the New Testament which is not concerned with the accuracy of past events for the sake of accuracy. Some of the material tells a story which has existential and theological significance. The biblical writers were not concerned about factual history as much as about the story of their own salvation. The fact that we have an account of something in the

New Testament does not immediately mean that what is recorded is historical fact. It may have a significance over and above or even apart from its historical dimension. On the other hand, this is not to say there is no accurate history in the New Testament. It is simply to say that not all of the New Testament is of that sort. We can only know which facts are historically accurate through critical research into the Gospel narratives themselves. The infancy narratives in the Gospels are considered by many not to be history in the strict sense.

Another way of posing the problem is to say that the Gospels themselves represent the theology of the early Christian community. The Gospels do not give us lives of Jesus. There was that phenomenon in the nineteenth century which scholars today refer to as "the quest for the historical Jesus." The quest was brought to a peak by Albert Schweitzer and has been renewed along different lines since then. One of the results of the nineteenth century quest was the realization that the Gospels are not biographies. They are not concerned with the *curriculum vitae* of Jesus.

To base the virginity of Mary upon the historical validity of the material in the infancy narratives of Matthew and Luke is a difficult task. This is not to say that the material is *not* historical; it is simply difficult to form an argument when the only basis is the historicity of this material. It is not likely that anyone would have been interested in Jesus' conception until after his resurrection. Then the people would have begun to ask the question: "Who was this man?" Then the traditions about his virginal conception would have developed. If the awareness of his virginal conception had existed during Jesus' own lifetime, it would be difficult to reconcile that awareness with the kind of Christology we find in the Gospel materials—a Christology which affirms the gradual unfolding of Jesus' mission and a developmental process of growing self-under-standing.[3]

It is not necessary to maintain the virginal conception in order to hold to the fact that Jesus was born of the Holy Spirit or that Mary conceived by the Holy Spirit. This kind of causality, the action of the Holy Spirit, does not demand a virgin birth. The Holy Spirit does not act apart from, but within, the natural course of events.

Jesus may well have been conceived both through human inter-course as well as through the action of the Holy Spirit. Divine activity does not preclude human or natural activity as well. God's creativity acts within the process of human procreativity. Jesus' divine sonship and his conception through the power of the Spirit do not require a physical miracle.[4]

A theology of celibacy or a theology of sexuality centered on the life of Mary would be a well-founded one. One looking to her physical virginity as an historically established fact is doomed to frustration. Mary is not necessarily an exemplification of virginity as I use the word. The question is then raised: what is the significance of this doctrine and what does it tell us about the life of Mary, who has been, is being, and will continue to be a model of the spiritual life?

Mary may or may not have been a virgin in the sense that I am using the word; she was, however, a chaste woman. She was a woman who was able to put her sexual life at the service of her relationship to God; she was a person whose sexuality did not prevent her from living a life of total dedication to God. In that sense she is seen in the history of spirituality as a supreme exemplification of the life of chastity. She was not celibate; she may not have been a virgin; but she is a supreme exemplification of the chaste life. Everything within her was ordered towards doing the will of God.

Luke's account of Mary's response to the angel Gabriel makes the point that the core of her response is in the context of her fidelity to God. The angel has communicated to her that she is to conceive although she is a virgin. Her final response is: "I am the handmaid of the Lord. Let what you have said be done to me" (Lk. 1:38). Mary does not consider her previous virginity to be an absolute in such a way that it would prevent her from being the handmaid of the Lord. She sees her mission at that point in life as doing the will of God. The totality of her life as it is seen in the scriptures, little though there may be, reveals that her life was lived out in the context of fidelity. Her response, "Let what you have said be done," is not unlike her son's later response, "Not my will but Thine be done." Nor is it unlike the way Jesus himself later teaches people to pray: "Our Father, thy will be done." This notion of doing the will of God is at the heart of the life of Mary. It is not her virginity but her faith that is significant.

It is difficult for people today to fully appreciate the notion of spiritual existence. Martin Heidegger has spoken of man as "being-toward-death." This is true; yet it is also true to say that man is "being-toward-God." To be a man is to be a daughter or son of God; to be a man is to be called by God; to be a man is to be a person whose being is basically oriented toward union with God. This is the kind of being that you and I have. This is holiness, sharing God's life. Holiness, of course, most appropriately applies to God alone. Yet man's being is that kind of being which is ordered towards union with God.

Mary in her life of dedication to God as a young Jewish girl gives witness to this life of holiness. It is not so much that she is "Virgin Mary" as that she is "Holy Mary." Whether or not her virginity remained throughout her life is not the question; she remained true to God throughout her life and therefore true to herself. She was a supreme exemplification of holiness. Holy Mary was the mother of Jesus of Nazareth.

Mary's virginity, then, is most appropriately understood in this context of chastity, faith, holiness, and prayer. She is the model of the prayer later to be taught by her son, "Thy will be done." She teaches us how to pray; she teaches that the apex of prayer is an act of faith. Whether we speak of Mary as a virgin or not is really not the important question. If we wish to interpret our understanding of virginity so that we see virginity not only in its physicality, but also in its holiness, Mary remains a supreme exemplification of the virginal life. The essence of virginity is union with God. Insofar as Mary is an exemplification of faith and holiness, she is an analogous exemplification of virginal living. In this sense, she always has been and will continue to be the virgin *par excellence*. She gives us true testimony as to what virginity really is, a life lived in search of and service of the Father.

Although I open to questioning Mary's physical virginity, I realize that the official opinion of the Roman Church still teaches it. I do not feel, however, that my opinion in any way destroys the significance of Mary in the life of the Church. I do feel, however, that her virginity cannot be the argument for virginity today. She may not have been a virgin. We can look to her, however, for a deeper understanding of chastity and faith. My discussion here is not intended to contribute to or resolve the question of Mary's virginity but only to point out the limitations of basing a theology of virginity today upon Mary's virginity *ante partum* as historical.

THE SIGNIFICANCE OF VIRGINITY TODAY

Celibacy and virginity are not the same in our culture as they were at one time in history. Yet they are visible expressions of a Christian system of values which will always speak to people and call them forth to fulfill their real human potential. Virginity, a celibacy which has never experienced genital love, does not necessarily excel a celibacy which has experienced genital love. Neither celibacy nor virginity are values in the same way that justice is. Justice is a value by definition because its opposite, injustice, is destructive of social life. Celibacy and virginity are not values in this sense because their alternatives are not destructive of human growth. Christian marriage is of as much value as celibacy; genital intercourse is of as much value as genital abstinence. Celibacy and virginity are not valuable by definition; like marriage, they become valuable because of the role they play in the life of a particular person. Celibacy and virginity give witness only insofar as a person in his or her totality gives witness and insofar as this particular dimension has become integrated into who that person is.

Many celibate men and women hold that virginity has a sacramental dimension, that virginity is a special sign, that it is an eschatological sign. This is true. But it is also true to say that genital union is sacramental. Sexual existence is also an eschatological form of existence. Every dimension in a Christian person's life can be both sacramental and eschatological. Human relationships ought to be signs of the possibility of eternal love. Genital union, by means of which two become one, can be a sign of that kind of love which lasts forever.

Marriage and virginity in themselves are not sacramental. In themselves they are not Christian ways of life. Insofar as they are

Christianized, they become sacramental. Christian marriage and Christian virginity are both sacraments of a value system whose basis is faith in God. Marriage and virginity are then potentially sacramental. Neither is immediately sacramental.

It is interesting to look at some of the statistics reported by Alfred Kinsey in his study of the sexual experience of the human female. He researched the sexual experience of those with no coital experience whose experience had involved at least the body contact of kissing. Kinsey found the following: [5]

100% — kissing
74% — deep kissing
72% — manual stimulation of the breast
32% — oral stimulation of the breast
36% — received masturbation
24% — performed masturbation
17% — contacted bare male genitals with her own
3% — received oral genital contact
2% — performed oral genital contact

Setting aside the question of the adequacy of the statistics, they are still revelatory. This is a report of the sexual experience of "virgins."

There is an understanding of virginity operative in our culture other than the Christian understanding, just as there is a concept of marriage in our culture other than the Christian concept. The doctrine of virginity in our culture is only physical, and not a physical expression of an interior life. It represents, in other words, a lack of integration. The people studied by Kinsey are only physically virgins. They are not necessarily interiorly virgins. The cultural understanding is that a person is a virgin if the penis has not penetrated the vagina. Herbert Richardson has written, "It is clear that the sexual competences required by American society are acquired through a long process of experimentation and 'line-drawing.' For 'dating,' including that long rationally sequentialized process of increasing sexual intimacy sometimes called 'petting,' is a highly stylized institution." [6] Culturally, virginity is more a question of "line-drawing" than it is of chastity.

Virginity understood only in its physical dimension is not virginity as a physical expression of a spiritual reality. Virginity culturally understood is not Christian virginity. A person is truly a virgin only insofar as his or her physical virginity is in accord with an interior life. The interior reality gives life to the physical virginity. If the interior reality is lacking, the external reality will never be significatory. Physical virginity, then, is not intrinsically and necessarily a sign. It is a sign in those people and in those situations where in fact it makes visible an inner reality.

A culture which does not respect spirituality is not going to respect virginity. To live in a secular society is more akin to living in the first centuries of Christianity than to living in medieval times. The height of Christian life in the first couple of centuries was the experience of martyrdom. Christian life then found itself in a social situation unfriendly to its values. The same is true of Christian life in America today. This is not to deny the positive potentiality within the process of secularization. It is simply to say, however, that one of the effects of this process is that it does not necessarily endorse spiritual values.

The society in which we find ourselves today, secular and technological, is hardly going to be appreciative of Christian virginity. American society endorses religion only insofar as it needs religion in order to maintain its own status and power. It endorses religion in the form of civil religion, the American way of life.[7] A nation which promotes its own civil religion is not going to be a nation which consciously promotes supra-national religious living. Civil religion might respect religious life in order not to make enemies of those religious people whom it needs in order to appear Christian.

A culture which rejects the value of Christian virginity is saying more about itself than it is about the virginal life. We are talking about a culture which is basically a culture against man.[8] We are talking about a culture which is in fact not Christian even though at times it may pretend to be so. The virgin certainly exemplifies a different way of understanding sexuality than the one which the culture supports. A culture which depends upon consumerism and advertising and which looks upon sexuality as a marketable commodity is not going to be a culture which is trying to promote a deeper appreciation of sexual life. It is a culture which uses the sexual for its own economic purposes.

I am not saying that a countercultural perspective necessarily leads to a positive appreciation of virginity. My own view is that virginity is a less significant aspect of the Christian life today than radical discipleship lived out in the context of political and social action. The kind of Christian response needed today is akin to that of the martyr in the early days of the Church. The emphasis on virginity in the history of Christianity accompanied monastic development. Monastic development, however, was very much a response to a culture which was friendly to Christianity. Monasticism was the response of people who wanted to live radical Christianity within a society that had begun to accept Christianity. Virginity, then, became one form of radical Christian response when martyrdom was no longer a possibility.

In our day, we are between a society which is openly hostile to Christian life, persecuting it, and a society which is accepting and supportive of Christian life. The relationship between state and church in our society places us very much between these two kinds of situations. Christian people in every age have to discern their own response to Christ in the context of the culture and society in which they find themselves. Martyrdom was one response; monasticism and virginity were others. The question is what the appropriate response of Christian life is today. What does it mean to be a disciple of Christ in Western society? What does it mean to live the radical life in our own day? Virginity is not necessarily a radical response although it can be a sign of a radical response if the life of the virgin is indeed radical.

Virginity is meaningful when it actually speaks. Virginity is meaningful if and only if it communicates a radically human value system. Many "virgins" who consider themselves virgins physically are not truly virgins. Likewise many who consider themselves Christian virgins are Christian virgins only nominally. Virginity will not communicate simply because it is genital abstinence; it will only communicate when it makes visible a value system which appeals to the deepest and highest dimensions of human existence. The question is not whether virginity is valuable; the question is what Christian virgins today are communicating. Rejection of virginity is not the fault of our society alone; Christians are also to blame.

For a person who fully appreciates the genital life, virginity is a sacrifice. This does not mean that it is negative or repressive. It means that in choosing virginity one is setting aside other deeply human and Christian experiences. I would like to explain this once again by using the analogy of vegetarianism. A vegetarian is not a person who does not like meat, a person who does not eat meat because he or she has no taste for it. He or she is a person who has experienced a positive motivation which lies underneath the vegetarian lifestyle. A vegetarian is a person who is motivated for other reasons than dislike of meat not to eat meat. In either situation, the person has made a positive choice about life which means that he or she is not going to fit into the culturally accepted way of life. A vegetarian as well as a virgin is a person who chooses to experience life differently. There is still value in the notion of virginity as a renunciation of sensual pleasure. This does not mean a negative attitude towards sensual pleasure. It means a choice of an ascetical lifestyle in order that one might experience one's culture in a way different from other people.

The theology of virginity can be understood in the context of the theology of celibacy. A life of virginity chosen for the sake of being celibate carries with it the same kind of motivation of which I spoke in the previous chapter. If there is value in celibacy, then there is value in virginity. This does not mean that all celibates are virgins. It does mean, however, that a person who has never experienced genital intercourse may choose at some time in his or her life to become celibate. This decision to become celibate involves for that person the vow to remain a virgin.

A question often raised is whether a person ought to experience genital intercourse before taking celibate vows to abstain from it. Should a celibate person have first a total experience of genital sexuality? This question is raised today both in society and in celibate communities. There are and will be different opinions. Some feel that it is foolish even to ask this question. Others feel it is foolish to give up something without experiencing it first. I offer my own opinion here.

Rollo May writes, "Where the Victorian didn't want anyone to know that he or she had sexual feelings, we are ashamed if we do not. . . . The Victorian nice man or woman was guilty if he or she did experience sex; now we feel guilty if we *don't*." [9] What is actually foolish, in my opinion, is to say definitively either that one should have genital relations or that one should not even consider having them. Sex is not the solution to the problems of human life. It is one area of human life that provides beautiful experience. There are many issues involved in the question, too many to say that one should have genital relations before making a final commitment to celibacy. Such an opinion sets aside the contextual and developmental aspects of our lives. A person cannot plan his life in such a way that he experiences all he might want before he makes a commitment. A time eventually comes in a person's life for making a final and permanent commitment. It may not come until the late twenties or early thirties, but it must come. The time comes in a person's life when he or she chooses to accept celibacy and then chooses to live out the celibate life in accord with that choice. If he or she has had genital intercourse prior to that commitment, fine; if he or she has not had genital intercourse, fine.

To say that a person should have genital relations before making such a decision indicates two unacceptable attitudes. To affirm that he should have genital sex first means either that he delay his decision and commitment until he has had the experience or that he have sex now before making that commitment. Neither of these is possible from a developmental point of view. The time comes in my life when I feel called to make or am desirous of making a decision about my life. That decision and the path that leads to it are parts of my own personal development. It is not something that I can always delay in order to increase my experience. I may want to get on with what I want to do with my life. I may decide to marry Joan and not feel that I want to wait until I fall in love with someone else in order to see whether I really want to marry Joan. The decision involves feeling convinced that this is it and what I want to do with my life. There is no reason to delay it.

To seek genital experience quickly before making the commitment is a naive attitude unaware of the nature of genitality itself. It reduces genitality to a thing that I can simply go out and find.

Genitality is not simply an experience but an interpersonal relationship. If the experience is going to be meaningful, it will be with someone whom I love. This means cultivating a relationship which takes time. The relationship also has no future if I have really decided upon a way of life that is not going to permit this kind of relationship. We cannot use persons for sexual experiments. Genital intercourse is not something that is mine alone. To seek sexual experience simply for the sake of the experience reduces sexuality to a very unintegrated element in one's personality.

Genital love is a gift which comes to a person in the context of an interpersonal relationship. It is not something that one can say he or she is simply going to experience. A person can seek genital relations, but genital love is a gift. The fact that a person has not had genital intercourse is not a reason for delaying the decision to be celibate. As long as a person feels his or her own motivation for choosing the celibate life is valid and he or she feels called at this particular time in his or her life to be celibate, the decision to enter into a celibate way of life may involve the decision to be a virgin. This decision is an even further exemplification of the value in the celibate way of life. A virgin is a supreme exemplification of celibacy. A virgin is a person who, not having experienced the full genital life, still sees so much value in the celibate life that he or she wants to make that choice and thus chooses virginal life as well. We must remind ourselves that neither celibacy nor virginity in themselves give the witness, only people do. It is not that virginity makes a person a sign of celibate love but that a person can make virginity such a sign.

It is important that we begin to de-mythologize the theology of virginity. It is important that we rethink the meaning and value of virginity in the light of current discussion. The real test to which the virgin is being put today is his or her attitude towards the sexual. The question is: "If you think so much of sexuality, why haven't you allowed yourself to enjoy it more?" This is the question which the virgin will have to answer. The response to this question cannot be Manichean and still be Christian. Virgins must ask themselves these questions: Would genital intercourse make one less holy? Is the saint one who foregoes genital love? One's answers to these questions will reflect whether one's own theology is a Christian appreciation of sexuality or a Manichean rejection of it.

The theology of spirituality underneath the theology of virginity cannot be based upon the fact that one cannot love both God and man. Some traditional theologies of virginity sounded as if they maintained that love when shared with more than one becomes less. God may be a jealous lover but he is also a divine lover. Having a human center does not mean the inability to have a divine center. Choosing the divine as the center of our lives does not negate having another person central to our lives. The theology of virginity cannot lead people to believe that they will *either* love God *or* other persons and the more they are committed to other persons the less committed they are to God. Christian love asks of us one thing—that we love both God and man. The Christian way of loving is able to reconcile these two so that in fact they become one act. There is a way of loving which does not divide us. Our theology of virginity cannot lead us to believe that loving someone in particular means not loving others or not loving God.

The theology of virginity must also remain in the context of a theology of asceticism. It is useless to talk to someone about the positive dimension of virginal love if one has no appreciation of the ascetical, mystical, and spiritual life. Just as people today need a positive appreciation of sexuality, many need a positive appreciation of spirituality. Just as many need a positive appreciation of genital love, so others need a positive appreciation of virginal love. One cannot accept asceticism today unless one sees freedom in the restrictions of the ascetical life. Many people at different times have asked me why I chose to give up what I had. I do not really feel that what I have chosen to give up is greater than what I have chosen to strive for. There is a freedom that comes from having the strength to live one's life on the basis of faith in God. To choose to become countercultural in an authentic way means choosing to live an ascetical life. To choose to be countercultural, according to enculturated people, will be to give up all that is valuable. Those who make that choice, however, feel that they are the ones who will gain.

Virginity must be placed in this context of asceticism. We must be aware, however, not to separate the asceticism of virginity from other forms of asceticism, if we are to be credible. A virgin who abstains from genital love but who never abstains from anything else is not going to be a living witness to his or her conviction of the value of ascetisicm. A man who has a cocktail before every evening meal but who refrains from making love after the meal is hardly a witness to the value of asceticism. The ascetical life is a stance taken by the total person and not simply restricted to the sexual sphere.

Another element besides the ascetical which we must keep in mind in re-thinking our theology of virginity is that sexuality is not the enemy of virginity. Physical pleasure is not the enemy of virginity. The physical aspect of virginity is not in itself its real power. Virginity is much more than a physical reality; it is a spiritual force. Spiritual deadness, not physical pleasure, is the enemy of the virginal life. If we could see more clearly the spiritual possibilities contained within sexuality, we could begin to realize that sexuality and virginity are not enemies but partners. Sexuality seeks the power of love; virginity seeks the same reality. In our whole discussion we are dealing with that underlying ambiguity which is inherently a part of humanity. Creation is good and yet sinful. Our Christian lives must recognize the essential goodness of created reality and also its distorted nature. This inherent ambiguity affects the totality of our lives in such a way that it prevents integration. Yet integration is what the Christian seeks. Integration does not come by condemning the sexual and glorifying the virginal. It comes from redeeming the sexual and appreciating the virginal, not one or the other but both. A virgin whose only goal is to avoid risk is not seriously undertaking the spiritual journey towards God. Man's journey towards God is a risky business and a virgin is a person who is willing to undertake these risks in order that he or she might become the man or woman that he or she can be before God.

The goal of man is both humanization and spiritualization in the sense in which Teilhard de Chardin speaks of these.[10] It is in this context that virginity must be placed. Virginity must not be seen as the enemy of sexuality because sexuality must be placed in the very same context. The question is: how can and does genital love contribute to the humanization and spiritualization of man? And the question is also: how does virginity contribute to that very same goal? Genital abstinence is intrinsically no more Christian than genital intercourse.

CONCLUSION

Virginity needs no justification today other than the validity of differences. Each person has the right to be different in order to discover more fully his or her self. Any ascetical practice is based upon this striving to discover one's self more fully. In one's upward and forward striving, choices will be made which are unsupported by secular culture at large. When it comes to living out differences that question the underlying values of the culture, the culture becomes intolerant. Yet religion strives to preserve the differences within the Body of Christ which contribute to its totality. It resists cultural imperialism. A countercultural asceticism is the milieu for man's striving after God, out of which milieu virginal life can emerge as a response to the Father.

To deny virginity in our own day would be either to deny celibacy or to reduce sexuality to an impersonal dimension of human life. Genital love is interpersonal and not simply a decision on the part of a person who wants an experience. The time comes in a person's life when he or she feels called to make a decision for celibate life, possibly prior to the experience of genital love. The person is not only going to choose celibacy; he or she will be choosing virginity as well. Human genitality is intended to be sacramental. A person does not express genitally what is not there to be expressed—namely vowed love between two persons. This love lasts, as Paul says, and is as strong as death, as the Song of Songs says. That is what genital love is all about. It is genital *love* as well as being *genital* love. Virginal love expresses another dimension of love. Genitality is a sacrament of an ongoing particular friendship between two. Virginity is a sacrament of ongoing universal love for all. This does not mean the two are exclusive. It simply means that different Christians choose to vow themselves and hence give public witness to different aspects of the mystery of love.

Virginity in the end is also a matter of experience. A person who has not experienced a reality is going to be limited in terms of being able to articulate its full meaning. A virgin will never completely understand genital love since he or she has not had a full experience of it. A non-virgin will never completely understand virginal love because he or she is lacking the experience of it. The experience in the end convinces and every experience is not open to each of us. Respect for other persons is the foundation for human growth and ways of life cannot be ruled out *a priori*.

Both genital love and virginal love are valid ways of loving. One is not superior to the other. Genitality and virginity contribute to building up the body of Christ. Both can be spiritualized; both can be simply external. The interior life of the man or woman gives substance to both genitality and virginity. It is not important whether Mary was or was not a virgin. That is not the question. She was and is a witness to chaste love, faithfulness to God, and the meaning of the interior life. Little is said about her in Scripture. The externals of her life need not be delineated. It is her interior life that was significant. That is summarized in one sentence. She is Holy Mary. We, too, are called to that same holiness and oneness with the Father through the work of the Spirit. Virginity is no more or no less than the interior life it expresses. It will continue to witness to the value of interiority. The moral ideal is neither celibacy, marriage, genitality, nor virginity. The moral ideal is life with Christ and through him union with God. The important question for all of us is not whether to marry or to be celibate; the important question is: where am I going and to what am I called?

PART TWO

6

Intimacy and Friendship

WE NOW BEGIN the second part of this book. The first part was more or less theoretical. The first two chapters were concerned with theories of sexuality from psychological and theological perspectives. Chapters three through five were concerned primarily with the theology of chastity, celibacy, and virginity. In general, I did not explore the practical questions and problems raised by chastity, celibacy, virginity, and sexuality, although at times I moved in that direction.

I have left the more practically oriented portion of this work until now. The real issue has been whether celibacy and sexuality are compatible. Now we face the implications of this.

This chapter discusses intimacy in particular. All people, not only celibate people, find the answer to their need for intimacy in friendship. The first section of this chapter discusses some of the psychological questions that accompany man's striving after intimacy through friendship. There is no effort to develop a complete psychology of friendship but simply an effort to make us more aware of the task involved. The second portion of the chapter attempts to give an appreciation of the value of friendship and intimacy from a Christian and theological perspective. The final section focuses on a central concern in the lives of celibate people seeking intimacy through permanent relationships, that of separation.

After affirming the value of friendship and discussing the complex task that is involved, the final two chapters of the book discuss the implications of this for a celibate's sexual life as well as for his or her spiritual life.

PSYCHOLOGY AND FRIENDSHIP

Intimacy in human living is important for personal growth, self-esteem, and for a feeling that life is worthwhile. Intimacy as I will use the word is the highest possible interpersonal experience, the experience of union or oneness with another. Because intimacy plays such a significant role in human life, friendship has always been given high regard by philosophers and theologians as well as psychologists. Because intimacy is so important, it is necessary to learn how to be friends with one another. Education in friendship is one of the needs of mankind today. I consider here only five elements that must be faced in any relationship: contracts, dependency, hostility, jealousy, and intimacy itself.

CONTRACTS: Contracts are important not only for married persons but also for celibate friends.[1] Contracts must be clear if a relationship between two persons or between a person and his or her community is going to grow. Kenneth Mitchell points to three different kinds: the formal, informal, and secret contracts.[2] The formal contract is public, the one of which we are most aware, the one we often take the most seriously, and the one which is most clear. We generally attach more importance to a formal contract than to the others. Yet the formal contract, although it is the one that receives the most public attention, is not more significant than the others.

In marriage, the formal contract is the public ceremony in which two people take each other for better or for worse. In celibate life the formal contract is a profession or an ordination ceremony. Whether people are celibate or married, vows contain clear promises, are surrounded by a ceremony, and are generally public. Between two celibate friends there usually are not formal contracts. We do not solemnize celibate friendship in this way although such friendships are still public. The relationship does not, however, presuppose a ceremony which makes public the commitment between the two. In this sense, friends outside of marriage do not make formal contracts.

Informal contracts, although less solemn, are frequently more important for the ongoing health of a relationship. Informal contracts are verbal; in that sense they are similar to formal contracts. They contain clear words; they are specific; they are not, however, public. They remain between the two people or between the person and the community. Such a contract exists between two people who plan to marry and decide not to have children during the first year of marriage in order to have time to adjust to the new way of life before undertaking the responsibility of raising a family. The two of them may decide between themselves to use the pill and practice birth control during the first year. This is a very specific and understood arrangement. Nevertheless, it is not made public. On the day of the solemn ceremony, the woman does not say, "I take you for better, for worse, in sickness and in health, and promise to take the pill." This is an understanding agreed upon between the two; it is a real contract. If the wife decides somewhere during the first year she would like to be pregnant, she is not free to disregard the informal contract. It is a contract which was mutually agreed upon. She cannot simply stop taking the pill in order to become pregnant and inform her husband that she has changed her mind. Violating informal contracts is a violation of the relationship, and infidelity as well.

Informal contracts also exist between people who are friends but not married. In celibate friendship, the informal contract is the only verbal contract that exists. Two friends may agree between themselves to be friends, to love each other, to vacation together. Informal contracts are quite specific. They are very important in any relationship. They specify the terms under which or within which the relationship is understood. They clarify the accepted expectations between the two persons. Informal contracts not only exist between celibate friends and married friends; they also exist between a person and a religious community. A person who chooses to live within community makes many private contracts with that community before he or she actually takes public and solemn vows. One could not take public and solemn vows unless many dimensions of the life had been previously clarified informally.

The secret contract is the least clarified and often the most significant. It contains the expectations that are not verbalized and frequently not conscious. Every person enters a situation or relationship with expectations. What Mitchell refers to as the hidden or secret contract, Levinson refers to as the psychological or unwritten contract. It is unwritten, unspoken, and largely implicit. It contains expectations which antedate a relationship. Whether I admit it or not, I enter into every relationship with prior expectations of which I may or may not be aware.

It is important that both partners in a relationship as well as both a person and a community in a relationship know and understand the mutual expectations. I recall once having invited someone to go out for an evening. When the time came, the person had invited another person to go along. My expectation, unclarified and unspoken, was that we would go out alone. The unspoken expectation led to disappointment, frustration, anger. We shall see later that anger is the beginning of the process of clarifying expectations.

Unspoken contracts and hidden expectations trouble religious communities and celibate relationships. Frequently the initial period of entrance into a community or into a relationship is a process of clarifying these expectations. It need not be a formal process such as a novitiate; it might simply be the time spent in adjusting to a new situation. The main task of this period is coming to an awareness of the unspoken contracts that exist and antedate my coming into this situation or relationship. It is a process of adjustment in which both parties adjust expectations.

The secret contract is troublesome since it is not in the open. Either party can deny that it actually exists. A person might actually be unaware of his or her expectations, and yet changes in secret contracts are a source of tension. Such changes are frequently one-sided since they have not previously been spoken. Yet a change in a secret contract is still felt as a betrayal. Whether between celibate or married friends or between a person and a community, it is important that secret contracts be discussed. The process of exposing hidden contracts is painful but necessary. If the contracts and expectations are not exposed, they cannot be faced.

Exposing a hidden contract may mean new investment. A person may undertake responsibility that he or she previously was not aware of. It may mean that a particular expectation has to be given up if two people cannot agree that they are willing to undertake the now clarified expectation and assume responsibility for it. Clarifying the expectation, then, is inevitably going to involve a change in the relationship. A change in the relationship does not mean a change for the worse. Clarified expectations generally mean change for the better, growth within the relationship. The change, however, may be painful.

The process of clarification leads to a discovery of those expectations of which I myself was unaware. I enter a situation in which I feel that my wife will butter my toast or in which I feel that my friend will spend his or her free time with me. These may be expectations of which I am unaware. Nevertheless, this hidden expectation determines whether intimacy and satisfaction can be achieved in any relationship. The achievement of a psychologically rewarding relationship involves the clarification of expectations and the discussion of contracts.

DEPENDENCY: There is both a good and a bad side to dependency which in itself is not destructive. Too often we identify dependence as a negative trait and independence as a positive one. The goal of human growth is both. Our culture regularly holds up independence as a sign of maturity. Not independence, however, but interdependence is a sign of a maturing person.[3] How interdependent one allows himself to be depends upon one's attitude towards dependency.

Dependence on others is a constant and necessary element in personal growth. Dependency upon another is a factor in interpersonal relationships. No person is ever completely independent nor is it desirable that any person be so. Complete independence or total self-sufficiency prevents a person from genuinely being able to receive. Dependency is not detrimental to self-actualization. Dependency needs are human needs like many other needs. If they are going to be healthfully handled, they must be positively accepted.

Many of us have experienced both extremes in handling feelings of dependency. We have experienced the overly dependent, possessive person who depends more upon us than we can comfortably accept and who makes demands we cannot meet. In a different relationship, we may have found ourselves becoming dependent and possessive ourselves. Over-dependence is not a healthy way to handle dependency needs. The phenomenon of over-dependence, however, does not negate the constructive dimension of dependency. The other extreme from over-dependence, total independence, is equally destructive. Maturity is a balance. In intimacy there is real dependency on both sides.

Dependency expectations are a part of psychological contracts. A friend is someone upon whom I can depend. A friend is someone whom I need not fear. A friend is someone with whom I can be vulnerable because I trust in the person's acceptance and understanding. A friend is someone with whom I can be dependent without being destroyed. Likewise, my friend is someone who can be dependent upon me and whose dependency needs I choose to fulfill. Working out a healthy degree of mutual dependence is no easy task.

There are two unhealthy ways of handling dependency needs—denial and possessiveness. To have feelings of dependency can be a threat to a person who then denies the dependency. Denial is strong in an overly independent person, the confident and composed person who gives the impression that he or she needs no one. Frequently this person is well respected because he or she embodies a cultural value—personal independence. This person, however, is unable to accept and express his or her own weaknesses. This person will inevitably frustrate a loved one because he or she will have to be in control.

An overly independent person is unable to share his or her weaknesses with another and limits the union that can take place between two people. This may be a man who is concerned about masculinity and unable to manifest femininity. This may be a person who is unable to say to someone else, "I need you." This may be a person unable to say, "I love you." It is important to be aware that there is nothing immature about weakness. The overly independent person is one who is not strong enough to accept his own imperfection and who does not permit himself to be dependent. A tendency is for an overly independent person to form a friendship with an overly dependent person.

The other extreme from independence is a person whose dependency is insatiable. He or she needs everyone to fulfill his or her needs, constantly makes demands, and becomes possessive. Such people form demanding, exhausting, and clinging relationships. It is not a mature giving-and-forgiving relationship. The tendency of this person is to form a friendship with a very independent person. The relationship eventually becomes frustrating as the dependent person demands more and the independent person refuses more. Both will be frustrated until they become aware of what they are doing.

It is very important for a person in authority to realize his or her own attitude towards dependency. Many structures as well as expectations refuse to permit a person of authority gratification of dependency needs. "Authority must be independent," the myth maintains. This is simply not true. A person in authority is a human person. Too often people complain that an authority is not human enough and yet do not permit him or her to be human. They do not permit a superior to show those most human of all qualities— dependency and weakness. They force the superior to deny his or her own need to be dependent. He or she then becomes increasingly independent and thereby increases dependency in others rather than freedom. The pathology exists on both sides. People do not permit persons in authority to be truly dependent and expressive of their own needs and authorities cannot permit themselves to be needy. The person in authority can be so threatened by dependency needs that he or she maintains independence and forces others into submissive roles. Their initiative and personal responsibility would be too much of a threat to their own independence.

A balance between dependence and independence has to take place within each person. In a relationship it cannot be one person who is independent and the other person who is dependent; within a community it cannot be one person who is independent and others who are dependent. The balance must take place within each person just as femininity and masculinity need to be accepted within each person.

HOSTILITY: Every person has a certain amount of anger within, which needs to be both accepted and expressed.[4] Yet hostile feelings are often more difficult to face than sexual feelings. There is probably more repressed anger than repressed sexuality among celibate people. It is easy for a celibate person who is striving to be deeply Christian to deny negative feelings. Intimacy itself is productive of hostility. Karl Menninger speaks of the love-hate relationship. Ambivalence is a fact of our interpersonal lives; we both love and hate people simultaneously. The two emotions, positive and negative feelings, co-exist. In an intimate relationship there is always the threat that we are going to lose our own autonomy, and this is a source of frustration and hostility. Losing ourselves in another person, the greatest act of love, can be a very central threat to a person's existence. The struggle between autonomy and intimacy must be faced in every interpersonal relationship. The closer we get, the more threatened we are. The more intimate we are, the more likely the flareup of anger. The more we love, the more important it is that we are able to face and express the anger.

Adults frequently find it unacceptable to express anger openly. Nevertheless, anger eventually comes out somewhere and influences the relationship. It cannot be denied if a healthy relationship is to develop. Admitting anger does not necessarily mean immediately expressing it; admitting the anger, however, is necessary to the constructive handling of it. It is worthwhile for every celibate person to take anger seriously. Because anger was considered one of the seven capital sins, we are afraid of it. Anger can be un-Christian; it can also be Christian. Jesus himself showed the ability to express anger when he felt it necessary.

There are many expressions in our language which give us a clue to the fact that there is unadmitted anger within. Some of these expressions are obvious and some more subtle. Some examples: "I am annoyed," "I am irritated," "I am sick and tired," "I am disappointed." All of these are less direct ways of saying, "I am angry," or "I'm damn mad."

Speech can betray anger to the person who is aware; so can behavior. Passive behavior is frequently one of the most overt signs of hidden hostility. The best example is "the silent treatment," wherein one partner within a relationship refuses to talk. Such silence is not the silence of the solitary person. It is the silence of an angry man or woman.

Along with verbal expressions and passive behavior, other phenomena such as sarcastic humor as well as the ordinary act of forgetting are expressive of hostility. A person who forgets an appointment often communicates something. All behavior communicates.

One of the most common ways of experiencing anger is depression, which is anger turned inward. Instead of saying "I am depressed," it is more honest to say, "I am angry." Many actually prefer depression because of an inability to face anger. Not only does depression indicate anger but excessive niceness can as well. The overly sweet and lovingly nice person is simply using what psychoanalysts call "reaction-formation." This is a way of coping in which a person acts the opposite of how he feels, being so threatened by a feeling that he converts it into the opposite feeling.

Physical symptoms can also be a sign of repressed hostility. Tension is frequently repressed anger. Headaches, ulcers, arthritis, high blood pressure, and hemorrhoids are related to how we handle hostility. Repressed anger affects the skin in itching or pruritis.

It is not my intention here to explore the topic of anger thoroughly but simply to make people aware that a denial of anger can be a negative factor in the growth of an interpersonal relationship. People must become aware of hostility that is inevitably a part of a close relationship. Hostility is not only a part of a relationship but can also affect sexuality within the relationship. There is nothing more hostile than the person who uses sex to express hostility. Refusing to have sex, engaging in extra-marital sex, as well as completely passive behavior during sex, are all ways of expressing anger. Sexual teasing and seductiveness are also ways of expressing hostility. The saying, "Fuck you!" has little to do with sexuality but a lot to do with hostility. There are also socially approved outlets for anger such as hunting, football, wrestling; hobbies such as gardening or driving a car.

An excellent outlet for anger is tears. The most frequent cause of crying whether as a child or as an adult is anger. Crying is a healthy outlet and it is unhealthy to hold back tears. Men in particular have to learn that tears are not unmanly. It takes strength to be able to cry. Not all crying is anger, but much of it is.

Although much is written about anger, few people suggest what one can actually do. Madow gives suggestions as to how to constructively handle it.[5] The first point he makes is that a person must recognize his or her anger and admit it to himself or herself. Then one can attempt to see where the anger comes from. Once you are aware that you are angry, it is important to try to pin down the cause or source of anger. Aware of the source, one can try to understand why he or she is angry. At this point a person can begin to deal with it. A direct expression of the anger might not always be the best solution. Nevertheless, the person can realistically look at the anger and come to some decision as to how he or she is going to express it. Often the solution simply lies in increased communication within a relationship. Expressing feelings, both positive and negative, is important if a relationship is going to grow.

Another important dimension of the problem of anger is simply dealing with other people's hostility. It is easy to say that it is important to express anger. None of us, however, likes to be the object of someone else's hostility. It is easy to say that we want the other person to feel free to express his or her anger; it is not easy, however, to accept the other person's anger. Manipulative behavior within a relationship frequently exists to prevent the other person from being able to express anger without guilt. All of these different elements—hidden hostility, expressing anger, permitting others to be able to express anger—are part of an intimate relationship. If two people, whether in marriage or in celibacy, want to grow closer together, they are going to have to face the threat that the growing intimacy will have to their own autonomy. There will be mixed communication saying, "I want to be closer," and at the same time, "I want more distance." If the two people are not able to handle this tension, there will be destructive manipulation. Ambivalence is a fact of life which all people, including celibate people, must face.

JEALOUSY: Jealousy is another factor which people have to face at one time or another in interpersonal life. It enters every person's life and it is not a question of feeling guilty about the jealousy but of constructively dealing with it. Jealousy is a phenomenon that arises primarily from the habit of making comparisons within human relationships.[6] This tendency to make comparisons exists among all of us. "Am I better than someone else?" "Am I more successful than someone else?" "Does someone love me more than someone else?" "My father is stronger than your father."

Making comparisons inevitably leads to feelings of inferiority. It is seldom that a person is threatened by someone who is perceived as not being comparable to himself. We compare ourselves to those people whom we suspect may in some way be better than we, who may be more liked than we are, or who may be more liked by someone in particular. Making comparisons, then, will almost always lead to a person's getting the short end of the stick. The feeling of inferiority as well as the feeling of jealousy continues until the person no longer makes comparisons. It continues until the person has enough self-strength and self-reliance so that he or she no longer needs to make such comparisons in order to feel secure. An antidote for jealousy is to improve one's self-image and increase one's self-reliance.

Comparative rivalry is something that a person usually learns early in life within the family. Each child has the desire to be the only child. Later the jealous person is the person who wishes that he or she were the only person in someone else's life or within some community. A jealous person wants to be a preferred person. Rivalry that is learned in the family centers around sibling rivalry. Parents often overlook such sibling rivalry and are unaware of the dangerous consequences to which it can lead. One will be able or unable to deal successfully with the kinds of rivalry that enter into later situations depending upon how rivalry was handled in the family. A child who is made to feel inferior or who is looked upon as inferior within the family will later have a very difficult time with jealousy. The person will have learned to estimate his own worth in terms of how he compares to others. The early years in school are also important. Destructive competition should be eliminated from families and schools if healthy psychological growth is to take place.

A jealous person is hypersensitive. Jealousy alters one's way of seeing and acting. A jealous person does not have complete control over his or her perception of reality, frequently seeing reality in a way that supports his or her mistrust or suspicion. A hypersensitive person is one who is always evaluating the external data in terms of comparison and rivalry. He or she lives on the defensive, is ready to attack imagined and trivial offenses, allows nothing to go unnoticed, and blows up explosively if one participant in the relationship looks at someone else. Jealousy can go to the extreme of possessiveness. The jealous person is easily hurt because he needs to be the center of attention. A person struggling for attention or popularity is underneath very jealous and insecure.

When jealousy enters a relationship, it should not be alarming. It is a natural enough phenomenon, but it needs to be handled constructively. The first thing is to recognize the jealousy, not to be ashamed of it, not to deny it. The two people have to be able to talk about it between themselves. If one person does not recognize the jealousy, it is important for the other person to confront the jealous partner. The problem cannot be handled until it is labeled.

Confronting jealousy does not destroy a relationship. It helps it grow. A person must maintain independence in the face of jealousy. If one allows the jealous person to be in control, it will lead to resentment on the part of the one being possessed. In either case, there is hostility involved that has to be faced. A person should not move in the direction of self-justification but should be willing to engage in open communication. One cannot prevent a jealous person from seeing the world in his own way. One can avoid, however, appeasing him by nurturing his need for continued assurance. The person is going to have to learn eventually to accept and to trust.

INTIMACY: If the above psychological realities are faced, intimacy is more likely—what Eric Berne refers to as "a game-free relationship." [7] There are other issues as well which enter into relationships which two people in their ongoing commitment to discover and accept each other have to face. Two other factors which I want to mention here are distance and privacy. A person has to establish distance in some relationships in order to maintain intimacy in others. A person also needs to have privacy if a relationship between two is going to grow. Intimacy does not grow in public although it needs to be public in order to grow. The privacy-publicity continuum and the distance-intimacy continuum are both elements in interpersonal life.

In addition to contracts, dependency, hostility, and jealousy, people must deal with the problem of distance if they are to have satisfying relationships. Healthy interpersonal living involves both distance and intimacy. A person who strives after intimacy with everyone experiences it with no one. In order to give and receive in some relationships, one is going to have to be more distant in other relationships. A celibate person striving after universal love must realize that this does not mean universal intimacy. Christian love and psychological intimacy are not the same. We are called upon to love all men and women. We are not called to psychological intimacy or Christian friendship with everyone. Growing deeply in a relationship and experiencing it more fully means that a person must set limits on his or her life. Intimacy requires disciplined living.

People differ as to their needs for closeness and their needs for distance. These differences between people must be respected. Setting distance in a relationship or setting limits on a relationship does not mean that you do not like someone or that it would be impossible to build in this particular relationship. It simply says something about one's own needs and one's own life. A person whose life is emotionally rich with satisfying personal associations finds less need to build in all the potentially intimate relationships in order to continue growing in those relationships where commitment already exists.

I speak of distance here because distance, like dependency, can too easily have a negative connotation. For a person striving after intimacy, distance smacks of coldness. The interpersonal life, however, is a vital balance, a balance between dependence and independence, between love and hate, as well as between distance and intimacy. One must have distance in some relationships in order to have intimacy in others.

Not only must I set limits on myself and establish distance; I must set limits in order to have privacy. I cannot be a public person all the time. Although a formal contract says something public about my private life, I still have a right to a private life. There is a whole area that the formal contract in celibate life does not negate and which is in fact preserved by the informal contracts within a community—the area of interpersonal intimacy. Just as personal living requires solitude, interpersonal living requires privacy. Friendship between two does not grow if the two are never alone together. This does not mean that friendship is exclusive; friends simply have a right to privacy that a community cannot violate.

Henri Nouwen writes about this problem in the life of the priest:[8]

How does the priest see himself in his relationship with his fellowman? How does he relate privacy to fellowship, intimacy to social intercourse? . . . Two things are necessary. First, that I must face my own inner privacy where I can hide from the face of the challenging world; and secondly, I must establish a hierarchy of relationships with this same world. In the inner circle of my life I find him or her who is closest to me. Around this circle of intimacy I find the circle of family and dear friends. Then, at a somewhat larger distance, I locate relatives, and acquaintances and, even further away, the associates in business and work. Finally, I am aware of the vast circle of people that I don't know by name but who in some vague way also belong to this world, which I can call *my* world. . . . It is exactly here that the priest has problems. Very often he has lost his private life, where he can be with himself; nor has he a hierarchy of relationships with guards on the thresholds. Being friendly to everybody, he very often has no friends for himself. . . . The priest, who is pleading for friends, needs his parishioners more than they need him. Looking for acceptance, he tends to cling to his counselees, and depend on his faithful.

I suspect that there is no human problem more anguishing and horrible than loneliness, which is not simply a part of celibate life but a part of life itself. We only overcome loneliness, to the degree that it can be overcome, by facing our need for intimacy and learning how to be a friend. Loneliness is one of the most anxiety-provoking experiences in celibate life, and yet the intimacy that is possible within celibate friendship is often not achieved.

There are many reasons for this. There exists confusion between intimacy and genitality for those who feel and fear that human intimacy implies genital love. Yet it is only the genital life and not human intimacy that is restricted by celibate men and women.

There are two facts of which we must be aware. The first is the valid distinction between intimacy and genitality, between what Harry Stack Sullivan calls intimacy and lust. The need for intimacy emerges with full force in preadolescence. It is at this time that loneliness first becomes really possible. The genital drive, or lust, usually emerges with full force at the time of adolescence. The task of early adulthood is to integrate these, but not to confuse them. A relatively non-genital but deeply human intimacy is possible.

The second fact of which we must be aware is that the distinction between intimacy and genitality does not mean a clear and distinct boundary between the two. We must not kid ourselves. Entry into the world of adult intimacy opens up the world of genitality. The experience of intimacy in the adult is not totally separable from genital feelings and anxiety. We should not be naive in thinking that a non-genital intimacy will be achieved easily.

I began my discussion of sexuality by distinguishing between affective and genital sexuality. There is a further distinction I wish to make. Celibate people need to be aware of the difference between intimacy, tactility, and genitality. All of these are aspects of our sexual lives. The need for intimacy is not the same as the need for touch or the need for genital sex although they are often experienced as the same. The worlds of intimacy and tactility are open to celibate men and women. Intimacy needs touch and touch leads to intimacy although they are not the same. Likewise touch can lead to genitality but need not do so. A tactual non-genital relationship is possible. It is only the genital world which is not fully open to celibate people.

Loneliness in the end is an inadequate response to one's striving for intimacy. Harry Stack Sullivan relates developmentally this striving as it involves the need for contact, then the need for tenderness, the need for adult participation in one's play, the need for compeers, the need for acceptance, and finally in preadolescence "the need for intimate exchange, for friendship." [9] All these needs add to the experience of loneliness but loneliness only becomes possible in its fullest form during and after preadolescence. Sullivan writes, "This new interest in the preadolescent era is not as general as the use of language toward others was in childhood, or the need of similar people as playmates was in the juvenile era. Instead, it is a specific new type of interest in a *particular* member of the same sex who becomes a chum or a close friend. This change represents the beginning of something very like full blown, psychiatrically defined *love*." [10] In adolescence the need for particular love shifts for most from someone of the same sex to someone of the other sex and the striving for intimacy goes on. Celibate people must face the need for particular love and both the emotional and spiritual tasks that it involves.

THEOLOGY OF FRIENDSHIP

We have looked briefly at some of the psychological dimensions of intimacy, and now we will look at some of the theological dimensions.

JOHN'S GOSPEL: Let us first look at how Jesus is portrayed as understanding friendship within the fourth Gospel. The fifteenth chapter of John is our primary source.

> I shall not call you servants anymore, because a
> servant does not know his master's business; I
> call you friends, because I have made known to you
> everything I have learnt from my Father (15:15).

There is a contrast in this passage between servant (*doulos*) and friend (*philos*), and Jesus prefers to describe his relationship with his disciples as one of friendship. He not only calls them friends, however, he tells them why he is calling them friends and thus reveals what he means by friendship. They are friends because he has completely opened himself to them. He has made known to them everything and shared with them everything that the Father has made known to him. There was complete openness and sharing on his part and now they are to be called friends. The Christian is a *doulos* from the viewpoint of service. He is also, however, a *philos* from the viewpoint of his relationship to Jesus. Jesus hides nothing from his disciples and thus they are his friends. This is the first quality of friendship—complete openness and self-disclosure.

Jesus continues:

> You did not choose me, no, I chose you (15:16).

Jesus considers these men to whom he is speaking to be his friends. He makes it clear to them that he chose them. He chose the ones to whom he would so totally open himself and reveal himself. Jesus did not just bump into someone and completely open himself to that person. He was selective. Nor was it simply that they chose him and so he responded with complete openness. His own decision was involved. Aelred of Riveaulx was to make a similar point later—the necessity of election as the beginning of true friendship.

> And I commissioned you to go out and to bear fruit, fruit
> that will last (15:16).

Jesus made a choice that he wanted to have this kind of relationship with these particular men. He did not choose, however, that the rest of their lives should then be completely focused on him. As soon as he says that he chose them to be his future friends, he says that he sent them out. He did not choose to keep them all to himself. The kind of relationship he is describing is not possessive. The relationship is oriented outwards. Jesus has no notion that because they are his friends, they do not have their own mission.

This same notion is found in verses 14 and 17. Jesus says, "You are my friends if you do what I command you." But, "what I command you is to love one another." The friendship is not focused simply on Jesus. It is true that Jesus expects them to do his will if they are to be his friends. It is not simply enough that he disclose himself to them. They have to respond, just as Jesus must respond to them when they so totally open themselves to him. Yet Jesus is asking a very generous thing of his friends. He does not say,

"What I command you is to love me completely and exclusively so that there is no other love in your life. Then you will be my friends." Rather his wish is that the relationship be centered outside themselves.

Jesus does not leave them in doubt at this point. He asks them to love one another but he has already said what love means.

> A man can have no greater love than to lay down
> his life for his friends (15:13).

A friend is someone for whom we would lay down our lives. This is symbolic of the extent to which Jesus wants this relationship of friendship to be taken. It is to be complete giving in every respect. It is not only total self-disclosure; it is also total sacrifice for one's friend to the point of death. Nothing is held back from someone whom you consider to be a friend. This is why it is important that careful choice be involved.

There is also the element of joy.

> I have told you this so that my own joy may be
> in you and your joy be complete (15:11).

Jesus wants them to be happy. He wants to share his joy and shared joy is more complete. You can almost hear him say, "A man can have no greater joy than to lay down his life for his friends." This same notion of Jesus' wanting to share his joy with his friends is found in 17:13. "While still in the world I say these things to share my joy with them to the full." When he communicates his own joy, the joy of his friends becomes more complete.

The joy is contrasted with sorrow, however, for friendship brings with it sorrow as well. In the next chapter Jesus is aware of his parting and what separation is going to mean.

> I tell you most solemnly
> you will be weeping and wailing (16:20).

Why? In a short time they are not going to see him anymore. They are not going to be with their friend. They will miss him. He tells them, "A woman in childbirth suffers. . . . So it is with you. You are sad now" (16:21–22). They will not be able to escape the pain of his absence. Yet that sorrow itself will someday become joy.

> You will be sorrowful,
> but your sorrow will turn to joy (16:20).

Friendship involves joy and sorrow for both Jesus and his friends. They were his friends and Jesus was hurt when they would not stay awake with him while he prayed. Likewise Peter loved Jesus and was hurt by Jesus when Jesus asked him three times if he loved him. We shall look at that incident later. We have already seen that friendship as Jesus sees it involves making a choice, complete self-disclosure, total giving, an outward-orientation, joy, and pain. It also involves real concern for one's friend—a fatherly or motherly kind of concern. Jesus found himself praying to the Father for them.

> Holy Father,
> keep those you have given me true to your name,
> so that they may be one like us.
> While I was with them,
> I kept those you had given me true to your name.
> I have watched over them and not one is lost
> except the one who chose to be lost (17:11–12).

Jesus' love for his friends included his desire to keep them true to the Father. In fact, if they could discover their own relationship with the Father, they would never be alone. The Yahwist's theology presented God as not wanting man to be alone. Now Jesus is aware of the problem of loneliness too. That is why he offers them their own relationships with the Father—that they might not be alone.

> I tell you most solemnly
> anything you ask for from the Father
> he will grant in my name (16:23).

Jesus had shared with them the most precious thing he could share—his love for the Father and the Father's love in return.

Listen; the time will come—in fact it has
already come—when you will be scattered, each
going his own way and leaving me alone.
And yet I am not alone,
because the Father is with me (16:32).

There is no greater love than the friendship of which Jesus speaks. And what are the effects of this kind of relationship? The deepest and most intimate union imaginable. Jesus is continually comparing his relationship to the disciples (what he calls friendship) to his own relationship to the Father. Human friendship is analogous to Jesus' relationship to the Father.

As the Father has loved me,
so I have loved you (15:9).

Jesus' love for his disciples (*philia*) is the same as the Father's love for Jesus (*agape*). In fact, in the verse above, the verb *agapo* is used for both. Jesus sees his relationship to his friends or disciples as both *agape* and *philia*—a point to which we will return later.

Jesus continues to describe his relationship to the Father in the same way he describes his relationship to his friends. He says, "Everything the Father has is mine" (16:15), just as he says, "All I have is yours" (17:10). The relationship of friendship is like the relationship between God and us. That is what is expected of friends—that they love one another as Jesus loves us. Friendship is an exemplification of divine love. And what kind of union is this? It is like being a vine and a branch. Jesus says, "You are my friends, I am the vine and you are the branches" (15:5 and 15). He envisages this as a really intimate union. It is to be as intimate as his own intimacy with the Father. "That they may be one like us" (17:11). This all leads to their actually being within one another. To be a friend is to be inside of me. "Make your home in me as I make mine in you. . . . Who remains in me, with me in him, bears fruit in plenty" (15:4-5).

What does Jesus mean by friendship? His attitude includes genuine choice, complete giving, self-disclosure, unpossessiveness, sharing joy and sorrow, motherly or fatherly concern, a sharing of the Father, and real life together or intimate union. John was a particular friend in Jesus' own life who is a supreme exemplification of the fact that Jesus loved in this way. At the Last Supper, this "disciple Jesus loved was reclining next to Jesus," and later "leaning back on Jesus' breast" asked Jesus the question about who it was who would betray him (13:21–25).

Jesus was concerned about his friends. Peter had denied him three times after having declared how much he loved Jesus. The last chapter of John's Gospel records how Jesus later questioned Peter three times as to whether he loved him. Jesus asked, "Simon, son of John, do you love me more than these others do?" Peter answered, "Yes, Lord, you know I love you," (John 21:15–17). The text is interesting because two different verbs are used in the Greek for love—*philo* and *agapo*. The first two times Jesus asks the question using *agapo* and Peter replies with *philo*. In the last of the three interchanges Jesus switches to *philo* as well.

verse 15	agapas me	philo se
verse 16	agapas me	philo se
verse 17	phileis me	philo se

There are those who emphasize the differences in the verbs. Some say Jesus is asking Peter for a higher kind of love of which Peter is unaware. There is really no ground for such an interpretation. John actually uses the words interchangeably throughout the Gospel. As far back as Origen and most recently with Spicq there is the tendency to emphasize the distinction. Most commentators, however, would not agree that any such point can be made: Cyril of Alexandria, Augustine, Erasmus, Lagrange, Moffatt, Bonsirven, Barrett, Hoskyns, and Brown.[11] As I have developed the theology of friendship above, the distinction is not valid.

The kind of relationship Jesus describes as *philia* is already an exalted understanding, a relationship that parallels the love of the Father, a relationship that actually is the work of the Father. For John, *philia* is *agape*. John could use either without intending a distinction since he continually does so elsewhere in the Gospel. They are the same. What is important is that the kind of love Jesus has for his disciples, which he calls friendship, is the highest kind of love possible—the kind the Father has and a greater than which there cannot be. True friendship is simply a love a greater than which there cannot be. This is John's teaching on friendship.

AELRED OF RIEVAULX: Aelred was a twelfth-century Cistercian monk, born 1110, who gave us a beautiful treatise on the subject of friendship.[12] It ranks along with Cassian's sixteenth conference on the same topic as one of the few formal treatments in the western theological tradition. Van Steenberghe's article in the *Dictionnaire de Spiritualité* on spiritual friendship basically presents Aelred's views. Aelred's discussion is valuable because it arises out of his own experience and his own solutions to problems. His own friendships with Waldef and Walter Daniel are well known. Waldef was Aelred's friend at the court of Scotland who later became a Canon Regular and still later a Cistercian monk when Aelred was abbot at Rievaulx. Walter Daniel was one of Aelred's monks and one of his intimate friends during the latter part of Aelred's life. Aelred's discussion of friendship is not simply theory. He basically sees friendship as both a creation of human effort and a gift of God. It is promoted by our own choice and effort as well as by God. Aelred brings us to our own interest about friendship among celibate people which is the topic of his *De Spirituali Amicitia.*

Aelred distinguishes charity, or love, from friendship. Charity is a more inclusive term. "Both enemies and friends are included in the former (love), while to those only to whom we entrust our heart and inmost thought, do we give the name of friend."[13] He also distinguishes true and false friendship as is common for most spiritual writers on the subject. True friendship endures. Flattery is its enemy. God is its source. "To distinguish between this false tie and true friendship, we may call the one carnal or worldly, as vice or the hope of gaining influence actuates it; the other we call spiritual, as harmony in life, in morals and ideals, inspires it."[14] A false friend, quoting Ecclesiasticus, is "a friend according to the time and not a possession in the day of tribulation."[15] You cannot count on him. "To have faith in one's friend gives security to friendship, which is, beyond doubt, one of its greatest blessings. But what security can there be in the love of one who is carried about by every wind? who acquiesces to every counsel? His affection can be likened to a soft lute which registers a variety of emotions through the day according to the whim of the one pressing it." [16]

True friendship is based on equality, sensitivity, and God. "We have still to speak of equality, which is another basic element in friendship. There can be no superior or inferior." [17] "Friends should have such understanding as to read at a glance whether the face of the other is overcast with sadness or serene with delight." [18] "Are all whom we love in this way to be admitted to the same degree of intimacy? The answer concerns itself with foundations. The house of friendship must be built solidly; therefore, it has need of a firm foundation. . . . The foundation of spiritual friendship is the love of God." [19] "Prayer for each other grows more frequent." [20]

Best of all is that the friendship lasts. "Once they have been made one from two, then since one cannot be divided, so friendship cannot be divided from itself. Hence a friendship that suffers a cleaving of the injured part never was true." [21]

Aelred places a high value on friendship. "Christ himself has given us the length to which friendship should go: 'Greater love than this no one has, that one lay down his life for his friends.' " [22] "There can be no genuine happiness without a friend. The man who has no one to feel glad of his success or to sympathize with him in sorrow, no one to whom he may pour out the perturbation of his mind, or with whom he may share such luminous thoughts as may come to him, that man can be likened to a beast." [23]

Such friendship does not simply happen. Our choice is involved in who will be admitted to this degree of intimacy. "One is not to receive into friendship all whom he might love, for not all are suited thereto. When a friend enters your life, you so unite your life to his as to become, in effect, one from two. You entrust yourself to him as to another self. You neither hide nor fear anything from him." [24] One must be discriminate in his choice since one does not change friendships overnight. Aelred in fact outlines four steps involved in the commitment that friendship implies. Choice was simply the first of these. "One should not in boyish fashion change his friends according to caprice. No one is more to be distrusted than he who has been disloyal to his friends, and nothing disturbs the soul so much as to be forsaken or impugned by a friend. Consequently, there is need of prudence in the choice and of great discrimination in the approval. When once he is admitted, he must be borne with so long as he does not recede irrevocably from the foundation. He is yours, you are his, to the extent of unity of mind, of affection, of will. Four steps there are then to the mount of affection: election, probation, admission, and the highest harmony in matters divine and human joined to affection and good will." [25]

Aelred discusses these four stages. "A friend must first be chosen, then tried, then admitted and thereafter treated as a friend." [26] There are certain people who are excluded in the first stage from the possibility of being friends. "In the election, we excluded the wrathful, the unstable, the suspicious, and the garrulous: not all, but those who were unwilling to order their passions." [27] After someone is chosen as a possible friend, the test comes as to whether he can really be the deep companion of which Aelred speaks. "We shall next consider probation. The friend must be tested in four things: faith, intention, discretion, and patience." [28] The person is then admitted to the stage of friendship and the highest possible intimacy and harmony follow.

There are certain things which are destructive of friendship and Aelred discusses these. When these are present, they prevent friendship from passing through the first stages or they are reason for dissolving the friendship. Such things are disclosing confidences, jealousy, and suspiciousness. Aered is a real enemy of disclosing the secrets of a friend. "To reveal the confidences of our friends is regarded as sacrilegious." [29] If we are in positions of authority and our friend complains about not receiving some position, Aelred comments, "The one inclined to complain of not being promoted to positions of responsibility would do well to ponder the choice of Peter over John. The fact that Our Lord gave primacy to Peter did not lessen His affection for John." [30] If it ever happens that a relationship has to be dissolved, this must be done carefully. "The friendship is not to be crushed at once, but is gradually to be dissolved, that no intolerable injury may come of it." [31]

Aelred's advice in this regard is very different from the advice

Francis de Sales gives in his discussion of friendship in the seventeenth-century work, *Introduction to the Devout Life*. Aelred says that if a friendship must be broken, it should be gradually dissolved so as not to leave injury. Francis de Sales advised that they be broken quickly. He writes:

Let him absolutely curtail all particular familiarity, all private conversation, amorous looks, smiles, and, in general, all sorts of communication and allurement, which may nourish this shameful, smoldering fire. At most, if he must speak to the other party, let it be only to declare, with a bold, short, and serious protestation, the eternal divorce that he has sworn. I call aloud upon everyone who has fallen into these wretched snares: Cut them! Break them! Tear them! Do not divert yourself in unraveling these criminal friendships; you must tear and rend them asunder. Do not untie the knots, but break or cut them.[32]

I quote Francis de Sales simply to give a different point of view from that of Aelred. There is a pluralism of theologies of friendship just as there is a pluralism of theologies of sexuality. I cannot take the time to elaborate the thought of Francis de Sales further here but his treatise is also worth reading.

Francis de Sales generally represents a more cautious attitude towards friendship while still appreciating its beauty. His own friendship with Jane Frances de Chantal is well known. Yet Francis, like Paul, is cautious because of the milieu in which he found himself. Late medieval and renaissance Europe had given rise to licentiousness in general and also among the clergy. There were many who were living like Corinthians. Thus his theology of spiritual friendship is more inclined to point to the dangers in particular friendships than the beauties in them. Actually Francis has had more of an influence on our own spirituality than Aelred. Aelred was writing in that period when the dangers of friendship were not the primary focus in such a discussion. Cassian earlier had a cautious theology of friendship. He forbade his monks, especially the younger ones, to go off together or to hold hands.[33] In the time between Cassian and Francis de Sales, false and true friendships were always distinguished but there was not the same fear.[34] As we can see, Aelred, like John, has high regard for particular love.

Friendship is particular love whereas love itself is universal. Not all whom we love are entitled to be called friends. But particular love such as this is a part of the life of a monk for Aelred. As in John's Gospel, friendship is divine and the highest kind of love.

JORDAN OF SAXONY: Aelred was a twelfth-century Cistercian; Jordan of Saxony a thirteenth-century Dominican (1190–1237). Aelred's reflections pertained especially to intrasexual relationships; Jordan's letters speak of heterosexual or intersexual relationships. The two of these portray the beauty in both kinds of friendship. Jordan's friendship with Diana d'Andalo is one of the better known relationships between men and women in spiritual history. His friendship with Henry of Cologne, who entered the Dominican Order with him, is also one of the historical examples of celibate friendship. He was the second Master General of the Dominican Order. He did not leave us a treatise on friendship as Aelred did. Rather, we have fifty of his letters to Diana, from which we can discover his attitude toward friendship, its relationship to the spiritual life, and its importance for celibate life. None of Diana's letters to Jordan have been preserved.

One discovers from reading the letters the humanness of their love and the genuine emotional and spiritual help they were to each other. Nor did they consider their love for each other to detract from their love for God. Three themes in the letters are: their constant presence to each other, their pain during absence or separation, and their mutual love of Christ. I will let Jordan speak for himself.[35]

Their constant presence to each other:

You are so deeply engraven on my heart that the more I realize how truly you love me from the depths of your soul, the more incapable I am of forgetting you and the more constantly you are in my thoughts; for your love of me moves me deeply and makes my love for you burn more strongly.[36]

O Diana, how unhappy this present condition of things which we must suffer: that we cannot love each other without pain and anxiety! You weep and are in bitter grief because it is not given you to see me continually; and I equally grieve that it is so rarely given me to be with you.[37]

Their pain of absence and separation:

Yet I cannot wonder that you are sad when I am far from you since, do what I may, I myself cannot but be sad that you are far from me.[38]

When I have to part from you I do so with heavy heart; yet you add sorrow to my sorrow since I see you then so inconsolably weighed down that I cannot but be saddened not only by our separation which afflicts us both but also by your own desolation as well.[39]

The longer we are separated from one another, the greater becomes our desire to see one another again.[40]

The basis of their friendship is Christ.

Yet whatever we may write to each other matters little, beloved: within our hearts is the ardour of our love in the Lord whereby you speak to me and I to you continuously in those wordless outpourings of charity which no tongue can express nor letter contain.[41]

Their particular and spiritual friendship was not incompatible with their call to universal love nor with their desire to love God. All three were well integrated. Friendship need not divide our attention. It can elevate our souls and deepen our persons. It is possible to love ourselves, to love persons of the other sex, to love persons of our own sex, to love God, and still be one person. True love does not divide; it unites. Spritual friendship is not that which lacks affection and emotion. It is that which is built upon a solid foundation, to use Aelred's expression, the foundation of a mutual love of God.

CONTEMPORARY REFLECTIONS: The traditional appreciation of friendship from John to Aelred and Jordan continues into our own time. Intimacy and friendship within celibate and religious life are important not only for human growth but for spiritual growth as well. Spiritual friendship is not platonic love in which there is no element of the erotic. Spiritual friendship is a deeply affective bond, but a bond which does not lose its basis in the spiritual life. Spiritual friendship is particular friendship in that all friendship is particular. Not all love is friendship, as Aelred pointed out in the twelfth century, but all friendship is love. Particular friendship became the subject of suspicion because particular friendship became identified with false friendship. All friendship is particular; not all friendship is exclusive. That is the quality which is an enemy to celibate love. Particular friendship acquired the connotation of exclusive friendship or genital friendship. As Quentin Hakenewerth observes, celibate friendship is both non-genital and non-exclusive.[42]

Hakenewerth points out the following six attributes as indicative that a friendship is becoming less in accord with the celibate life: a) when the expression of the love gravitates toward the genital as the vehicle of union; b) when one or both resent the sharing of love with others; c) when one considers the other person as his or feels bound to regard the other person as the number one person in his life; d) when one begins to expect or demand certain responses; e) when one's commitment to the members of his religious community suffers because of his emotional involvement; and f) when the friendship causes loss of interest in prayer.[43]

There is always tension in life; the possibility of a tension-free life is a myth. Tension arises from friendship as we integrate it into the total thrust of our life. There are three sources of tension in particular that arise from friendship: the tension between this particular friendship and one's larger community; the tension between the friendship and one's ministry; the tension arising from the sexual dimension of the friendship. These tensions should not make one fearful of friendship nor lead one to run from it. They are natural frustrations which have to be faced. Celibate friendships are not easily acquired. We have to work to gear them in a celibate direction; they do not simply arise as non-genital, non-exclusive, non-possessive, well-integrated relationships. They become that way through emotional and spiritual work.

The tendency to become genital is nothing other than the affective quality of human relationships. The tendency to be possessive and resent sharing with others is simply the jealous quality of friendships. With increased psychological awareness today, as I pointed out in the first part of this chapter, these elements within friendship can and must be handled: the contract, healthy dependence, the need for distance, jealousy, hostility, the need for privacy. All of these are dimensions of intimacy which must be faced along with many more. They are not realities from which to run but realities through which we grow. Becoming chaste implies taking risks. It also implies being realistic about where the relationship is going. It is generally clear whether the two are growing in their love for each other as well as in their love of celibacy or whether the mutual love moves them farther and farther from an appreciation of celibacy. It is clear whether or not the spiritual life is being shared or whether it is only affection that is shared. Growth together demands prayer together as well. Aelred was wise in this regard. Some friendships may have to be dissolved but these should be few, and then they must be ended carefully and gradually. The two should challenge themselves to grow in their love for each other as well as in their love for their communities and their love for Christ. The process of becoming true friends is not an easy task even in marriage. It demands genuine communication as well as a mutual love of God.

Gerald Vann writes:

Just as foolish direction can ruin a young man's health, both physically and psychologically, in the sacred name (in this case the *sacré nom*) of asceticism or religious fervour; just as a false theory of obedience can give him a wholly wrong outlook on life by training him to identify the ideal with the unnatural; just as he may have his youthful gaiety extinguished in him for the sake of a stuffy decorum, or his individuality quenched by the imposition of a common pattern, a sort of pseudo-personality; so too his emotional nature, his heart, may be wholly repressed and smothered, the lid firmly screwed down, while all his energies are directed to the avoidance of any wrongdoing, so that he ends in a sort of irreproachable vacuum. (Sometimes this last is justified on the grounds of playing for safety: but safety for what? and at what price? In the last resort it is better to run the risk of an occasional scandal than to have a monastery—a choir, a refectory, a recreation room—full of dead men. Our Lord did not say 'I am come that ye may have safety, and have it more abundantly'. Some of us would indeed give anything to feel safe, about our life in this world as in the next, but we cannot have it both ways: safety or life, we must choose.)[44]

Intimate friendship is part of any doctrine of the spiritual life and we have famous examples from spiritual history. There are famous friendships between men: Jesus and John, Basil and Gregory Nazianzen, Anselm and Gilpert Crispin and Lanfranc, Bernard of Clairvaux and William of Thierry, Aelred and Waldef, Jordan of Saxony and Henry of Cologne. There are the famous friendships between men and women: Francis of Assissi and Clare, Catherine of Siena and Raymond of Capua, Jordan of Saxony and Diana, Francis de Sales and Jane Frances de Chantal, Vincent de Paul and Louise de Marillac, John of the Cross and Teresa of Avila, Teilhard de Chardin and Leontine Zanta.[45] Such friendships will always have their dangers but they are also a source of beauty, growth, and a high degree of love. There is no pretending we love everyone in general if we cannot love anyone in particular.

The rule of Taizé reads, "Our celibacy means neither breaking with human affections, nor indifference, but calls for the transfiguration of our natural love. . . . There is no friendship without purifying suffering." [46] The love of friendship is not easy but it does help to make life worthwhile. Growth in love involves all that the emotional, intellectual, and spiritual lives can provide. It is necessary for those who claim to take as their primary command to love one another as their Lord has loved them. Our lives will then not be like the religious man whom Thomas More reported as saying, "I have with me in my convent innumerable brothers, but not a single friend." [47]

THE SIGNIFICANCE OF SEPARATION

Separation is a problem within celibate life although not a problem exclusive to celibacy. It is important to be aware of both its psychological and theological dimensions. The psychological process is grief. We usually think of the experience of death when we think of grief. Death, however, is simply one form of separation. There are many other manifestations as well: divorce; separation due to a military assignment; children growing up and leaving home; friends moving away from each other. Absence and death are similar—in both cases one experiences a loss of someone loved.

Sometimes separation can be anticipated since the loss of the loved person is something of which one is aware ahead of time, whereas death is often a sudden loss for which there can be little preparation.[48] When separation can be anticipated, grief begins prior to the actual departure of the loved person. The anticipatory grief reaction begins before the separation, continues during it, and comes to completion only after the actual separation. What I am discussing here is the phenomenon of separation and not death as such. Nevertheless, much of the literature on grief comes from a study of death in particular.[49]

There are many characteristics of the grief reaction and the separation process. There are ten different symptoms that occur frequently in the literature on grief and separation: anxiety, loss of meaning, acute pain, the need to cry, hostility, guilt, depression, withdrawal, the need to talk about the lost person, and somatic symptoms.

Psychologically, separation is one of the most difficult realities that will be faced by celibate people striving after intimacy since intimate friendship in the celibate's life does not involve the commitment to each other of physical presence for life. The interpersonal contract between two celibates is not to be a couple in the same way that two married people become a couple. Separation is not only a psychological issue, however; it has spiritual and theological significance as well. Separation can be a revelatory experience and a deepening of the Christian life. At that time, possibly more than any other, we realize dependency and therefore dependency upon God as well. At that time in a person's life, one realizes he or she cannot live except by faith. The psychological experience is that I would not choose to go on. Somehow, unbelievable as it might be, and though my experience seems to reveal the contrary, it is true that all things work unto good for one who loves God. One year later, one can realize that death leads to new life.

In separation, God reveals to us that there are two sides to life. Every friendship involves pain and joy. It is the Christian who is able to stand at the foot of the cross, the foot of his *own* cross, with tears in his eyes, and yet with hope for a new resurrection and with faith in rebirth. Thus one can stand at the foot of that experience, agonizing though it might be, with tears in one's eyes, but with the conviction that there is more to come, possibly more pain to come before new life emerges, but that someday new life will be there. In that sense Christianity is the basis for a sense of humor because a Christian realizes that there is more to life than that which meets the eye. There is more to reality than my present experience. God is with us even though, in my present experience, I experience only emptiness. To be a Christian is to experience the paradox of death and separation while believing in resurrection and rebirth. The Christian revelation is a reflection upon our own experience that growth never comes without pain, struggle, and suffering.

In the experience of separation, we also discover the Christian theory of personality. The experience of no longer being physically present to a close friend reveals to me that this other person is indeed part of me. We can no longer talk about ourselves as if my self is this body or this flesh in this space. We come to the realization that a person is very much a center of relationships and that people who enter into my life are realistically parts of me. Most of us have no trouble in saying that a hand, finger, or hair is a part of us. Yet, who would not give up a hand to remain with someone he loves? Our experience is that a friend is more a part of us than the physical parts of our body. It takes the experience of separation (the experience of being torn apart) before we realize it is not "I" but this other person who lives within me. "I" as person is more than my self alone. I will close this section on the theology of separation and friendship with Augustine's experience of the loss of a close friend:

My heart was made dark by sorrow, and whatever I looked upon was death. My native place was a torment to me, and my father's house was a strange unhappiness. Whatsoever I had done together with him was, apart from him, turned into a cruel torture. My eyes sought for him on every side, and he was not given to them. I hated all things because they no longer held him. Nor could they now say to me, 'Here he comes,' as they did in his absence from them when he lived. . . . Only weeping was sweet to me, and it succeeded to my friend in my soul's delights. . . .

I marveled that other men should live, because he, whom I had loved as if he would never die, was dead. I marveled more that I, his second self, could live when he was dead. Well has someone said of his friend that he is half of his soul. For I thought that my soul and his soul were but one soul in two bodies. Therefore, my life was a horror to me, because I would not live but as a half.[50]

CONCLUSION

There is no need to write a conclusion for this chapter. It simply points to both the significance and the complexity, both psychologically and theologically, of the value of intimacy and friendship in the lives of celibate men and women. Just as spirituality is not separable from sexuality in the life of a chaste person, so spiritual or Christian friendship is not separable from the sexual dimension of those relationships. It is to that sexual dimension in the life of a celibate person that we now turn.

7

The Sexual Life
of a Celibate Person

ALBERT PLÉ writes, "The man who enters a life of consecrated celibacy enters a condition in which, nowadays especially, his whole emotional life is going to be profoundly affected." [1] Celibate people must be realistic about the emotional facts of life. The decision to be single is a decision to set aside the conjugal way of developing friendship but is not a decision to remain emotionally unfulfilled. Emotional and sexual fulfillment are possible within the celibate life although manuals on celibacy frequently leave this dimension undiscussed. Man is a unified being. His spiritual life affects his emotional life and vice-versa. The two cannot be separated for a person attempting to live an integrated life. My purpose in this chapter is to look at some aspects of celibate sexuality.

SEXUAL AWAKENING

The final goal of psychosexual development is the mature capacity to love which is necessary for both celibacy and marriage. Psychosexual development involves a number of different abilities among which I list the following:
1) the capacity to love myself
2) the capacity to love persons of the other sex

3) the capacity to love persons of my own sex
4) the capacity to love God
5) the capacity to love in a non-possessive way
6) the capacity to express love physically
7) the capacity to communicate tender and warm feelings
8) the capacity for genital love and orgasm
9) the capacity to distinguish sexual desire and sexual love
10) the capacity to integrate sexual desire into a loving relationship.

Teilhard de Chardin speaks of personality development as a process of centering.[2] He speaks of three phases in personality development, centration, excentration, and super-centration, which are concerned with the three dimensions of personality—individuality, sociality, and spirituality. A healthy person is self-centered, other-centered, and God-centered. The task of personality development is to integrate all three. Psychosexual development is the history of this capacity to love myself, others, and God in a freeing way.

A part of this process of psychosexual development is the history of sexual desire itself. Sexual desire is not love in itself nor is it sufficient for intimacy in an ongoing relationship. Love requires more from two people than sexual attraction provides. Nevertheless, for mature love, sexual desire needs to be integrated into our loving relationships. Sexual desire should increasingly become a part of those relationships where there is a commitment to intimacy and fidelity.

At a certain time in sexual development there emerges an awakening in one's life of very intense sexual feelings accompanied by an intense genital desire and a feeling of urgency. This is usually, but not necessarily, adolescence or puberty and is one of the sources of anxiety that accompanies adolescence. Not all people stay sexually awake at this time since the sexual awakening at puberty can be handled by repression as often happens with many celibate people for whom the awakening occurs later. Ethel Nash speaks of an unmarried counselee who experienced her first sexual awakening at thirty-four.[3] Although sexual awakening is generally thought of as occurring at the time of puberty, it often occurs later.

The awakening is accompanied by increased capacity and desire for orgasm.

The goal of psychosexual development, however, is not orgasm. It is the capacity to love. This awakening is one step along the way to developing the capacity to love. We often have an unhealthy attitude towards sexual awakening no matter at what age it occurs. We speak of the adolescent years as being dangerous years because of this. It is true that sexual awakening is accompanied by intense anxiety whether this be the anxiety of adolescence or the anxiety reaction of a delayed sexual awakening. No matter at what age it occurs, however, it is a rewarding experience and should not be repressed. Delayed sexual awakening is not often discussed; it is generally considered sufficient to discuss adolescence and puberty.

I am concerned about the effects of sexual awakening for a person who is considering or who has already chosen celibate life. Intense sexual desire makes a person question the celibate way of life. One of the effects of the sexual awakening is to feel pulled or pushed towards genital activity. If genital intercourse takes place, there will be the effects that accompany this experience, which can include intense anxiety, dissatisfaction with the experience, and the tendency to repeat the experience in the near future.[4]

No matter how one handles the awakening, there is the task of integrating this new potentiality into one's capacity to love. This is a most important task at this time. Until this is accomplished, there will be anxiety and fear. Until the task of establishing controls is taken care of, a person will fear relationships as well as enter into immature relationships. Emotional involvement rather than personal commitment will be the basis for relating. Until a person is able to handle sexual feelings and integrate them, he or she will have available only adolescent relationships. If a person experiences genital intercourse at this time, there are other factors to take into consideration. He or she is going to feel a loss of control; increased physical need; the possibility of increased genital behavior, whether masturbatory or homosexual or heterosexual; and guilt feelings.

Sexual awakening usually comes at puberty but can occur later due to successful repression. At puberty it accompanies the physiological changes which create increased genital potential and also tension. This tension finds itself expressed in nocturnal wet dreams, masturbation, and intercourse. It can be experienced by a person as falling in love since the capacity to distinguish sexual desire and love has not yet matured. Many adolescent relationships emerge at this time when people do feel they have fallen in love.

If the sexual awakening occurs later, earlier repression now fails for varying reasons: increased physical contact in relationships, an entrance into a more intimate relationship, curiosity, freedom that exists away from parental controls, or an accidental experience which brings to life genital forces. This is something that should be welcomed. The question raised is how to deal with this phase of sexual life and not to resort once again to repression. If we identify sexual desire as sinful, repression is almost inevitable.[5] Sexual desire and feelings are not immoral. What one does with these feelings might be.

Anxiety and panic can accompany sexual awakening and the first experience of genital intercourse. I only gradually learn that I can control my sexual behavior.[6] Sexual feelings need not control me; they need not be acted out inappropriately. Feelings are meant to be felt, and sexual feelings are no exception. They should not be repressed. Allowing ourselves to feel the feelings, however, is not the same as acting them out. There are times when I feel that I will rape the next person who walks into my room. I have, however, raped no one yet. There are times when I feel like killing someone. I have killed no one yet. I only gradually learn that I can allow myself to feel these feelings and still be in control of my behavior. To the degree that I am able to control (not repress) myself, to that degree I will allow myself to feel more and more feelings. Self-control enables me to feel, and allowing oneself to feel is the middle ground between repression and destructive behavior. Nathaniel Branden writes:

A rational man neither represses his feelings nor acts on them blindly. One of the strongest protections against repression is a man's conviction that he will not act on an emotion just because he feels it; this allows him to identify his emotions calmly and to determine their justifiability without fear or guilt. It is an interesting paradox that repression and emotional self-indulgence are often merely two sides of the same coin.[7]

HETEROSEXUAL FRIENDSHIP

When I speak of celibate friendship, I am not speaking of platonic relationships which do not involve affective and erotic dimensions. Emotionally intimate friendship is usually affectionate. The question is whether a deeply affectionate but non-genital relationship is possible, and a celibate person says that it is. This does not deny the necessity of limits. If I "French kiss," my genitality will be so stirred that it will be difficult not to continue further in a genital direction. If I invite a close friend to my bedroom to share discussion, turn off the lights, and light a candle, the erotic feelings can more easily take over. A bedroom is not the atmosphere for developing celibate intimacy between a man and a woman. An affective relationship between a celibate man and a celibate woman needs more than sexual attraction. Sexually inexperienced people sometimes mistakenly feel that this is enough on which to build. In solid fact, more is necessary for an enduring friendship.

A difficult relationship to maintain is that between two people only one of whom is celibate. Two celibate people see their relationship in the context of a common commitment. In the other relationship, one of them is more free to think in terms of marriage as a possible future even if this is only subconscious. Such a relationship is not fair to a non-celibate person unless he or she is also committed to some form of the single life. A non-celibate person will be more actively engaged in building relationships where marriage is a possibility. A relationship between a celibate person and a non-celibate person should be honest from the very beginning in this regard in case one person's goal is celibacy and the other's is marriage. There is no substitute in any relationship for honest communication.

Although we are brought up to think that love means marriage, this is not the case. A loving relationship of friendship need not culminate in marriage even though this is what the culture expects. The celibate accepts that any relationship he or she develops must be within the terms of the commitment to celibacy. Their love does not lead to marriage. The Yahwist's theology of sexuality saw partnership between the sexes as good. The two are made to be together and to share together. A monosexual world limits the growth of a person. We need relationships with the other sex in order to come to that full human growth which we desire as Christian men and women.

Sexual feelings are present in many interpersonal relationships and should not be frightening. Sexlessness and coldness are not the measures of holiness. Friendship between the sexes involves sexual feelings, yet genitality does not become a primary mode of communication. A celibate person lives with sexual emotions. When he loves, he feels the love. We are going to be excited about the loved one; we are going to be thinking about the loved one. Not all sexual feelings indicate love, but love usually involves sexual feelings. I do not mean simply affective sexuality but genital sexuality as well. Genitality is involved in a sexual response. Such genital excitement is healthy and need not be feared. It is a part of the personal response of a sexual person to another sexual person for whom one cares deeply.

Expressing heterosexual affection is not inappropriate as long as it is within the limits set by the relationship itself. Affection can be expressed in smiles, hugging, holding, kissing. Genital feelings may well be there. A mature person knows when he is communicating affection and when he is arousing genitality. Both dimensions of sexuality, affectivity as well as genitality, are involved. The celibate person is free to express the affection and is not to be frightened by the genital. Nor does he direct the relationship towards genitality.

The question is posed today whether genital expression is compatible with celibate love. Feeling comfortable with both our sexuality and our celibacy, we should be able to face this question and discuss it. The basic argument in favor of genital love for a celibate person is something like this: the decision a celibate person makes about his or her life is to be single and to remain unmarried. At one time sexuality was seen as necessarily procreative and valid only in marriage, an institution which could serve the raising of the children. Sexuality today is not seen as necessarily procreative. It need not, therefore, be restricted to marriage. The decision not to marry is no longer a decision not to have genital relations. Genital love, however, still belongs within one, ongoing, permanent, faithful commitment in accord with Christian ideals. Nevertheless, such a commitment need not be found in marriage alone; it can also be found among celibate people. Since genitality need not be restricted to marriage, it is appropriate for the celibate to express love genitally without failing in his or her decision to be single for the sake of the kingdom.

My own opinion is that celibate people choose to forego genital love. This is not because we now transfer a negative attitude toward sexuality to a negative attitude toward genitality. Genital love is beautiful and enjoyable. But celibate love is not genital love. Nor is celibacy primarily genital abstinence. Someone may well abstain from genital love and still not be celibate. The life of a — celibate involves concentration on forms of loving other than genital. Genital love requires commitment to physical presence with another person.

Genital interaction eventually leads to either exclusiveness, or marriage, or superficiality, or promiscuity. It becomes exclusive because of the intensity of the emotional involvement through continued genital interaction, which unity usually leads to marriage. The alternative to such emotional attachment is to remain casual (superficial) in genital experiences, which is especially difficult for women. Nor is it the Christian understanding of the sacramentality of genital life. A casual attitude towards genitality sustains only a superficial relationship and also moves in the direction of promiscuity. One becomes promiscuous in order to satisfy what is felt or a need not yet transcended. If two celibate people genitally involved with one another separate for the sake of the apostolate, they are going to need other genital relationships if they have not yet transcended experiencing their genitality as a need. Genitality will be satisfied only in exclusivity, marriage, superficiality, promiscuity, or by transcending genitality as a need. Only the latter is compatible with celibate life.

One might argue that the genital relationship lies within the limits of the Christian understanding, in one relationship, in an intimate relationship which is his or her private life, and is in no way destructive of his or her celibate goals; yet the celibate person says something public about his or her private life, and there will be tension between the two.

In addition, intimate genital attachment creates an exclusivity within the relationship that makes life in community more difficult. The goal of a celibate person is celibate love and genital love does not serve this goal. Sexual love can; genital love does not. It would be the exception if, in some case, genital love worked to the advantage of celibate love. Only after counseling, prayer, and spiritual direction could one conscientiously make such a decision.

There is another aspect, however, to the question of a celibate having genital intercourse. We have considered the aspect of its legitimacy in terms of the celibate ideal. Not all people, however, live the ideal. This does not mean that we water down the ideal. Those people who argue for the legitimacy of genital love are changing the understanding of the celibate ideal. There are those, however, who accept that this is the ideal and have found themselves at times not living it—either through an experience of genital intercourse or in a genital relationship not yet outgrown. This is a pastoral question.

The question is: what is a proper attitude and response towards oneself or someone else who has or is experiencing difficulty in this way? If a celibate comes to me having had or presently having genital relationships, there are two sets of questions I keep in the back of my mind. The first is: what does this mean in the total context of this person's life, this particular relationship, and the commitment to celibacy? what does the genital expression really mean? The second set of questions is: what is the nature of the relationship we are talking about? is it an expression within a transient relationship or an expression within a significantly deep relationship which is important to the person's own life?

It is important to explore what the genitality means for this particular person. Is the person seeking intimacy? Is the person experiencing a struggle in his (or her) striving after masculinity or femininity? Is it an expression of anxiety that lies somewhere else within the person at this time? Is this a sexual awakening? If this is a striving after intimacy, the person must become aware that genitality is not necessary for intimacy. The counselee should also see that this is a problem which can easily enter into a close relationship and especially in an early phase of a relationship. If this is a sexual awakening for the person, there are further questions and ramifications to be considered. It is also possible that what was once integrated has now become a problem area. The counselee should not become afraid and run.

The most significant task in such counseling is to insure that the person does not feel cheap or that he or she does not feel a failure. The counselee may well need to reconstruct his or her self-esteem if he or she is going to continue in the celibate life. Overdependence on the genital aspect may be a lack of self-esteem. To make a person feel cheapened by this action is to increase rather than alleviate the problem. The counselee should not be led to believe that the celibate life can no longer be lived, that he or she is no longer a celibate person, that his or her relationship to God has been destroyed. The person has experienced life in a new way and now has to set about the task of integrating this into his or her celibate commitment. It might mean that the counselee will change his or her decision about the celibate life in the end, but it is not immediately apparent that this is the direction in which to move.

The counselee must continue the process of integrating his or her sexuality, his or her sexual feelings, new sexual experiences, into his or her Christian life. It may be that this process of integration needs both therapy and spiritual direction. There are some dimensions of the integration that counseling and therapy can facilitate; there are other dimensions which spiritual direction can facilitate. Encourage a person to engage in both unless he or she is involved with a director or therapist who is skilled in both the emotional and the spiritual dimensions of life. The task, however, is one of continued integration. Continued integration does not mean permission for continued genital expression. It means integrating one's feelings about this expression and the difficulty one is having in such a way that nongenital love becomes possible.

Another task is to resolve the tension between the private and public life. This may take some time. One should not feel guilty if it is not immediately resolved or if integration is not immediate. The counselor cannot tolerate irresponsibility in this regard; nevertheless the person should not feel hypocritical if he or she is conscientiously undertaking the task of trying to grow in the celibate life.

The sexual life is at the core of the private life of a person and yet vows make it public. One must have continual respect for a person's private life and the privacy of a relationship. Approach him or her as a person and not as someone who has failed in a commitment. Celibacy is something we grow into; it is not simply given. We face new questions about our celibate life every day. The counselee must not give up on interpersonal relationships at this time. If he or she does, his or her interpersonal life may be permanently damaged. The person should now be more in tune with his or her genitality and more aware of physiological reactions. The person can approach future relationships more aware. I emphasize the need a person has for positive support at this time. Too often the person finds himself or herself in a loving relationship that cannot be shared with other celibate people. The less he is able to share his celibate life with his community, the more he will move in the direction of sharing his life and his problems outside the celibate community.

In this regard, the ideal is not being changed. There will always be the tension, to use Freudian terms, between the ego ideal and the id. Not being perfect does not invalidate the striving after perfection. Striving for perfection means that we are not yet perfect. This is the eschatological tension in an individual celibate's life between the ideal of celibacy and his present growth. We must accept our humanity and be realistic about our expectations. At the same time we do not set aside our striving after the ideal. The ideal is still non-genital. The person learns each day that the celibate life is a beautiful life and that we have to continue to learn how to live it.

The task of integrating sexuality into celibate living is not new to our day. I am continually amazed as I read the problems of early monasticism. Louis Bouyer, in commenting on the ideal of Antony, who was born around 251 A.D., the founder of anchoritic monasticism, states, "Monastic life is essentially progressive. Later on, the canonists would tend to see it only as a state of life, defined once for all by the vows. But at this stage, the vows were still unknown and the monastic life seemed, on the contrary, to be a commitment to detachments and correlative ascents which were to have no end here below." [8] The celibate life is a process of development and not an accomplished state. We are called forth to continually further growth. Let me report two brief stories from the sayings of the Fathers.

Two brethren made their way to the city to sell their handiwork: and when in the city they went different ways, divided one from the other, one of them fell into fornication. After a while came his brother, saying, 'Brother, let us go back to our cell.' But he made answer, 'I am not coming.' And the other questioned him, saying, 'Wherefore, brother?' And he answered, 'Because when thou didst go from me, I ran into temptation, and I sinned in the flesh.' But the other, anxious to help him, began to tell him saying, 'But so it happened with me: when I was separated from thee, I too ran into fornication. But let us go, and do penance together with all our might: and God will forgive us that are sinful men.' And they came back to the monastery and told the old men what had befallen them, and they enjoined on them the penance they must do. But the one began his penance, not for himself but for his brother, as if he himself had sinned. And God, seeing his love and his labour, after a few days revealed to one of the old men that for the great love of this brother who had not sinned, He had forgiven the brother who had. And verily this is to lay down one's soul for one's brother.[9]

And an old man said, "Judge not him who is guilty of fornication, if thou are chaste: or thou thyself wilt offend a similar law. For He who said, 'Thou shalt not fornicate' said also 'Thou shalt not judge.' " [10]

HOMOSEXUAL FRIENDSHIP

Friendship not only exists between the sexes, but also within a sex, where sexual attraction and erotic feelings are also present. Such friendship is not homosexual in the sense that it is primarily based on sexual feelings; no friendship is based on sexual attraction alone. Friendship differs from a sexual liaison. Nevertheless, the sexual aspect is still present in friendship even though it is not primary. A friendship is not best understood by designating it either heterosexual or homosexual because the sexual dimension is not the only nor even the primary aspect of friendship.

Friends offer sustenance during weakness, sympathy amid sorrow, and sacrifice for the sake of the other. I use heterosexuality and homosexuality to describe the sexual quality of relationships without saying that the sexual quality is the most significant aspect.

In this chapter my concern is the sexual life of a celibate person and hence the sexual dimension of Christian friendship as well. I am not talking about those relationships which are not examples of Christian friendship.

Homosexual friendships are an important dimension of any person's life. Celibate homosexuality, in the positive sense of that word, remains non-genital. Closeness can cause genital reactions, but a celibate relationship does not move in that direction even though the feelings are there. The feelings are not to be denied or repressed; they are to be felt. Celibate people confronted for the first time with homosexual and homogenital feelings sometimes panic. Homosexual panic and pseudo-homosexuality are not pathological homosexuality in the clinical sense.[11] The first experience of homosexual feelings can cause anxiety and fright. In a state of anxiety, one may judge oneself to be homosexual in a pathological sense rather than realizing the normality of the feelings. Homosexual feelings are an aspect of celibate life since celibates have close and loving relationships with members of their own sex. Environment can give strength to the homosexual dimension of the personality by bringing together members of the same sex for periods of time to the exclusion of the other sex. There is no reason to fool ourselves about this. Celibate people are sexual beings like everyone else. When affectionate and genital feelings enter homosexual friendship, one should recognize and accept their presence. This does not mean the relationship is unhealthy.

Much of what I have said about heterosexual relationships could be repeated here. The two are not totally different. Friendship between people of the same sex involves affective and erotic aspects. Limitations need to be placed on homosexual friendships lest they too become genital. These relationships as well as others require honest communication. The fear of mistakes exists in homosexual relationships as well as a fear of homosexuality itself. These relationships involve risk as well as demand responsibility. The ideal of celibate love is to be pursued. I would say the same about homogenital relations as about heterogenital relations for celibates, both with respect to their unacceptability and with respect to a healthy attitude towards oneself or another who has or is experiencing difficulty.

Some celibates fear relationships between men and women because they fear the sexual issues involved. Those who fear these relationships need to be aware that men and women can and do sleep with their own sex as well as with members of the other sex. Restricting relationships to one's own sex does not solve the problem of what a celibate does with sexuality. The celibate life is a risk that mature people undertake who attempt to both face and limit their sexual life in accord with certain spiritual values and Christian goals. Although lessened restriction on interpersonal relationships is open to possible dangers, celibates must face and not fear this fact. That which is important is sincerity and maturity on the part of the people who are striving to find God in a celibate way.

My discussion of homosexual friendship to this point has been more a question of men and women who are more heterosexual in their preference for sexual love but who still are capable of deep relationships with their own sex. There are also, however, homosexual men and women in celibate life. Geoffrey Moorhouse records the affirmation of one celibate homosexual in his *Against All Reason*: "I should never have got married even if I had not become a religious. I am completely homosexual." [12] There is no reason why homosexual men and women cannot live the celibate life as genuinely and profitably as heterosexual men and women and still enjoy friendship both with their own sex and with the other sex. I speak here, of course, of healthy homosexuals. Homosexual affection can be as celibate as heterosexual affection. Norman Pittenger states the issue about homosexuality quite clearly in an excellent discussion on homosexual affection. He writes:

The wrongness in homosexuality is to be found in exactly the same place as the wrongness in heterosexuality—that is, not in the condition, not in the accompanying desire for and practice of physical contact, but insofar as the homosexual, like the heterosexual, fails to be a responsible person, refuses to exercise control over his actions, and lacks real respect for the one whom he loves, or thinks he loves. [13]

Immature relationships can occur among adult celibates which re-enact the preadolescent homosexual chum stage or the adolescent heterosexual crush state.[14] These affective relationships are not adult friendships. A characteristic of the adolescent is his ability to abandon an intense relationship with the same facility with which he initially established it.[15] These relationships are not mature in that they do not involve genuine commitment to the other person and are not experiences of free intimacy.

Celibacy raises definite questions about homosexuality. There are those people whose preference in sexual love is always homosexual. For others, there are homosexual feelings, experiences, and love which emerge in certain situations. Freud pointed to the fact that when people tend to associate more exclusively with their own sex the homosexual dimension emerges with strength simply because our sexuality is now being channeled in the direction of those people with whom we relate and with whom we have the opportunity to relate. Freud writes:

It is possible to point to external influences in their lives, whether of a favorable or inhibiting character, which have led sooner or later to a fixation of their inversion. (Such influences are exclusive relations with persons of their own sex, comradeship in war, detention in prison, the dangers of heterosexual intercourse, celibacy, sexual weakness, etc.) [16]

Freud is referring to a situational kind of homosexuality. Our previous exploration of sexual attraction as related to external stimuli would confirm this observation of Freud's as well. Others besides Freud have pointed to this same fact.[17]

Celibacy is one of the situations which can give rise to forms of homosexuality. Celibacy is not a homosexual way of life, but common sexual sense would tell us that celibate people must realistically face the homosexual dimensions of life. This does not imply a lack of health on the part of the people nor a lack of health on the part of the way of life. Homosexuality can be proportionate to the unavailability of heterosexual partners. Albert Ellis writes, "Human beings are born with an ambisexual tendency, which allows them to be raised to be heterosexuals in most instances, but which is sufficiently liable to permit homosexuality to develop under somewhat unusual circumstances and in many individual cases under fairly usual conditions." [18] Circumstances affect our way of relating sexually. More intimacy between the sexes is possible in many celibate communities. Many, however, still find themselves in more of a monosexual than a bisexual environment. Homosexual feelings as well as homosexual experiences may enter and need to be understood. These are not a manifestation of pathology. As celibate people there is no need to deny our own homosexuality, which is present in all people.

When we talk about homosexuality, we need to rid ourselves of cultural prejudice. In all professions there are those who are homosexual. (I am talking about healthy homosexuality.) When I talk about the sexuality of the celibate way of life, I am not saying that celibacy is a homosexual way of life. It is not a homosexual way of life but does give rise to homosexual dimensions which need to be faced.

Homosexuality also has to be seen in both an affective and a genital way. Affectivity cannot be totally separated from genitality. These two dimensions of our sexuality frequently involve each other. Homosexual affection frequently moves into the direction of homogenital feelings. Nouwen writes, "The experience of homosexual feelings in a certain period of life, or in a temporary fashion, or in certain situations, is a perfectly usual, healthy, and normal thing. Involvement in a homosexual act or different homosexual acts during a period of life is not fatal in the sense that one is now doomed to be a homosexual for the rest of his life. More dangerous than the experience is the anxiety and fear related to it and the avoidance of asking for help and advice." [19] Nouwen points here to the real problem of homosexuality, whether in celibate communities or in our culture. This is the problem of anxiety, depression, and guilt which is not caused directly by homosexual feelings but by one's attitude or view towards them. Too often people view the homosexual dimension of their personalities as catastrophic. In such cases it is the attitude, discomfort, and self-rejection which are unhealthy.

There are three steps that can lead to a destructive attitude towards one's homosexuality. These are progressively to move from the awareness, "I have homosexual feelings and homosexual experiences," to "I am homosexual," to "I am sick." The first level of awareness is healthy; it is facing the homosexual dimension which is a real part of all life. To take the second step and come to the conviction that because I have these feelings or experiences I am homosexual is not the inevitable conclusion. I have pointed out previously how difficult it is to classify sexual behavior as simply heterosexual or homosexual. Kinsey speaks of a seven-point scale. Sullivan speaks of forty-five patterns of sexual behavior. To describe oneself flatly as homosexual or one's sexuality as homosexuality is frequently an oversimplification. Nevertheless there are those for whom sexual attraction does arise for the most part only from those of their own sex. To go from this awareness to the final statement that I am therefore sick is destructive. To have homosexual feelings, experiences, and relationships is not to be homosexual. To be homosexual, however, if that is what one is, is not to be sick. This does not deny that there are sick forms of homosexuality (inability to relate to the other sex) but it does mean that homosexuality is not necessarily sickness, as we found in the work of Hooker, Hoffman, and Weinberg.

Arnold Buss, in his discussion of abnormality and deviancy, writes, "The three criteria of abnormality are discomfort, inefficiency, and bizarreness." [20] A homosexual person need not experience discomfort if he does not allow his homosexuality to disturb his sexual identity, if he does not confuse homosexual dimensions of his sexuality with being pathologically homosexual, and if he is able to comfortably accept the degree of homosexuality operative in his personality. Getting to this level of comfort can be difficult and stormy as is the process of growth for all of us. Homosexual people, however, can achieve this comfort level. Men and women need this particular awareness when joining celibate communities since they are frequently going to find themselves in situations which upset their sexual lives, give rise to homosexual dimensions, and require adjustment even for a mature person in order to achieve the comfort level necessary.

The second criterion listed by Buss, that of inefficiency, does not necessarily apply to homosexual people. As Hooker and others have pointed out, the homosexual person can operate efficiently in society and at work, and is normal in every other area of his or her personality. Buss himself writes, "The sexual deviant rarely suffers discomfort, and his unusual sexual outlet does not usually interfere with his job or the efficient playing of his various non-sexual roles. The essential criterion is bizarreness. Society trains its members . . . to regard heterosexual behavior between adults as normal and any other sexual outlet as disgusting and deviant." [21] It thus seems that homosexuality is abnormal primarily by social definition. There is no need for one to personally feel that he is necessarily sick because he is homosexual. A person, as he or she experiences the homosexual dimensions of personality more fully, should deepen his or her self-awareness, his or her feelings, perhaps along these lines: I have homosexual feelings; I am both a heterosexually and homosexually oriented person, with aspects of my personality motivated in both directions as well as in others; I am a healthy person and not sick, seeking to actualize my human potential as a person.

Before one can become a healthy person, one needs to overcome the resistances that he or she puts in the way of accepting and owning his or her homosexuality, the resistances which are quite understandable due to the social disapproval placed on homosexual behavior. The Dutch psychiatrist W. G. Sengers, as reported by Henri Nouwen, points to the deep-seated resistance against accepting existing homosexual feelings. "Only when this resistance is gone and the homosexual feelings can become available to one's self is one able to relate realistically to them." [22] Sengers discusses different levels of resistance and Nouwen points to two of them. "The first level includes a radical resistance in which man completely denies his homosexual inclinations, not only to others but primarily to himself. By doing this, man cuts himself off from his own most personal, intimate, and creative feelings and forces himself to 'evacuate' to the safe place of cerebral life. Once man does this, he tends to become a rigid and impersonal man who impresses others as being very distant and who seems to have everything under control. It is obvious that this kind of denial does great harm to the personality, easily creates emotional poverty, and makes social life a very 'dry' reality." [23]

The second level of resistance is to communicating one's homosexual feelings to another. The first level does not allow me to admit them to myself and the second level does not allow me to admit them to others. "The homosexual knows and understands his feelings but is tortured by the fear that anyone else should know them. . . . This can lead to an obsession with the homosexual condition. In that case the homosexual becomes so preoccupied with the fear of becoming known as a homosexual that his sexual feelings are constantly in his mind and become like an isolated power which haunts him day and night and sexualizes his total existence." [24]

The so-called traditional Christian attitude towards homosexuality is beginning to change.[25] There is a pluralism in this regard just as there is a pluralism of theologies of sexuality. The most prevalent attitude stemmed from the story of Sodom and Gomorrah's condemnation for the sin of homosexuality, which is an inaccurate interpretation of the story. The people of Sodom were not punished because of their homosexuality but because of their inhospitality. Likewise, the texts which refer to homosexuality in the New Testament are being more carefully studied.

We no longer have, however, sufficient theological grounds for perpetuating a destructive attitude. This does not mean that some homosexual relations are not unhealthy, unchristian, and sinful. It simply means that homosexuality can exist in healthy, Christian, and graced forms. Any biblical discussion would have to give due consideration to the texts which point out Jesus' love of John, Lazarus, and Peter, as well as his love for Martha, Mary, and Mary Magdalene. In this regard it is also important to be aware of the Old Testament attitude which comes through in the relationship between David and Jonathan:

After David had finished talking to Saul, Jonathan's soul became closely bound to David's and Jonathan came to love him as his own soul. Saul kept him by him from that day forward and would not let him go back to his father's house. Jonathan made a pact with David to love him as his own soul; he took off the cloak he was wearing and gave it to David, and his armour too, even his sword, his bow and his belt. Whenever David went out, on whatever mission Saul sent him, he was successful, and Saul put him in command of the fighting men; he stood well in the people's eyes and in the eyes of Saul's officers too (1 Samuel 18:1–5).

Jonathan then gave his weapons to his servant and said, 'Go and carry them to the town.' When the servant went off, David rose from beside the hillock and fell with his face to the ground and bowed down three times. They then kissed each other and both shed many tears. Then Jonathan said to David, 'Go in peace. And as regards the oath that both of us have sworn in the name of Yahweh, may Yahweh be witness between you and me, between your descendants and mine forever.' David then rose and left, and Jonathan went back to town (1 Samuel 20:4–43).

Saul and Jonathan are then killed in the fight with the Philistines. David grieves over Saul and his son Jonathan:

Saul and Jonathan, loved and lovely, neither in life, nor in death, were divided. Swifter than eagles were they, stronger were they than lions.

O daughters of Israel, weep for Saul who clothed you in scarlet and fine linen, who set brooches of gold on your garments.

How did the heroes fall in the thick of the battle?

O Jonathan, in your death I am stricken, I am desolate for you, Jonathan my brother. Very dear to me you were, your love to me more wonderful than the love of a woman.

How did the heroes fall and the battle armour fail? (2 Samuel 1:23–27).

Any theology of homosexuality must include a discussion of relationships such as the above. There are different ways of being homosexual and different ways of being heterosexual. Christian understanding praises relationships seen in the context of love, fidelity, permanence, and living in Christ through the Spirit.

MASTURBATORY ACTIVITY AND FANTASY

The word, *masturbation*, comes from two Latin words, *manus* and *turbatio*, which mean *hand* and *agitation* or *excitement*. Masturbation is not necessarily self-abuse. Few would deny that self-abuse is emotionally and spiritually destructive. The question is whether what we usually think of as masturbatory is actually abusive of personal spiritual growth. Words which do not evoke the same negative feeling are self-stimulation, auto-eroticism, or solo-sexuality. How does self-stimulation fit into the life of a Christian and the life of a celibate?

The best way to begin is to make some necessary distinctions with reference to the kinds of masturbatory activity. Irene Josselyn writes, "If an adult male masturbates with female articles of clothing or an adult female masturbates with bottles or other articles that appear to be the equivalent of a penis, it is usually considered significant of disturbance exceeding that which is involved in more common patterns of self-stimulation to produce the gratification masturbation offers." [26] One has to distinguish the method of masturbation, the frequency of masturbation, and the situation of the person if we are going to understand the implications of masturbatory activity. There are many different reasons for self-stimulation. An adolescent might masturbate out of curiosity. A married man separated from his wife might masturbate because he is accustomed to genital relations. Someone might masturbate in order to get to sleep.

I distinguish four kinds of masturbation. The first is the infantile masturbation of which Freud speaks.[27] A child finds gratification in exploring his or her genital area. This is exploration before puberty and simply a part of normal growth. We usually do not think of this kind of masturbation when we discuss the question. The next type is adolescent masturbation which accompanies puberty. The majority masturbate during this period. An adolescent boy can be absorbed with the mystery of an erection and spontaneously experiment in order to discover its meaning. At this time masturbation can become an easily acquired habit.

Most discussion centers around the masturbation of puberty. Nevertheless, there is also adult masturbation, masturbatory activity which would not be expressed in this way if other channels were possible. There are many examples of adult masturbation: university students who have chosen not to marry might masturbate in order to avoid unwanted pre-marital intercourse, a widow or widower who finds herself or himself without the same genital life as before, one separated from a spouse for a period of time in the armed forces or in prison. The question here is one of genital and physiological tension which might need release especially if the person were accustomed to genital relations prior to the separation. A similar situation exists for celibates who have chosen that genital intercourse will not be their mode of interpersonal communication. For many single adults, occasional masturbation is an outlet for tension. Adult masturbation differs from adolescent masturbation in that the adult person has integrated his or her sexuality into his or her life more than the adolescent has, and the adult would express his or her genitality with someone he or she loves rather than alone if that were possible.

The fourth kind of masturbation I call abusive masturbation, the kind of which we frequently speak. We assume that most masturbatory activity is destructive. The cases I have referred to above, however, are not abusive or destructive. An example here might be a person who prefers masturbatory genitality to intercourse or masturbatory genital activity that is disintegrating rather than integrative.

There are many distinctions to keep in mind: different kinds of masturbation, reasons, frequency, methods. The question is whether the masturbatory activity helps to integrate or disintegrate the person—how does it function in the total well-being of the person?

We have a negative conception of masturbation within the writings of the past couple centuries. Tissot, in the middle of the eighteenth century, wrote his *Onan, A Treatise on the Diseases Produced by Onanism.* He attributes epileptic seizures, gonorrhea, and insanity to masturbation. He held that the loss of one drop of seminal fluid causes more bodily damage than the loss of forty drops of blood. This kind of unscientific thinking has given rise to prejudice. Henry Varley, in the nineteenth century, conveyed to us the Victorian attitude. In 1883, he delivered a lecture on the destructive sin of self-abuse. Masturbation causes weak lungs and gives one a tendency toward colds, indigestion, and depression. Today we smile at such an understanding. Yet not long ago these myths prevailed and many people feared the effects. If we look more carefully at the facts, masturbation is harmless on the physical plane.

Psychological disturbance may cause masturbation but masturbation does not cause psychological disturbance. Masturbation may be symptomatic but not causative. McCary writes, "The only conflicts that masturbation engenders stem from poor sex education and guilt on the part of the parents, other teachers, and peers who pass on to those young people whom they instruct their disturbed attitudes toward a perfectly normal act. Certainly it is advisable that if an individual has anxieties concerning masturbation, and self-stimulation causes him extreme guilt, he should avoid it until the underlying psychological problem is corrected. Similarly, if one has extreme and severe guilt about head scratching, one should also avoid head scratching until the underlying psychological difficulty in this instance is rectified." [28]

Psychological problems caused by masturbation do not arise from the masturbatory activity but from the individual's attitude towards it. Those who do not practice masturbation or suppress the tendency might equally move in the direction of emotional difficulty. If an individual's thinking about sexuality is clouded with guilt, fear and confusion, his attitude is detrimental. Only if masturbation is the exclusive sexual release when heterosexual relations are possible is it pathological. When masturbation is preferred to intercourse, something is wrong.[29]

Adolescent masturbation as well as many adult forms of masturbation may be healthy.[30] The criterion is whether the masturbation is destructive due to our own attitudes and feelings. The question then is what are its effects on oneself, on one's interpersonal relationships, and on one's spiritual life. The masturbatory activity must be integrated into the life of the person in such a way that it is not destructive, whether this means overcoming it or continuing it in a more constructive way.

Physical harm does not come from masturbation nor does psychological harm, although psychological harm can come from an unhealthy attitude. The question remains whether spiritual harm comes from masturbation and this raises the question of morality which influences a person's attitude. In this regard there has been a change away from the traditional view. This does not mean that the traditional view is no longer being taught; it means that there are varied opinions in this regard.

Norbert Brockman, in his survey of contemporary attitudes toward masturbation, identifies four different statements of current positions within the Roman Church.[31] I quote these because they are well stated:

Masturbation is objectively a serious sin. Except in rare cases, it is also subjectively sinful, and the average person who gives in to masturbation, either as a teenager or as an adult, commits sin. Through confession and the sacraments, a person of good will can obtain the grace to overcome this habit, if he is willing to mortify himself and to avoid occasions of sin.

This position is a statement of the traditional understanding. The next statement represents what can be called "the diminished freedom position":

Masturbation is far from being a simple sexual sin, but is part of the complex process of maturation. While it is always objectively sinful, habitual masturbation usually involves a significant diminishing of freedom, so that in many cases it is unwise to consider the person who has this problem as being morally responsible, at least in regard to serious sin.

The third position Brockman refers to as "the fundamental option view." It states:

While masturbation is a moral question, for the average person it is not necessarily to be regarded as seriously sinful. A particular individual action has meaning insofar as it makes incarnate and intensifies the fundamental moral choice that man must make between God and creatures, which ultimately means self. It is difficult to imagine that an act of masturbation could be regarded as such a fundamental choice.

The final position which Brockman points out is "the neutral attitude":

Masturbation is such a normal part of growing up that the only serious evil that can be attached to it arises from the unfortunate guilt feelings that come from early training and negative attitudes toward sexuality. Masturbation represents a phase through which a person grows toward interpersonal relationships.

These are opinions present in the church today. One's attitude toward masturbation is affected by one's opinion of its morality. The opinions are not only four attitudes toward masturbation but are different theologies as well. One's moral evaluation reflects one's theological understanding. My own opinion is that masturbation is more a question of maturity and integrated sexuality. Sexual maturity does not imply that a person does or does not masturbate.

In one person it might be mature; in another person it might be immature and unintegrated. Fantasy which generally accompanies masturbation is the same. It is not necessarily immoral.

Although I do not consider masturbation intrinsically immoral, it does raise moral questions. It should be understood within a moral context lest we segment human life. The goal of human life is to become an integrated person, integrated emotionally and sexually, spiritually and morally, and intellectually. An act is not simply physical when it is human; insofar as it is human, it has ramifications beyond physicality alone. Likewise, we cannot consider any human act totally separate from morality. This would segment the person into moral, physical, and emotional domains rather than integrate them. Thus masturbation does raise moral questions. McCary speaks of the psychological danger, although remote, that sex might become a solitary rather than a shared experience.[32] Certainly this is a question that the person must raise for himself in terms of his own growth. Does masturbation lead me in the direction of narcissistic rather than interpersonal sexuality? In general, however, adult masturbation is not selfish. Masturbation is not in complete accord with the goal of sexuality, which is other-oriented love. Nevertheless, in the case of a man separated from his wife while in prison, masturbation is not infidelity. Masturbatory activity has to be understood in the light of one's struggle to become who he or she can be. It is as false to say that masturbation is always wrong as it is to say that it is never wrong.

I will now make some remarks about self-abuse. As I mentioned earlier, masturbation is not necessarily self-abuse. It is probably inappropriate and unhealthy for us to continue to think of it that way. When it is abusive of the self, it is questionable on both psychological as well as moral grounds. Of the four kinds of masturbation which I mentioned, I regard only the fourth as immoral. Besides masturbation, however, there is a sin of self-abuse. The sin, however, is a much more profound one than the physical act and its physiological gratification. We need a broader understanding. I can also abuse myself through repression. Insofar as masturbation is immoral because it is abusive, there are other actions which are as abusive as the physical act of masturbation. Insofar as any sexual expression is destructive of our physical, emotional, or spiritual growth, it is abusive. Insofar, however, as it is constructive and contributes to our physical, emotional and spiritual life, it is mature. Insofar as any sexual expression impairs my self-respect and my self-acceptance, it is inappropriate.

Masturbation is a phase in adolescent sexual growth and a later potentially healthy genital outlet when intercourse is not possible. It is an acceptable aspect of ongoing psychosexual life. As far as Christian life is concerned, it is to be integrated into our life in Christ. The question is how it affects the life of chastity to which all of us are called. We must keep in mind the various forms of masturbation as well as the various forms of chastity. Chastity raises different questions in different situations. I can speak of adolescent chastity, adult chastity, conjugal chastity, pre-conjugal chastity, and celibate chastity. The questions that my particular state in life raises for me may be different from the questions raised by another state of life or phase of growth. The questions I ask of my sexual activity are asked from the viewpoint of what it means to be a chaste person. The question for us at this point is how masturbation fits into the life of a celibate.

Celibacy, as we explored it, is an ideal. Although we are all called to perfection, perfection is a process. It is not something we attain by our own powers; it is a gift of God. It is not something we are given all at once; it is given in stages. Perfection is a gift that comes in the form of human growth. In that sense, chastity is a process and an unfinished one. We are not yet completely chaste because we have not yet been given the gift of complete chastity. This does not mean that we can ignore our own responsibility. Nevertheless, we also have to accept the fact that we have not yet been given the perfection of the gift. Chastity is a process, an unfinished one, life-long. It is something we long for; it is something we pray for. Celibate chastity, as an ideal, is seldom perfectly realized in the concrete. Yet it must be continually sought and held up as an ideal. The ideal of celibate chastity is to love God, his creatures, and all of creation. Celibate chastity is to be one with God and one with his universe. The prayer of the Christian is the prayer of Jesus that we might all be one as he and the Father are one.

Celibate love foregoes genital sexuality in order to be single for Christ. If one is going to be interpersonally free as a single person, genital abstinence contributes to this goal. The celibate struggles to forego genital love in his interpersonal life and thus to transcend experiencing genitality as a need. Masturbation, however, is genital activity. For this reason, it is something that a celibate person wants to grow beyond. As genital activity, it is not bad, not unhealthy, not harmful, not immoral, even for a celibate. Nevertheless, it represents the fact that a celibate has not fully outgrown his need for genital expression, which he or she is choosing to outgrow. Masturbation, for the celibate, although not immoral, falls short of the ideal. The ideal, while few achieve it or are given it, is to pass beyond auto-genitality as well. To feel guilt about this is to enter into a more destructive process than the masturbation itself, which is not in itself destructive. A celibate's guilt over masturbation often reflects a deeper guilt about sexuality itself. A mature celibate who has an accepting attitude toward sexuality is not going to feel guilt over sexual or genital expression.

Masturbation is not completely appropriate for the celibate; neither is it sinful. It is simply a fact of his or her life which he or she accepts insofar as it is there. It is something which one hopes someday to grow beyond. Masturbation is not a chaste action for a celibate insofar as it is not an exemplification of celibate chastity. Those sexual expressions are chaste which communicate spiritual values. Masturbation seldom reflects, however, the spiritual values of the celibate person. In that sense, it does not witness to a life of chastity. This does not mean one needs to be embarrassed about it. We are only embarrassed about it to the degree that we are embarrassed about being sexual beings. We no longer define the celibate person as an asexual being. We do not deny sexuality in choosing celibacy. Masturbation is not a sign of the perfection we as celibates strive to live; neither is it sin. It is simply imperfection —that which we all are and yet strive to overcome.

Masturbation points to the unfinishedness of the process of spiritualization. To be unfinished is not to be immoral nor irresponsible. It is, however, to be challenged toward further growth. We must accept unfinishedness but not choose to remain there. There will always be the tension between accepting ourselves where we are and striving after the ideals of Christian life. Such is the process of divinization. The process of divinization is the continual cooperation of the person with God. God initiates and the person grows. We should not be ashamed of our present stage of growth nor should we stagnate there. Masturbation is an element in a celibate's own personal life which reflects a genital need he hopes to outgrow, not because genitality is at all inappropriate but because it does not particularly serve him in his celibate life.

The fundamental question chastity poses is how does our sexuality serve my relationship to God and my relationship to my fellow men. In the light of this, the significance of masturbation diminishes. There are so many other realities about which we are to be concerned. Nevertheless it does not become totally insignificant because it symbolizes that we are not yet what we have chosen to be. The question upon which a celibate bases his life is his life of charity. Is my sexual life aiding it or impeding it? Insofar as my sexuality is aiding it, it is serving the very purpose of sexuality itself.

THE CHANGE OF LIFE

There are many aspects of sexuality and many phases of psychosexual development which I am not discussing. I do not want, however, to give the impression that sexual development comes to an end after sexual awakening and the period of integration following it. A significant phase in later psychosexual development is the "change of life," sometimes called the "climacteric" or, in women, the "menopause."

Menopause is that time in a woman's life when the ovaries cease to produce eggs, the production of female sex hormones lessens, and menstruation comes to an end. This is not the only change in life that a sexual person undergoes; it is simply one of the many changes in life. It is associated with traumatic struggle and has come to be known as *the* change of life. Menstruation does not stop all at once. As menopause approaches, a monthly period or two may be missed. It may be prolonged or become very short. Finally the time of no period arrives. In women for whom menstruation began early, menopause generally begins late, and in those who started to menstruate late, menopause begins early. This time in a woman's life generally begins between the ages of forty-five and fifty; many, however, do not approach menopause until the early or mid-fifties; in some it begins earlier than forty-five. The symptoms of menopause, if they exist at all, may last for less than a year or up to two or three years. Once a woman has stopped menstruating for six consecutive months—or, at most, a year—she can be fairly certain that ovulation has ceased.

A myth connected with menopause is that it is inevitably traumatic and will lead to emotional instability. Three-fourths to four-fifths of women pass through this time of life with no discomfort at all. The vast majority do not experience menopause as a time of real difficulty. In those who do exhibit the symptoms, medicine can relieve them rather easily. A woman who has been nervous most of her life will probably have a more difficult time. Nervousness is one of the symptoms of menopause, and it is understandable that an already nervous person will experience more difficulty. The majority of women, however, need no medical treatment of any sort. A few require psychiatric care.

The symptoms of menopause are varied and not all women who manifest some symptoms manifest all of them. The more common are hot flashes, nervousness and irritability, fatigue and sleeplessness, headaches, and the tendency to increase in weight. As I said, most women do not exhibit these. For those who do, most of the symptoms can be alleviated by the taking of estrogen, which should be taken only on the advice of a physician. Many women unnecessarily look to this time with anxiety and tension because of the fears associated with it.

A couple of suggestions could be made to celibate women as well as to others. A celibate woman should be in touch with a physician with whom she can discuss an approaching menopause. It is also good to read something on menopause in order to be aware of the changes in your body that will begin to take place.[33] It is very good at this time to have outside interests. A married woman should have something outside of her family; a celibate woman should not withdraw from ministry. With the proper education, menopause need not be something to worry about.

The question is raised whether a man goes through a similar

physiological change and not all agree, although an increasing number affirm that the man does.[34] Many men undergo a similar time in their lives about the age of fifty-five, a time later than women. The decline in genitality occurs much more slowly in the male. A state of semi-erection may last for several years and be adequate for sexual relations. A man can manifest some of the symptoms of nervousness, irritability, and increase in weight at this time. As a man grows older and approaches the time of his climacteric, there is a reduction in size and firmness of the testicles; the production of sperm and the force of ejaculation decrease; longer time is required to effect an orgasm. Erection becomes less frequent and vigorous, and erectile power eventually diminishes until it is lost. There is also a decline in the production of the male sex hormone. A man associates his sexuality and manhood very much with his penis and dreads the failure of this organ and the impossibility of reaching erection. This is one of the fears in the adult male. His masculinity is very much related to his erectile power and the power to produce orgasm. The coming to an end of this can be difficult for the man to accept. Nevertheless, as with women, if properly approached, the time need not be traumatic.

In addition to the myth that there will be trauma as the physiological and genital dimensions of sexuality change, there is the myth that this is the end of one's sex life.[35] This is simply not the case. There is no reason why a woman should not continue genital relations. Sexual desire does not change just because menstruation comes to an end. A woman can expect her sexual desire to remain the same from about thirty to sixty despite menopause or hysterectomy. Genital intercourse diminishes in frequency with age but does not cease. The average frequency of coitus for the majority of men over sixty-five is four times a month. There is also a recurrence of masturbation at this time among twenty-five percent of the men. Not only does sexual activity not cease, it provides needed comfort that can be a source of assurance that, although the period of intense genital involvement is gone, the person is still cared for and loved. Great psychological benefit can be attained from sexual affection even though the genital aspects diminish. Simone de Beauvoir unmasks the myth that old age diminishes sexual desire.[36] The physiological changes that accompany this time of life do not mean an end to sexual desire; they simply mean the end of procreative sexuality.

This period is a time of change; it is, however, but one change among the many changes that take place in the course of one's sexual life. At this time, although genital sexuality lessens, affection can grow. De Beauvoir writes that a person whose genital functions have diminished is not therefore sexless. Sexuality does not come to an end with diminishing genitality. It can reach fulfillment in old age where affective relationships and maturity of love peak. Psychosexual life moves back and forth between the affective and the genital, one being more prominent at one time and the other being more prominent at another. The so-called latency period is a coming to be of the affective life of the person. Puberty is a coming to be of the genital life. After puberty, there is a return to the socialization of a person's sexuality and its integration with the genital life. After the climacteric, there is a diminishing of the genital life which accompanies the cessation of physiological processes.

It is important for a celibate person to have continual awareness of his or her developing sexuality. This time of physiological change need not be feared. Neither is it a time when sexual desire decreases and the living of the celibate life in this area becomes easy. Sexual desire in celibate people continues at this time and there may be a recurrence of masturbation. All of this simply points to the importance of sexual self-understanding. This time in one's sexual life brings with it the chance to bring one's sexuality to genuine maturity along with increasing spiritual maturity.

CONCLUSION

There is much more that could be said about celibate sexuality. Our awareness of the sexual life of celibate people is important and will continue to grow. Celibate sexuality is primarily affective sexuality, social sexuality as we discussed in chapter two. It is the goal of celibate love to socialize and universalize one's affectivity in the direction of compassion, which is the supreme sign of an integrated sexual life. Affective sexuality finds its primary manifestation in friendship of which celibate friendship is an important example. Friendship implies intimacy, but intimacy does not necessarily imply genitality. Celibate sexuality strives after non-genital intimacy and tactility in the struggle to become a celibate person.

8

The Spiritual Life
of a Celibate Person

THIS CHAPTER requires volumes in order to be the least bit
adequate, and I make no pretense of adequacy; I only share a
perspective on the spiritual life which I hope some will find of
value. The spiritual life is the core of the celibate life. It is in the
context of the spiritual life and one's journey to God that celibacy
is best understood, and it is to that dimension of personality that
we now turn.

ON BEING A SPIRITUAL PERSON

In addition to psychosexual history, a person has a psycho-spiritual history as well. A personal autobiography includes a spiritual
autobiography. It is of benefit to look at the moral, religious, and
spiritual development that accompanies childhood, adolescence,
adulthood, and old age just as we look at the sexual, social, and
intellectual dimensions of these periods. Accepting ourselves as
spiritual beings is as important to our personal growth as is
acceptance of ourselves as sexual beings. The two are not exclusive
of each other. Just as people attempt to deny their sexuality, so
people can deny or repress spirituality.

Being sexual involves many aspects of personality: affectivity,
sociality, genitality, femininity, masculinity, heterosexuality, homo-

sexuality, sexual identity, and love. The exploration of spirituality is equally complex. It involves religious experience rather than sexual experience, religious identity rather than sexual identity, religious awakening rather than sexual awakening. It involves raising one's consciousness to God's presence in history, in the world, and in one's own life. Its goal is also the capacity to love. Only by integrating the sexual and the spiritual and all that is within us can we develop the mature and tremendous capacity to love ourselves, others, mankind, and God. A repression of any capacity within the person can cripple the capacity to love. Psychology helps us in this task; so does religion.

Religious education is an ongoing process as is sex education. There are three events or phases in spiritual development of which I will speak. These are: the religious or spiritual awakening, religious or spiritual identity, religious or spiritual commitment.

A sexual awakening is that time in a person's life when his or her sexuality comes to life with full force; it wakes up. Personality growth not only gives rise to a sexual awakening; it gives rise to a spiritual awakening as well. Spiritual life has a long history that begins in childhood, passes through an adolescent phase, matures, and continues into old age where it bears real fruit. In the development of the spiritual, there is the emergence of an intense spiritual desire. It can emerge gradually. It can be a unique experience. It can be a conversion. It can be followed by repression if a person is unprepared to deal with it. It can be accompanied by intense anxiety, fear, or inner peace. It is an experience of God although not always identified that way at first. We are not always aware of what is happening, and yet we face the task of integrating this new potential into our self-understanding. There is no particular time in our lives when this occurs.

Once a person has become spiritually aware, he or she sets about the task of feeling comfortable with this newly discovered dimension of his or her life. In the task of sexual identity I come to accept myself as a sexual person of a certain sex. In the task of spiritual or religious identity, I begin to see myself as a spiritual person within a particular religious tradition with spiritual needs. I accept myself as a man or a woman of God. I am a religious person, a holy person, a person called by God from an earlier way of living to a new life.

The struggle of man's journey towards union with God varies, and it is discussed by spiritual writers who chose to share their spiritual autobiographies with us. Our lives are not their lives, however. We each have our own journey. Teilhard writes that each person traverses a specific path.[1] The goal of both the sexual life and spiritual life is union of the individual with God and with others.

The task of identity is not only sexual identity and vocational identity. It involves religious identity as well. This task is delayed for many people and many times never fully resolved. It is an important task for celibate life. A celibate person cannot feel comfortable about his or her celibacy until he or she has faced what it means to be a spiritual person. The spiritual life is the core of celibate living, and spiritual identity must precede and accompany celibate identity. The issue of celibate identity is how to integrate sexual, vocational, and spiritual identity into the life choice. In choosing to be celibate, a person is saying something about all three: his or her sexuality, his or her ministry or profession, his or her belief in God. Each of these must be faced as the celibate person moves towards making this decision. The task of religious identity moves a person in the direction of a decision which is a response to being called. I decide to be a religious person and decide to be so in such-and-such a way. I may decide to be a celibate person; I may decide to enter into Christian marriage; I may decide to be Buddhist. All of these alternatives confront me as I decide what religious existence means for me and how I am going to live out the spiritual and religious dimensions of my own life.

Commitment or decision is an important task in becoming a spiritual person. The spiritual awakening brings spirituality to the level of awareness. Spiritual identity brings it to the level of self-acceptance. The commitment or decision brings it to the level of responsibility. Rollo May writes, "Decision . . . is responsive to and responsible for the significant other-persons important to one's self in the realizing of the long-term goals."[2] In any way of life, there are "significant others" to whom we become responsible after our decision is made. After this decision, future decisions are not simply mine alone. My life is not simply mine alone. In making a decision I enter into people's lives in a certain way and become responsible. This responsibility may be to a husband, to a wife, to members of a religious community, to friends, and to others; and I cannot deny the responsibility to them. Celibate people in community might feel that their commitment is primarily to God or between God and themselves. This is an attitude of American individualism and privatized religion. Celibate people have significant others to whom they are responsible just as married people do. Healthy celibate life is committed to people as well as God. A celibate commitment is not between God and myself alone.

Rollo May discusses the decision-making process.[3] He concludes that the human person has the ability "to transcend the concrete situation of the immediate self-oriented desire and to live in the dimensions of past and future, and in terms of the welfare of the persons and groups upon whom his own fulfillment intimately depends."[4] A human person has the capacity to make a life decision. In fact, such life decisions are necessary. They enable us to give our lives meaning. Until such a commitment, there is no direction to our lives. Without such direction, there is no meaning. Commitment, far from preventing human growth, facilitates it. It is this meaning for which people long. Yet they cannot have it until they commit their lives to something or someone.

The fact of evolution and development in psychology leads people to think that it is foolish to make a decision at one time in a person's life to which he or she is committed for the rest of his or her life. How can I commit myself to something and bind myself to it? This denies future freedom and later experience. Life decisions, of course, should not be made at an immature age nor made immaturely. They are not foolish, however; they give people direction. A commitment is not made in order to avoid life but in order to live it deeply. Evolution and development do not imply a total lack of permanency and stability. Evolution and development are not chaos and randomness alone. For Teilhard they are directional and, on the human plane, self-directed.

Teilhard de Chardin has pointed out that not to decide is, in fact, to decide.[5] A person who decides to avoid making any permanent commitment in his life is already limited by this decision not to make a permanent decision. It is impossible to avoid making decisions which affect our lives. To avoid them leads to disintegration and instability. Life choices may become destructive and incapable of being dealt with in a way other than by a change of that decision. Life choices, however, which are made by mature people at a mature age generally imply the personal resources on the part of that person to deal with later elements that were not anticipated at the time of the decision.

A person grows and matures and eventually the time comes to make a decision that will affect one's life. What does he want to do with his one and only life? Until he makes this decision, his life will not have meaning. The time comes when the decision must be made if the person is going to grow and mature. We look at alternatives; we question and doubt; eventually we make a decision. This does not mean that the other alternatives are not desirable. Every choice is a sacrifice. I simply stop looking at the alternatives and begin living one of them. Life now takes on a new character. I begin to live out the decision I made and to understand the implications of it.

Our culture does not make life choices easy and generally militates against them. Yet they are important for human growth. One chooses a direction for one's life in order to live less superficially. We can live only one of our possible lives. I only realize the implications of any decision after it is made and never fully at the time of the choice. Only life reveals that. Many choices are available, but only one can be lived in depth. It goes without saying that such a commitment should be freely arrived at. It also goes without saying that these commitments will always have their times of stress and tension. The celibate life as well as the married life can come to an end under too much stress. Prolonged tension destroys a commitment. A commitment, in order to be responsible, must include the capacity to handle reasonable tension.

I have mentioned three elements of the spiritual life: religious awakening, religious identity, religious commitment. All come together in the process of a person's coming to be. They become part of one's self-understanding and one's self-concept. Religious commitment, whether as celibate people or as married people, is part of who we are. Sexual, professional, and religious choices come together to give our lives direction. Celibacy can only be understood and lived in the context of spirituality. It is basically not concerned with our sexual lives; it is concerned with our relationship to God, to fellow men, and to fellow women. To choose celibacy is to choose to live a spiritual existence. Celibate chastity integrates sexuality into that choice. Celibacy is not something I am once and for all but something I continually become. Growth and process imply both direction and unfinishedness. There is a certain direction toward which I move, union with God and others, while realizing I am not yet there. Kierkegaard liked to say that purity of heart was to will one thing.[6] Teilhard's concept of purity was a single-mindedness of direction.[7] Bonhoeffer saw purity of heart as single-minded obedience, a call to discipleship, and costly grace.[8] A spiritual person, as Augustine exemplified, is restless until he rests in God.[9] A celibate chooses to live and witness in an undivided way to man's search for God. Spiritual living continually calls me forward.[10]

DISCIPLINE

Christian life, celibate or married, requires discipline in order to be lived fully. Self-discipline is an important ingredient in spiritual living and spiritual living is an important dimension of life. In addition to the importance of spiritual awakening, identity, and commitment, there is the ongoing task of daily spiritual living. Discipline contributes to the daily growth of a person.

Discipline is destructive if pursued in excess or as an end in itself. In itself, it is an occasion for pride; yet it is not something to be proud of. Its goal is growth in justice, charity, and humility, and is constructive to the degree to which it promotes these. Thomas Merton writes, "My purpose is simply to reaffirm that without discipline the monastic quest, which seeks typically to explore regions of faith, of love, of experience and of existence beyond the limits of ordinary Catholic routine, can never lead to anything serious." [11] Discipline is in excess if it enhances one dimension of a person but harms another dimension. Discipline which is destructive of emotional or physical health is destructive no matter how spiritual the goal. The goal is always the integration and wholesomeness of the person.

Self-abnegation, as Nathaniel Branden points out in discussing the psychology of self-esteem, can be used by religious people to achieve a sense of worthiness which is pseudo self-esteem.[12] Karl Menninger points out in *Man Against Himself* how ascetical practices can be an unhealthy manifestation of man's aggressiveness turned against himself rather than outward in a constructive fashion.[13] Self-discipline, although it might frequently function in a negative way in emotionally immature people, can be a positive force. Self-denial is a dangerous tool for an emotionally immature person but a real potential for an emotionally mature one. Frank Goble, in his outline of Maslow's psychology, writes, "Self-actualizers cannot avoid discipline." [14] A self-actualizing person is motivated by values after which he strives and to which he is loyal.

Discipline is better when self-imposed than when external. Merton writes, "True discipline is interior and personal." [15] Gandhi points this out in his own ascetical life:

Inhibitions imposed from without rarely succeed, but when they are self-imposed, they have a decidedly salutary effect.[16]

Self-imposed discipline is usually not destructive, although of concern to one's spiritual director, who attempts to discern its actual function.

Discipline serves a life based on values. This is true not just of the spiritual life. Artistic life needs discipline. A musician practices daily in order to perfect his art. A dancer cannot neglect regular exercise if he is going to be able to dance well. Years of discipline precede one performance of a ballet. Intellectual life also requires intellectual exercise. A scholar undertakes the discipline of learning the languages he needs to do his work well. Physical health requires physical exercise. Growth in any area of life is not automatic. Even emotional growth is facilitated by the disciplines of individual therapy and group process. Those who seek emotional growth undertake regular sessions as individuals or in groups and the tasks which confront one in these sessions are not easy but are chosen for the sake of growth. Accepted rules and qualified personnel are a part of interaction in therapy groups. Self-discipline is not negative for someone seeking to grow, although the growth, whether artistic, emotional, intellectual, physical, or spiritual, is not easy.

Asceticism as self-imposed discipline or active self-purification is a constructive and necessary factor in spiritual growth—as constructive and necessary as self-discipline in any area of human life.[17] Dan McGuire, in his discussion of the ascetical theology of Merton, relates asceticism to the process of self-discovery, the recovering of the true self, and the beginning of divine fulfillment. He writes, "Asceticism is a striving for the freedom of an authentic Christian life." [18] It would be of benefit to discuss not only the ideal of spiritual exercise but the spiritual exercises themselves. Nevertheless we cannot do this. We can say only that such practices as abstinence, fasting, and meditation play a vital role in the Christian life. Spiritual direction or guidance and spiritual or religious counselling are also necessary. All these help the Christ in us come alive.

Asceticism, from the perspective of Christian theology, is understood in the light of eschatology. In earlier years an individualistic eschatology permeated both Catholic and Protestant circles. In Catholic theology, eschatology was concerned with death, heaven, hell, and purgatory. The individual was concerned with saving his own soul. The doctrine of merit entered in. On a popular level, semi-Pelagian attitudes affected the understanding of Christian life. The eschatological perspective of the New Testament, however, is quite different. New Testament eschatology is more communal and social. It focuses on the future destiny of man. Its central concept is God's kingdom. Our task is building up the body of Christ. This eschatological function requires asceticism—an asceticism, however, which is not an end in itself nor concerned with the sanctity of the individual. It is an asceticism for the sake of the kingdom.

Today we speak of the asceticism of communication and dialogue, the asceticism of nonviolence, the asceticism of political and social action, as well as the asceticism of the simple, chaste, and responsible life. We are primarily concerned with the asceticism, the discipline, and the life of celibate chastity in this book. Celibate chastity is only one small part of the whole of Christian life, however, and cannot be seen apart from the larger context. Neither celibate life nor married life can be separated from the asceticism of communication, nonviolence, political action, simple living, and responsibility to Christ. It cannot be separated from the asceticism of growth which is the hallmark of a Christian striving for perfection. This upward striving is better understood today as striving for growth and maturity. Growth includes spiritual growth. Maturity includes self-discipline. The command of Jesus to all Christians is: Be mature as your heavenly Father is mature (Mt. 5:48).

SOLITUDE

Solitude is necessary for both the private life and the spiritual life of a celibate person. Many people today are afraid of being alone. Solitude helps us face this fear; it helps us face ourselves. Celibacy is a positive choosing of solitude. Celibacy comes from the Latin word meaning *alone*. The celibate chooses solitude because he or she can grow within it. He or she feels called to a more solitary life than many people have the opportunity to live.

It is important to clarify how I am using the word "solitude." Solitude is not withdrawal; it is not rebellion; it is not private religion; it is not a return to the womb. Solitude is not necessarily being a hermit. One of the best essays on the philosophy of solitude is that by Thomas Merton.[19] He writes:

Why write about solitude in the first place? Certainly not in order to preach it, to exhort people to become solitary. What could be more absurd? Those who are to become solitary are, as a rule, solitary already. At most they are not yet aware of their condition. In which case, all they need is to discover it. But in reality, all men are solitary. Only most of them are so averse to being alone, or to feeling alone, that they do everything they can to forget their solitude. How? Perhaps in large measure by what Pascal called 'divertissement'—diversion, systematic distraction. By those occupations and recreations, so mercifully provided by society, which enable a man to avoid his own company for twenty-four hours a day.[20]

The solitary side of a person refuses to live by being amused. It resists the tyranny of diversion. In solitude, as well as with others, one can face himself, others, and God. True solitude—not the anti-social solitude of withdrawal, not the anti-establishment solitude of rebellion, not the anti-catholic solitude of private religion, not the immature fear of life which longs to return to the womb, but the solitude of a man or woman who wants to grow and to love and to be—the solitude of one who faces the risk of life by facing himself. True solitude confronts the irrational element within one's self and one's universe in the face of which faith becomes a possibility.[21] Solitude facilitates facing life in such a way that faith is an appropriate response to life.[22]

It is not that some men are solitary and others are social. All men are both solitary and social and all must face both. Solitude in itself is a social reality in that it is shared by everyone. Merton writes:

What the solitary renounces is not his union with other men, but rather the deceptive fictions and inadequate symbols which tend to take the place of genuine social unity—to produce a facade of apparent unity without really uniting men on a deep level. Example—the excitement and fictitious engagement of a football crowd.[23]

The solitary side of life seeks union with others just as the social side of life does. It simply seeks union in a different way. The goal of solitude as well as of intimacy is love. Both find their fullness in the life of charity—the supreme hallmark of the spiritual life. Traditional spiritual theology sees charity as the goal of the spiritual life and this insight remains unchanged in contemporary asceticism. If solitude does not lead to love, it is not true solitude. Its goal, as well as the goal of the whole spiritual life, as well as the goal of sexuality, is compassion. Compassion is identity with mankind and the task of identity is not constructively resolved until this takes place. My universality is the ultimate goal of both sexual and spiritual identity. The task of identity is to realize that I am one with all, that *Atman* is *Brahman*, that God is in me and I in Him, that we are all one as the Father and his Son are one, as vine and branches are one, as a body is one although it has many members. Merton writes, "Compassion teaches me that my brother and I are one." [24] Luke's counterpart to Matthew is, "Be compassionate as your Father is compassionate" (Lk. 6:36).

Within a sexual environment based on orgasm, the celibate is a failure and a contradiction. Within a social environment based on diversion, a solitary man or woman is likewise a failure and contradiction. Merton writes:

In the eyes of our conformist society, the hermit is nothing but a failure. He has to be a failure—we have absolutely no use for him, no place for him. He is outside all our projects, plans, assemblies, movements. We can countenance him as long as he remains only a fiction, a dream. As soon as he becomes real, we are revolted by his insignificance, his poverty, his shabbiness, his total lack of status. Even those who consider themselves contemplatives often cherish a secret contempt for the solitary. For in the contemplative life of the hermit there is none of that noble security, that intelligent depth, that artistic finesse which the more academic contemplative seeks in his sedate respectability.[25]

The solitary is first of all one who renounces this arbitrary social imagery. When his nation wins a war or sends a rocket to the moon, he can get along without feeling as if he personally had won the war or hit the moon with a rocket.[26]

The monk is compassionate in proportion as he is less practical and less successful, because the job of being a success in a competitive society leaves one no time for compassion.[27]

A solitary person has his eccentricities. These are not impediments, however, to human maturity. He realizes not only his obligation to human maturity but to spiritual maturity as well. Solitude must be based on prayer and meditation. Just as its social goal is compassion, so its spiritual goal is contemplation. Compassion and contemplation are elements of mature Christian living. "Without solitude of some sort there is and can be no maturity," Merton writes.[28] Solitude not only contributes to psycho-social growth and psycho-spiritual growth; it forms along with intimacy the private life of man. The private life of a celibate person is as important as is his public life. His public life is lived out in community and ministry; his private life is discovered in intimacy and solitude. All four of these are of importance if we are to be mature. Solitude forces a person to face his or her true self. Louis Bouyer writes, "Solitude alone allows a man to discover, and so to face, all the obscure forces that he bears within himself. The man who does not know how to be alone, does not know either (and secretly does not wish to know) what conflicts there are in the depths of his heart, conflicts which he feels that he is incapable of untangling, even of touching. Solitude is a terrible trial, for it serves to crack open and burst apart the shell of our superficial securities." [29]

Although we often associate solitude with hermitage, solitude is not isolation. There is a solitary dimension to all of us. There is a priceless solitude in celibate life. Merton points out that there is solitude in cenobitic life.[30] Solitude is found in interior peace and quiet. It exists within as well as without. Its interiority is silence. It is not necessarily loneliness although it may sometimes be experienced that way.[31] Silence itself is social.[32] It is a form of human communication. It is communication with self, others, and God. There is the silence of listening—to self, to others, to God. There is the silence of awe—for art, for nature, for God. There are realities for which the only appropriate form of communication is silence. There is the silence beyond words—as in mystical union or in sexual union. We are reminded of the lovers in the Song of Songs who after every possible extravagance of language realize the insufficiency of words. Love requires silence together and silence can communicate love—whether the love of holding hands, the love of just being near, or the love of just being. The aspiration of the solitary side of life is to just be. All I want to do, God, is just to be!

JOY

One cannot write of the spiritual life without writing of joy. Joy is at the heart of spiritual living. The sexual dimensions of life are accompanied by intense pleasure, the spiritual dimensions by intense joy. In our day, with the necessary re-thinking of celibacy, we focus on the problems of celibate life. We need this awareness in order to be realistic about the life we choose. Yet our focus is out of proportion if we fail to speak of the joy of celibate life as well.

There are three spiritual joys which are the heart and soul of celibacy. The core of celibacy is not living an austere life nor abstinence from sexual life. Celibacy means friendship, ministry, and prayer. Intense joy comes from each of these three: prayer so intense that it bursts forth in dance, ministry so rewarding that it leads to a loss of self-consciousness and the feeling of simply being, friendship so beautiful that it shines forth in laughter, kisses, and tears.

Thomas Aquinas shares his own insight on joy in four articles in his *Summa*. He asks whether joy is an effect of love, whether it is compatible with sorrow, whether it can be complete and full, and whether it is a virtue.

Thomas holds that love is the cause of joy. With keen experiential insight he writes:

"Joy and sorrow proceed from love, but in contrary ways. For joy is caused by love, either through the presence of the person loved, or because the proper good of the person loved exists and endures in him; and the latter is the case chiefly in the love of benevolence, whereby a man rejoices in the well-being of his friend, though he be absent. On the other hand sorrow arises from love, either through the absence of the person loved, or because the loved person to whom we wish well is deprived of his or her good or is afflicted with some evil." [33]

How true to our own feelings! Who among us has not experienced both joy and sorrow in love? Who has not experienced the joy of being with the person we love? Who has not rejoiced in the joy of a friend even though our friend is not with us? Who has not experienced the pain of separation and a friendship of absence? Who has not hurt, even in the presence of his friend, because his friend was hurting?

The above quotation already answers the question whether joy can be mixed with sorrow. Not only can it be, it is. Joy which comes from love is often mixed with sorrow either due to absence or separation or due to a person's hurt or affliction. Even the joy which comes from enjoying God himself is mixed with sorrow here and now because God is not fully present to us. The lives of the saints witness to this. They long for ever closer union with God. This is not due to any lack on God's part but due to the fact that He is not yet fully present to us. Thus the sorrow of absence and separation also enters into our love of God himself.

The perfection of joy is complete union, but our union with God is not yet complete. It reaches perfection in mystical experiences when one experiences unity with God. There is the counterpart of this ecstacy in our sexual lives when we experience oneness. This oneness, however, in both spheres, does not last forever. It is temporary and not eternal. Friendship with God, as well as with men and women, is a mixture of absence and presence. Hence joy is never complete. There are experiences of sexual and mystical union, but these are not everlasting. It is this for which we long, when our joy will be complete, when we will all be one and together will be one with God. Eye has not seen nor has man experienced the joy that awaits us! We constantly live in the eschatological tension of the already and the still to come.

Once again we have moved into the next question Thomas raises—whether joy can be complete and full. Our joy will never be perfect here and now because it does not last. This does not mean that our experience is not an experience of perfect joy. It simply means it is not a perfect experience of joy because it does not endure. Thomas basically says that the joy of a creature is finite. Joy will be complete when there is no longer desire. But this does not happen to any of us in our present living. It is always possible to grow closer to God and closer to others. We are not yet one. Perfect joy is an attribute of the future. Celibacy is a sign of this coming kingdom insofar as it is a sign of joy. Joy is a sign of the already present God as well as the future presence of God. Our presence to one another and our presence with God is an evolving reality. Presence brings joy. Being fully present to another is full joy.

The final question for Thomas is whether joy is a virtue. It is not so much a virtue, he says, as an effect, the effect of love, which is also called charity.[34] Hence joy is one of the effects of a life of love, or as Paul says, one of the fruits of living in the Spirit. According to Paul, the Spirit brings love, joy, peace, patience, kindness, goodness, trustfulness, gentleness, and self-control (Gal. 5:22).

Discussions on celibacy cannot neglect joy. Friendship involves its high points as well as low points. Prayer has its bright days as well as dark nights. Ministry has moments of satisfaction and dissatisfaction. These three are the sources of the joy that makes celibate life worth living. We have to learn how to grow in all three—the art of prayer, the art of ministry, and the art of friendship—in order to find the joy which awaits us.

CONCLUSION

It is obvious that there is much more that can be said of the spiritual life. The relationships between celibacy and community, celibacy and ministry, and celibacy and prayer could all be further explored. The thrust of this chapter has been simply to point out that the spiritual life is actually the soul of celibacy and that affective relationships and friendships, are not something other than, but a part of, the spiritual life of man.

Conclusion

IT IS DIFFICULT to write a conclusion, but here are a few basic convictions:

Sexuality and spirituality are not enemies but friends. A development of one does not mean a denial of the other. Both flow forth from the innermost center of human life. Our goal is not to choose between them but to integrate them, to be both spiritual and sexual, holy and sensual, at one and the same time. We as Christians believe in incarnational spirituality and that the future life will be an embodied way of being. Living "in the Spirit" and "in Christ" does not mean an alienation of ourselves from our own physicality.

It is possible and necessary, therefore, to speak of celibate sexuality. This does not mean that we have as of now explored fully this notion. A celibate person is not asexual. He or she has a full sexual life which needs to be understood in order to have a richer understanding of Christian sexuality itself as well as in order to assist people in living celibate life.

Just as it can be said that sexuality is beautiful and Christian, so it can be said that sexuality is dangerous. These are the two awarenesses within which the Christian lives out his or her sexual life. We must be realistic as well as positive. The Yahwist is aware of the Canaanite degradation of sexuality. Paul is aware that it can lead us to live like Corinthians. The history of Christianity also gives testimony to these dangers. The history of celibacy itself, in the late Middle Ages and during the Renaissance, became the story of sexual irresponsibility. Sex *is* a danger. It has the power to overtake the person. It can deaden us to living in the Spirit as well as bring us to fuller life. We as celibate people cannot be naive as we accept the sexual dimensions of celibate life. Healthy integration cannot become an excuse for sexual license.

The sexual life of a celibate person is going to manifest itself primarily in the affective bonds of permanent and steadfast human friendships which are exemplifications of God's way of loving. Through a re-discovery of friendship within the Christian tradition and through an integration of community, friendship, ministry, and prayer, the present discussion of celibacy can lead to a revival of a truly Christian value, the value of friendship, which is a service for the entire Christian community.

In future discussions of celibate friendship we need to be aware of both the "success stories" as well as the "failures." Again this points to the prudential vital balance we need in our awareness of the questions connected with this issue. Affective relationships, although beautiful, are not easy and painless. We need to be aware of the possibility of these in order to support our hope and we also need to be aware of those friendships which have not worked out in order to be realistic in what we encourage. I would like very much to have included case studies in this work but decided that this would be for a different or later treatment. The questions I have raised, however, must be given flesh and blood as we pursue these issues further during the coming years.

The understanding of the Christian sexual life as a delicate balance is based upon sound psychology, sound theology, and the insight of Thomas Aquinas, who sees the sexual life of a Christian (chastity) as a mean between two extremes, both of which are destructive. A rejection of the sensual is just as much a deviation from the life of virtue as is making the sensual the end of life itself. Choosing to live life in this balanced and virtuous way is risky and requires the faith that God will grace us on our way, which grace cannot be an excuse for irresponsibility. The Christian is not the one who always chooses the safest way. Insensitivity is as unspiritual as is promiscuity.

There is need for a renewed spirituality which re-thinks the spiritual life along other than monastic categories in such a way that it is equally available to the conjugal life and the celibate. The core values in this spirituality are community, friendship, ministry, and prayer, which provide a context for understanding the Christian life, whether married or celibate, and enable celibate and married people to define themselves not against each other but in their relatedness within the one body of Christ.

The Christian way of living necessitates a return to affective prayer, which has always been vital to Christian growth as outlined in the Catholic mystical tradition. An effort to deal with the spiritual aspects of the affective life opens us to the need for an affective and experiential love of God as well. Prayer can be discursive, affective, and contemplative, the higher forms of which require a synthesis of the emotional and spiritual lives. Friendship leads to a discovery of mystical prayer and teaches us, in the school of love, the beauty of dependence, which opens us to our ultimate dependence upon God Himself. An exploration of celibate sexuality need not destroy the spiritual life of Christian men and women; it should enhance it as it did throughout the history of spirituality.

Celibacy is an ideal and a challenge. It is an ideal to be striven for, an ideal which we may never achieve as we seek to actualize our human potential, an ideal that cannot be achieved without God's grace. It is not only an ideal, however; it is also challenge. To live celibate love incarnationally day by day in a secular world amid an alien value system is not easy and verges on the heroic. I say this not only of celibate life; Christian marriage is also an ideal and a challenge. Any form of Christian life verges on the heroic in a world which not only does not value but often scorns permanent commitments, whether in single life or in married life.

The goal of celibacy is fuller life and life in Christ, which is the goal of life itself. The goal of celibate life is to achieve the radical freedom of the daughters and sons of God, to achieve radical oneness with the Father, to obey radically His Word and call, and to be radically available as God's person to do His work in the world. Christian celibacy is Christocentric and must be christologically based not on the celibate life of Jesus of Nazareth, but upon Jesus of Nazareth as fully man, as man of faith, as God's man, as God's presence in history, as revelatory event, as corporate person, and as the Christ who calls us and invites us to live as He did and does. Celibacy and sexuality both have the same ultimate goals— the fullness of life. It is not a question of one or the other, celibacy or sexuality, but of an integration of both, of being a sexual celibate at the service of God's Kingdom.

Glossary

THIS IS A LIST of words which I use in a way that sometimes differs from ordinary usage:

Affective Sexuality—the affectionate, emotional, social, non-procreative dimension of sexuality, which includes the sexual qualities of compassion, gentleness, sensitivity, tenderness, and warmth, achieving its highest expression in friendship.

Bisexuality—a) the acceptance and integration rather than dichotomization of feminine and masculine sexuality within the psychic life of a person, whether male or female; b) the acceptance and integration rather than dichotomization of heterosexual and homosexual sexuality within the psychic life of a person, hence the ability and capacity to love and relate sexually to both sexes.

Celibacy—a positive choice of the single life for the sake of Christ in response to the call of God.

Chastity—that Christian virtue which integrates the totality of sexuality into our lives as Christian men and women, which strives to unify the sexual and spiritual dimensions of a person whether single or married, which universalizes affectivity in the direction of compassion and elevates genitality to a sign of God's love for man

228

by limiting it to a faithful and permanent interpersonal commitment.

Femaleness—the sense or felt quality of belonging to the female sex or of being a woman, which quality is biologically and psychologically determined, and compatible with psychological bisexuality. Not to be confused with femininity.

Feminine—a culturally defined quality and socialized sex role associated with the adjectives artistic, considerate, impulsive, intuitive, and sensitive, which does not exclude masculinity in a healthy sexual person, although often seen culturally as the antithesis of masculinity.

Genital Sexuality—the biological, physiological, physical, procreative dimension of sexuality, which includes the sexual quality of arousal and achieves its highest expression in orgasm.

Heterosexuality—the ability and capacity to love and relate sexually to a person of the other sex.

Homosexuality—the ability and capacity to love and relate sexually to a person of one's own sex.

Love of Friendship—interpersonal intimacy, whether celibate or conjugal, in which there is the faithful and unconditional acceptance of another person for life.

Maleness—the sense or felt quality of belonging to the male sex or of being a man, which quality is biologically and psychologically determined, and is compatible with psychological bisexuality. Not to be confused with masculinity.

Masculine—a culturally defined quality and socialized sex role associated with the adjectives adventurous, assertive, competitive, dominating, and rational, which does not exclude femininity in a healthy sexual person, although often seen culturally as the antithesis of femininity.

Monosexuality—the ability and capacity to relate sexually to and love only one sex, whether one's own sex or the other sex; exclusive homosexuality or exclusive heterosexuality, and hence pathological.

Sexual Identity—the psychological process which accompanies puberty and lasts through the twenties, which primarily involves the sense of belonging to one's own biological sex as well as an acceptance within one's self of the opposite sex, also including an acceptance of one's sexuality in all its dimensions. Hence an affirmative response to one's own body and sexuality and an acceptance of one's bisexuality, not only one's femininity and masculinity but also one's heterosexuality and homosexuality.

Sexuality—the dimension of personality that makes one male or female, capable of affective bonds and procreative activity, as well as intrinsically structured for an "other," including affective, genital, feminine, masculine, heterosexual, homosexual components, achieving its highest manifestation in interpersonal love.

Virginity—both a physical and spiritual way of living in which a person who has not had genital intercourse chooses to integrate genital abstinence for life into his or her response to God.

Notes

INTRODUCTION

1. For a good brief introduction to Hinduism, see K. M. Sen, *Hinduism* (Baltimore: Penguin Books, Inc., 1970). Also Thomas Hopkins, *The Hindu Religious Tradition* (Encino, California: Dickenson Publishing Co., Inc., 1971); *The Hindu Tradition*, ed. by Ainslie Embree (New York: Vintage Books, 1972).

2. See Mohandas Gandhi, *Autobiography: The Story of My Experiments With Truth* (Boston: Beacon Press, 1968). Also see Louis Fischer, *Gandhi, His Life and Message for the World* (New York: Mentor Books, 1954) and Louis Fischer, *The Life of Mahatma Gandhi* (New York: Collier Books, 1966). Also see Gandhi's, *The Love of Continence: Brahmacharya* (Bombay, India: Bharatiya Vidya Bhavan, 1964).

3. See E. Burtt, *The Teachings of the Compassionate Buddha* (New York: Mentor Books, 1963); E. Conze, *Buddhism: Its Essence and Development* (New York: Harper and Row, 1959); Richard Drummond, *Gautama the Buddha: An Essay in Religious Understanding* (Grand Rapids: Wm. B. Eerdmans, 1974); S. Dutt, *Buddhist Monks and Monasteries of India* (New York: Fernhill House, 1962); James Mohler, *The Heresy of Monasticism* (Staten Island: Alba House, 1971), pp. 1–14; and Richard Robinson, *The Buddhist Religion* (Belmont, California: Dickenson Publishing Co., 1970).

4. Josephine Massingberd Ford, *A Trilogy on Wisdom and Celibacy* (South Bend, Indiana: University of Notre Dame Press, 1967), p. 50.

5. See William S. LaSor, *The Dead Sea Scrolls and the New Testament*

(Grand Rapids, Michigan: Wm. B. Eerdmans Pub. Co., 1972); A. R. C. Leaney, *The Rule of Qumran and Its Meaning* (Philadelphia: Westminster Press, 1966); James Mohler, *The Heresy of Monasticism* (Staten Island: Alba House, 1971), pp. 15–27; Shemaryahu Talmon, "The New Covenanters of Qumran," *Scientific American*, 225 (1971), pp. 73–81.

6. Henry C. Lea, *History of Sacerdotal Celibacy in the Christian Church* (London: Watts and Co., 1932). Also see Josephine Massingberd Ford, *op. cit.*; Roger Gryson, *Les origines du celibat ecclesiastique* (Gembloux: J. Duculot, 1970); and E. Schillebeeckx, *Celibacy* (New York: Sheed and Ward, 1968), pp. 19–72.

7. See Schillebeeckx, *op. cit.*, pp. 56–67.

8. See 1972 *Catholic Almanac* (Huntington, Ind.: Our Sunday Visitor, 1972), based on the statistics from the Vatican's *Annuario Pontificio*.

9. Max Thurian, *Marriage and Celibacy* (London: SCM Press, 1969).

10. For further information on Taize, see *The Rule of Taize* by Roger Schutz (New York: The Seabury Press, 1974). Also Donald Bloesch, *Centers of Christian Renewal* (Philadelphia: United Church Press, 1964). Also John Heijke, *An Ecumenical Light on the Renewal of Religious Community Life—Taize* (Pittsburgh: Duquesne University Press, 1967); Geoffrey Moorhouse, *Against All Reason* (Harmondsworth, England: Penguin Books, 1972), pp. 3–20.

CHAPTER 1

1. See Peter Ellis, *The Yahwist* (Notre Dame, Indiana: Fides Publishers, Inc., 1968) for further background and bibliography.

2. Gerhard von Rad, *Genesis* (Philadelphia: Westminster Press, 1961), p. 80, comments on this text by saying, "Man is created for sociability." Dietrich Bonhoeffer, *Creation and Fall* (New York: Macmillan Co., 1969), p. 62, comments by saying, "Sexuality is nothing but the ultimate realization of our belonging to one another."

3. A theology of sexuality that does associate sexuality and propagation is the Priestly account in the first chapter of Genesis. The author is generally considered to be a priest writing in the sixth century B.C. The theology of the Yahwist is older as well as more often quoted in the New Testament. Thus we actually find two theologies of sexuality in Genesis 1–11. Pierre Grelot, *Man and Wife in Scripture* (New York: Herder and Herder, 1964), pp. 32–39, also distinguishes between these two. For another opinion about the non-procreative sexuality of Genesis 2, see Otto Piper, *The Christian Interpretation of Sex* (New York: Charles Scribner's Sons, 1941), pp. 40–51.

4. One could develop further the Yahwist's positive theology of woman. The Yahwist sees the woman as of equal dignity with man. She is man's partner. Thus again the Yahwist's theology is distinct from the Canaanite's fertility cult degradation of women.

5. See Robert Gordis, *The Song of Songs* (New York: Jewish Theological Seminary of America, 1961), p. 1.

6. W. Sibley Towner, "The Song of Songs, Yesterday and Today," address given December 9, 1971, at the Schools of Theology in Dubuque, Iowa.

7. See Gordis, *op. cit.*, as well as the commentary in *The Interpreter's Bible*. Also Roland Murphy, *Seven Books of Wisdom* (Milwaukee: Bruce Publishing Co., 1960), pp. 67–86.

8. H. H. Rowley, "The Interpretation of the Song of Songs," *The Journal of Theological Studies* 38 (1937), p. 345.

9. See Willoughby Allen's *Gospel According to Matthew*, ICC (New York: Charles Scribner's Sons, 1907). Also David Hill's, *The Gospel of Matthew* (Greenwood: The Attic Press, 1972).

10. Pierre Benoit, "Qumran and the New Testament," *Paul and Qumran*, edited by Jerome Murphy-O'Connor (Chicago: The Priory Press, 1968), p. 9.

11. Jacques Dupont, *Mariage et divorce dans l'Evangile* (Bruges, Belgium: Abbaye de Saint-André, 1959); Thomas Fleming, "Christ and Divorce," *Theological Studies*, 24 (1963); pp. 106–120; Wilfred Harrington, "The New Testament and Divorce," *Irish Theological Quarterly* 39 (1972), pp. 178–187; Quentin Quesnell, "Made Themselves Eunuchs for the Kingdom of Heaven," *Catholic Biblical Quarterly* 30 (1968), pp. 335–358. For a still different interpretation of the eunuch logion, one which places it in the context of celibacy and which follows the views of Josef Blinzler and Rudolf Schnackenburg, see the doctoral dissertation by Donald Trautman, *The Eunuch Logion of Matthew 19:12—Historical and Exegetical Dimensions as Related to Celibacy* (Rome: Catholic Book Agency, 1966).

12. See Joseph Blenkinsopp, *Sexuality and the Christian Tradition* (Dayton, Ohio: Pflaum Press, 1969), esp. chap. V. Also Tom Driver, "Sexuality and Jesus," *New Theology No. 3*, edited by Marty and Peerman (New York: Macmillan, 1966), pp. 118–132. And William Phipps, *The Sexuality of Jesus* (New York: Harper and Row, 1973). Also see Nikos Kazantzakis, *The Last Temptation of Christ* (New York: Simon and Schuster, 1966).

13. Edgar J. Goodspeed, *The Meaning of Ephesians* (Chicago: University of Chicago Press, 1933), 79–81. For further introduction to the Pauline

epistles, see: Gunther Bornkamm, *Paul* (New York: Harper and Row, 1971); H. J. Schoeps, *Paul* (London: Lutterworth Press, 1961). For exegesis of I Corinthians 7, see, among others: H. L. Goudge, *First Epistle to the Corinthians*, Westminster Commentaries (London: Methuen & Co., 1903), pp. 52–65; Robertson and Plummer, *First Epistle of St. Paul to the Corinthians*, ICC (Edinburgh, T. & T. Clark, 1953), pp. 130–162.

14. Louis Bouyer, *The Spirituality of the New Testament and the Fathers*, vol. I of A History of Christian Spirituality (New York: Desclee Co., 1963), p. 468.

15. *Ibid.*, pp. 469–470.

16. Augustine, *The City of God*, vol. II of The Nicene and Post-Nicene Fathers, First Series (Buffalo: The Christian Literature Co., 1887), Book 14, Chapter 18.

17. Augustine, *Against Julian*, vol. 35 of The Fathers of the Church (Washington, D.C.: The Catholic University of America Press, 1957), Book 3, Chapter 21, paragraph 42.

18. *The City of God*, Book 14, Chapter 18.

19. Augustine, *The Good of Marriage*, vol. 27 of the Fathers of the Church (Washington, D.C.: The Catholic University of America Press, 1957), Chapter 3.

20. *Against Julian*, Book 3, Chapter 21, paragraph 42.

21. *Ibid.*, paragraph 43.

22. *Ibid.*, Book 3, Chapter 25, paragraph 57.

23. Augustine, *Sermons on the New Testament*, vol. 1 of A Library of Fathers (London: Oxford, 1844), Sermon I (LI of the Benedictines), paragraph 22.

24. *Against Julian*, Book 3, Chapter 21, paragraph 43.

25. *Sermons on the New Testament*, Sermon I, paragraph 23.

26. *The Good of Marriage*, Chapter 3.

27. *Ibid.*, Chapter 10, paragraph 11.

28. *Against Julian*, Book 3, Chapter 21, paragraph 43.

29. *The Good of Marriage*, Chapter 6, paragraph 5.

30. *Ibid.*, Chapter 7, paragraph 6.

31. *Sermons on the New Testament*, Sermon I, paragraph 22.

32. *The Good of Marriage*, Chapter 11, paragraph 12.

33. *Ibid.*, Chapter 10, paragraph 11.

34. *Sermons on the New Testament*, Sermon I, paragraph 24.

35. *The Good of Marriage*, Chapter 7, paragraph 6.

36. *Ibid.*, Chapter 6, paragraph 6.

37. For the influence of Stoicism on early Christianity, see Edwin Hatch, *The Influence of Greek Ideas On Christianity* (New York: Harper and

Row, 1957); John McKenzie, *The Power and the Wisdom* (Milwaukee: Bruce Publishing Co., 1965); John T. Noonan, *Contraception* (Cambridge: Harvard University Press, 1965).

38. Peter Brown, *Augustine of Hippo* (Berkeley: University of California Press, 1969), p. 389.

39. Derrick Bailey, *Sexual Relation in Christian Thought* (New York: Harper and Brothers, 1959), p. 59. See pp. 50–59 for material on Augustine.

40. *Ibid.*, p. 284.

41. *Ibid.*, p. 285.

42. *Ibid.*, pp. 285–286.

CHAPTER 2

1. Sigmund Freud, "Instincts and Their Vicissitudes," *The Complete Psychological Works of Sigmund Freud*, vol. 14 (London: Hogarth Press, 1964), p. 119. For more thorough discussions of Freud, see: Reuben Fine, *The Development of Freud's Thought* (New York: Jason Aronson, Inc., 1973); Calvin Hall, *A Primer of Freudian Psychology* (New York: Mentor Book, 1954).

2. Sigmund Freud, "The Sexual Life of Human Beings," *The Complete Introductory Lectures on Psychoanalysis* (New York: W. W. Norton and Co., 1966), p. 313.

3. See Sigmund Freud, "Three Essays on the Theory of Sexuality," *The Complete Psychological Works of Sigmund Freud*, vol. 7, especially the third essay, especially pp. 217–19. Also available in paperback, *Three Essays on the Theory of Sexuality* (New York: Avon Books, 1971), pp. 118–121.

4. For further discussion of Adler see the "Introduction" by Heinz Ansbacher to Adler's *Superiority and Social Interest* (Evanston: Northwestern University Press, 1964). Also Ansbacher, "The Structure of Individual Psychology," in *Scientific Psychology: Principles and Approaches*, ed. by Benjamin Wolman (New York: Basic Books, 1965), 340–65. Also Hall and Lindzey's *Theories of Personality* (New York: John Wiley and Sons, 1957), 114–56. For original material: Alfred Adler, *The Practice and Theory of Individual Psychology* (London: Kegan Paul, Trench, Trubner and Co., 1924); Alfred Adler, *Superiority and Social Interest* (Evanston: Northwestern University Press, 1964).

5. Madelaine Ganz, *The Psychology of Alfred Adler and the Development of the Child* (London: Routledge and Kegan Paul, 1953), p. 10.

6. Adler, "Advantages and Disadvantages of the Inferiority Feeling," *Superiority and Social Interest*, p. 52.

7. Adler, "The Differences Between Individual Psychology and Psychoanalysis," *Superiority and Social Interest*, p. 216.

8. Adler, "On the Origin of the Striving for Superiority and Social Interest," *Superiority and Social Interest*, pp. 34–35.

9. Adler, "Religion and Individual Psychology," *Superiority and Social Interest*, p. 285.

10. For a good introduction to Viktor Frankl, see his *Man's Search for Meaning* (New York: Washington Square Press, 1965), and *The Doctor and the Soul* (New York: Bantam Books, 1967).

11. *Man's Search for Meaning*, p. 106.

12. Adler, "The Sexual Function," *Superiority and Social Interest*, p. 223.

13. *Man's Search for Meaning*, p. 177.

14. This point is well made by Robert Francoeur, *Utopian Motherhood* (Garden City: Doubleday and Co., 1970), pp. 221–264. Also Abel Jeanniere, *The Anthropology of Sex* (New York: Harper and Row, 1967).

15. Sigmund Freud, "The Development of the Libido and the Sexual Organizations," *The Complete Introductory Lectures on Psychoanalysis* (New York: W. W. Norton and Co., 1966), p. 321. Also see Freud's *Three Essays on the Theory of Sexuality* (New York: Avon Books, 1971), pp. 98–99 and 107–08. Further references to these essays will be to the Avon edition.

16. *Three Essays on the Theory of Sexuality*, pp. 98–99 and 107–108.

17. *Ibid.*, pp. 71–72.

18. Freud, "The Libido Theory," *Collected Papers*, vol. 5 (New York: Basic Books, Inc., 1959), p. 134.

19. "The Development of the Libido and the Sexual Organizations," *The Complete Introductory Lectures on Psychoanalysis*, p. 328. Also see pp. 326–28 and *Three Essays on the Theory of Sexuality*, pp. 107–113.

20. Abraham Maslow, *Motivation and Personality*, (New York: Harper and Row, 1970), p. 191.

21. Herbert Marcuse, *Eros and Civilization* (New York: Vintage Book, 1962), especially pp. 69 and 75.

22. Erik Erikson, *Childhood and Society* (New York: W. W. Norton and Co., Inc., 1963), especially chapters one and seven.

23. For a critique of Freud's stages of psychosexual development and an attempt to re-interpret them in the context of a competence model, see Robert W. White, "Competence and the Psychosexual Stages of Development," *Nebraska Symposium on Motivation*, vol. 8 (Lincoln: University of Nebraska Press, 1960), pp. 97–141. See especially his criticism of Freud's handling of latency, pp. 127–133.

24. *Complete Introductory Lectures on Psychoanalysis*, p. 326. *Three Essays on the Theory of Sexuality*, pp. 70–71.

25. Rollo May, *Love and Will*, (New York: W. W. Norton and Co., 1969), p. 318. Also see Harry Stack Sullivan, *The Interpersonal Theory of Psychiatry* (New York: W. W. Norton and Co., 1953), pp. 245–262.

26. *Three Essays*, pp. 98–99.

27. Teilhard de Chardin, *Human Energy* (New York: Harcourt Brace Jovanovich, 1970).

28. Harry Stack Sullivan, *The Interpersonal Theory of Psychiatry*, pp. 266–267.

29. *Ibid.*, pp. 263–296.

30. *Ibid.*, p. 290.

31. See Frank Goble, *The Third Force—The Psychology of Abraham Maslow* (New York: Grossman Publishers, 1970). Works by Abraham Maslow: *Motivation and Personality*; *Religion, Values, and Peak Experiences* (New York: Harper & Row, 1970); *The Farther Reaches of Human Nature* (New York: The Viking Press, 1972); *Toward a Psychology of Being* (New York: Van Nostrand Reinhold Co., 1968). Maslow himself uses "the third force" as an expression. See *Toward a Psychology of Being*, pp. 189–214.

32. For further discussion of these characteristics, see *Motivation and Personality*, pp. 149–180. Also *Toward a Psychology of Being*, pp. 135–145.

33. I discuss the basic needs as identified in *Motivation and Personality*, pp. 35–104. Also see Goble, *The Third Force*, pp. 36–51.

34. *Motivation and Personality*, p. 99.

35. *Ibid.*, p. 23.

36. *Ibid.*, pp. 105–107.

37. *Ibid.*, pp. 187–188.

38. *Ibid.*, 189.

39. Maslow, "Neurosis as a Failure of Personal Growth," *Humanitas*, 3 (1967), pp. 153–169.

40. Rollo May, *Love and Will*, p. 311.

41. Irene Josselyn, *Adolescence* (New York: Harper & Row, 1971), p. 104.

42. *Motivation and Personality*, p. 107.

43. Robert Stoller, *Sex and Gender* (New York: Science House, 1968), pp. 39–64.

44. Maslow, *The Farther Reaches of Human Nature* (New York: The Viking Press, 1972), pp. 160–162.

45. Stoller, *op. cit.*, p. 29.

46. Jeanne Humphrey Block, "Conceptions of Sex Role: Some Cross-

Cultural and Longitudinal Perspectives," *American Psychologist*, 28 (1973), p. 512.

47. *Ibid.*, p. 517.

48. *Ibid.*, p. 520.

49. James McCary, *Human Sexuality* (New York: Van Nostrand Reinhold Co., 1967), p. 210.

50. For a discussion of Teilhard de Chardin's theory of personality, see my *Personality-in-Process and Teilhard de Chardin* (Dubuque: Aquinas Institute Library, 1970), unpublished. I hope within the coming year to have a book ready for publication on this topic. Key essays by Teilhard on this topic can be found in his *Human Energy*.

51. Jeanniere, *The Anthropology of Sex*, p. 128.

52. Ignace Lepp, *The Psychology of Loving* (Baltimore: Helicon, 1963), p. 15.

53. Nathaniel Branden, *The Psychology of Self-Esteem* (New York: Bantam Books, Inc., 1971), p. 207.

54. Stoller, *op. cit.*, pp. xiii, 3–23, 65–85, 262–268.

55. Bardwick, *Psychology of Women* (New York: Harper & Row, 1971), p. 216.

56. *Ibid.*

57. *Ibid.*, p. 217.

58. Charles N. Cofer and M. H. Appley, *Motivation: Theory and Research* (New York: John Wiley and Sons, 1965), p. 815.

59. White, *op. cit.*, p. 101.

60. Cofer and Appley, *op. cit.*, pp. 769–75.

61. Leon Festinger, "The Motivating Effect of Cognitive Dissonance," *Assessment of Human Motives*, ed. by G. Lindzey (New York: Rinehart and Co., 1958), p. 69. Also see Festinger's *A Theory of Cognitive Dissonance* (Evanston, Ill.: Row-Peterson, 1957).

62. Festinger, *op. cit.*, p. 70.

63. Cofer and Appley, *op. cit.*, pp. 821–825.

64. *Ibid.*, p. 823.

65. Frank A. Beach, "Characteristics of Masculine 'Sex Drive,' " *Nebraska Symposium on Motivation*, ed. by M. R. Jones, vol. 4 (Lincoln: University of Nebraska Press, 1956), p. 5.

66. Charles N. Cofer, *Motivation and Emotion* (Glenview: Scott, Foresman and Co., 1972), pp. 48–52. Cofer and Appley, *op. cit.*, pp. 822–824. F. A. Beach, *op. cit.*, pp. 1–32.

67. Eric Berne, *Principles of Group Treatment* (New York: Oxford University Press, 1966), pp. 283 and 311.

68. Del Martin and Phyllis Lyon, "The New Sexuality and the

Homosexual," *The New Sexuality*, ed. by Herbert Otto (Palo Alto, Calif.: Science and Behavior Books, Inc.), p. 200. This volume is a series of essays by twenty-four authors edited by the Chairman of the National Center for the Exploration of Human Potential, La Jolla, California.

69. Maslow, *The Farther Reaches of Human Nature*, p. 361.

70. The quote is from Martin Hoffman, "Homosexual," *Psychology Today*, 3 (1969), p. 43. The article is an interview in which Hoffman discusses his book, *The Gay World* (New York: Bantam Books, 1969), pp. 160–161 for the same material as in the above quote. Also see Evelyn Hooker, "The Adjustment of the Overt Male Homosexual," *Journal of Projective Techniques* XXI (1957), p. 18.

71. Albert Ellis, *Homosexuality: Its Causes and Cure* (New York: Lyle Stuart Inc., 1965), pp. 78–79.

72. See Alfred Kinsey, *Sexual Behavior in the Human Male* (Philadelphia: W. B. Saunders Co., 1948), pp. 636–659, for his discussion of the heterosexual-homosexual balance and the seven point scale.

73. Evelyn Hooker, "Homosexuality—Summary of Studies," *Sex Ways —in Fact and Faith*, ed. by E. Duvall and S. Duvall (New York: Association Press, 1961), p. 167.

74. Morton Hunt, *Sexual Behavior in the 1970's* (Chicago: Playboy Press, 1974).

75. Sullivan, as I mentioned earlier, speaks in terms of the lust dynamism and the need for intimacy as distinguishable tendencies in the person. In discussing the possible ways of integrating these two tendencies, he writes, "The theoretical patterns of manifestation of the two powerful integrating tendencies, the need for intimacy and lust, may be classified: 1) on the basis of the intimacy need and the precautions which concern it—as autophilic, isophilic, and heterophilic; 2) on the basis of the preferred partner in lustful integrations, or the substitute therefor—as autosexual, homosexual, heterosexual, and katasexual; 3) on the basis of genital participation or substitution—as orthogenital, paragenital, metagenital, amphigenital, mutual masturbation, and onanism." He proceeds to discuss each of these. The detail goes beyond the scope of this work. My only point is to show that Sullivan would agree with others in saying that one cannot speak of homosexuality as a simple category of behavior. See *The Interpersonal Theory of Psychiatry*, pp. 290–296.

76. *Ibid.*, p. 294.

77. *The Gay World*, especially pp. 154–163.

78. George Weinberg, *Society and the Healthy Homosexual* (New York: St. Martin's Press, 1972).

79. Martin and Lyon, *op. cit.*, p. 210.

80. Henri Nouwen, *Intimacy* (Notre Dame, Ind.: Fides, 1969), p. 41.
81. Stoller, *op. cit.*, p. 157.
82. *Ibid.*, p. 159.

CHAPTER 3

1. Ashley Montagu, *Touching—The Human Significance of the Skin* (New York: Harper and Row, 1972), p. 273.
2. *Ibid.*, pp. 16–42, for discussion of the importance of licking among pre-humans.
3. *Ibid.*, pp. 43–91.
4. Anna Freud, *Normality and Pathology in Childhood* (New York: International Universities Press, 1965), p. 155–56. Ashley Montagu, *op. cit.*, pp. 92–109, and 290–293.
5. Montagu, *op. cit.*, 176–179, and 245–251.
6. *Ibid.*, pp. 185–209, 277–287, 333–334.
7. Margaret Mead and Frances Cooke Macgregor, *Growth and Culture: A Photographic Study of Balinese Childhood* (New York: G. P. Putnam's Sons, 1951), pp. 41–50 on child rearing. Also Montagu, *op. cit.*, pp. 134–138.
8. Montagu, *op. cit.*, p. 284.
9. W. Caudill and D. W. Plath, "Who Sleeps by Whom? Parent-Child Involvement in Urban Japanese Families," *Psychiatry*, 29 (1966), p. 344.
10. *Ibid.*, p. 363.
11. Montagu, *op. cit.*, pp. 299–312.
12. *Ibid.*, pp. 194–209, 283–290.
13. *Ibid.*, pp. 31, 35, 42, 184, 249, 334.
14. Ortega y Gasset, *Man and People* (New York: W. W. Norton and Co., 1957), p. 72.
15. Martin Heidegger, *Being and Time* (New York: Harper and Row, 1962), p. 81. Part in parentheses mine.
16. See E. F. O'Doherty's discussion of chastity in *Vocation, Formation, Consecration and Vows* (Staten Island: Alba House, 1972), pp. 125–134.
17. Thomas Aquinas, *Summa Theologica*, II-II, q. 141, a. 4.
18. *Ibid.*, q. 151, a. 3.
19. Albert Plé, "Celibacy and the Emotional Life," *Clergy Review*, 55 (1970), p. 39. Also see his *Chastity and the Affective Life* (New York: Herder and Herder, 1966).
20. Aristotle, *Politics*, 1, 3. Aquinas, *ST*, I-II, q. 56, a. 4, ad 3.
21. *ST*, I-II, q. 56, a. 4, ad 3.
22. *Ibid.*, q. 34, a. 1.

23. *ST*, II-II, q. 142, a. 1. The Latin which I translate as "insensitivity" is "insensibilitas." It basically means an anti-sensible or anti-sensual bias. Some translate it as "insensibility," but that is not as common in speech. An excellent example is frigidity, but that word alone is too narrow. I prefer insensitivity; in the widest sense, an insensitive person is a non-feeling person.

24. Adrian Van Kaam, *The Vowed Life* (Denville, New Jersey: Dimension Books, 1968).

25. Rollo May, *Love and Will*, p. 123.

26. *Ibid.*, p. 313.

CHAPTER 4

1. Dietrich Bonhoeffer, *The Cost of Discipleship* (New York: Macmillan, 1972), especially 105–114.

2. Adler, *Superiority and Social Interest*, pp. 23–28, 66–70.

3. Max Thurian, *Marriage and Celibacy* (London: SCM Press, 1959), p. 44.

4. Karl Barth, *Church Dogmatics*, III, 4 (Edinburgh: T. & T. Clark, 1961), pp. 160–240, 595–647, especially 181ff.

5. See John Cobb, *God and the World* (Philadelphia: Westminster, 1969), for his expression of God as the call forward.

6. Marshall McLuhan and Quentin Fiore, *War and Peace in the Global Village* (New York: Bantam Books, 1968). Marshall McLuhan and Harley Parker, *Through the Vanishing Point* (New York: Harper & Row, 1968).

7. Karl Rahner, "The Celibacy of the Secular Priest Today: An Open Letter," *Servants of the Lord* (New York: Herder and Herder, 1968), pp. 149–172.

8. *Ibid.*, p. 172.

9. William Lederer and Don Jackson, *The Mirages of Marriage* (New York, W. W. Norton & Co., 1968), p. 15.

10. *Ibid.*, pp. 126–129.

11. *Ibid.*, pp. 203–204.

12. *Ibid.*, pp. 114–125.

13. Maslow, *Motivation and Personality*, pp. 105–107, 186–192.

14. Lederer and Jackson, *op. cit.*, pp. 75–78.

15. John Cassian, *Conferences* (The Nicene and Post-Nicene Fathers), Second Conference, Chapter 16.

16. This is Louis Bouyer's comment on the persistence of the solitary life even after the rise of cenobitic life. *The Spirituality of the New Testament and the Fathers* (New York: Desclee Co., 1963), p. 326.

CHAPTER 5

1. Frederick Jelly, "Mary's Virginity in the Symbols and Councils," *Marian Studies*, 21 (1970), pp. 69–93. Austin Vaughan, "Interpreting the Ordinary Magisterium on Mary's Virginity," *Marian Studies*, 22 (1971), pp. 75–90.

2. Piet Schoonenberg, "The Dutch Catechism Defended," *Herder Correspondence*, 4 (1967), pp. 94–95. Piet Schoonenberg, "The Dutch Catechism Controversy," *Herder Correspondence*, 4 (1967), pp. 156–161.

3. Raymond Brown, *Jesus—God and Man* (Milwaukee: Bruce Publishing Co., 1967). Oscar Cullmann, *The Christology of the New Testament* (Philadelphia: Westminster Press, 1963). Reginald Fuller, *The Foundations of New Testament Christology* (New York: Charles Scribner's Sons, 1965). Ferdinand Hahn, *The Titles of Jesus in Christology* (New York: World Publishing Co., 1969). Piet Schoonenberg, *The Christ* (New York: Herder and Herder, 1971).

4. For a more detailed discussion of the question of Mary's virginity, see Raymond Brown, "The Problem of the Virginal Conception of Jesus," *Theological Studies*, 33 (1972), 3–25, later printed in his *The Virginal Conception and Bodily Resurrection of Jesus* (New York: Paulist Press, 1973). Also see John Craghan, "Mary's Ante Partum Virginity: The Biblical View," *American Ecclesiastical Review*, 162 (1970), pp. 361–372. John Craghan, "The Gospel Witness to Mary's Ante Partum Virginity," *Marian Studies*, 21 (1970), pp. 28–68. Vincent Taylor, *The Historical Evidence of the Virgin Birth* (Oxford: Clarendon Press, 1920). Hans Von Campenhausen, *The Virgin Birth in the Theology of the Ancient Church* (Naperville, Ill.: A. R. Allenson, 1964). Cletus Wessels, "Our Lady and the Incarnation," *Marian Studies*, 17 (1966), pp. 46–64.

5. The statistics I report are for those born in 1910 or after. See Alfred Kinsey, *The Sexual Behavior in the Human Female* (Philadelphia: W. B. Saunders Co., 1953), pp. 227–281, especially 251–259. The charts for the above statistics, pp. 280–281.

6. Herbert Richardson, "The Symbol of Virginity," in *The Religious Situation: 1969*, ed. by Donald Cutler (Boston: Beacon Press, 1969), p. 796.

7. Robert Bellah, "Civil Religion in America," in *The Religious Situation: 1968*, ed. by Donald Cutler (Boston: Beacon Press, 1968), pp. 331–356.

8. Jules Henry, *Culture Against Man* (New York: Vantage Books, 1963).

9. May, *Love and Will*, p. 40.

10. Teilhard de Chardin, *The Divine Milieu* (New York: Harper and Row, 1960).

CHAPTER 6

1. Much of the present day study of psychological contracts pertains to marriage. It is important to utilize these studies in our understanding of friendship as well. Some introductory material includes: Harry Levinson *et al.*, "The Unwritten Contract," *Men, Management, and Mental Health* (Cambridge: Harvard University Press, 1962), pp. 22–38; Kenneth Mitchell, "The Secret Contracts of Marriage," *The Menninger Quarterly* 23 (1969), pp. 13–22; Nena and George O'Neill, *Open Marriage* (New York: Avon Books, 1972), pp. 51–63.

2. Mitchell, *op. cit.*, pp. 13–22.

3. Levinson, *op. cit.*, pp. 39–56. Also John Bowlby, *Separation: Anxiety and Anger* (New York: Basic Books, Inc., 1973), esp. pp. 109–244.

4. There is much written on anger today. For an introduction, see Leo Madow, *Anger* (New York: Charles Scribner's Sons, 1972). Also George R. Bach and Peter Wyden, *The Intimate Enemy* (New York: William Morrow & Co., 1969); Lederer and Jackson, *The Mirages of Marriage*, pp. 79–84; Karl Menninger, *Love Against Hate* (New York: Harcourt, Brace & World, 1942), *Man Against Himself* (New York: Harcourt, Brace and World, 1938).

5. Madow, *op. cit.*, pp. 107–124.

6. Marguerite and Willard Beecher, *The Mark of Cain* (New York: Harper and Row, 1971). Ignace Lepp, *The Psychology of Loving* (Baltimore: Helicon, 1963).

7. Eric Berne, *Games People Play* (New York: Grove Press, 1967), pp. 15–20, *Principles of Group Treatment* (New York: Oxford University Press, 1966), pp. 230–232, 310–311, *The Structure and Dynamics of Organizations and Groups* (New York: Grove Press, 1966), pp. 146–148.

8. Nouwen, *op. cit.*, pp. 131–133.

9. Sullivan, *op. cit.*, p. 291.

10. *Ibid.*, p. 245.

11. Ray Brown, *The Gospel According to John XIII–XXI* (Garden City: Doubleday, 1970), pp. 1102–1112. Edwyn Hoskyns, *The Fourth Gospel* (London: Faber and Faber, 1948), pp. 557–558.

12. See Louis Bouyer, *The Cistercian Heritage* (Westminster: Newman Press, 1958), pp. 125–160. Also A. Fiske, "Aelred of Rievaulx's Idea of Friendship and Love," *Citeaux*, 13 (1962), pp. 5–17, 97–132. Also Amedee Hallier, *The Monastic Theology of Aelred of Rievaulx* (Spencer, Mass.: Cistercian Publications, 1969). For the text of Aelred from which I will be quoting, see Aelred of Rievaulx, *Of Spiritual Friendship* (Paterson, N.J.: St. Anthony's Guild Press, 1948).

13. Aelred of Riveaulx, *op. cit.*, p. 18.

14. *Ibid.*, p. 19.

15. *Ibid.*, p. 20. Quoting Ecclesiasticus 6:8. See Ecclesiasticus 6:5–17 for the complete text on friendship.

16. *Ibid.*, p. 52.

17. *Ibid.*, p. 72.

18. *Ibid.*, p. 90.

19. *Ibid.*, p. 46.

20. *Ibid.*, p. 90.

21. *Ibid.*, pp. 57–58.

22. *Ibid.*, p. 34.

23. *Ibid.*, p. 29.

24. *Ibid.*, p. 47.

25. *Ibid.*, pp. 47–48.

26. *Ibid.*, p. 59.

27. *Ibid.*, p. 59.

28. *Ibid.*, p. 60.

29. *Ibid.*, p. 51.

30. *Ibid.*, p. 83.

31. *Ibid.*, p. 55.

32. Francis de Sales, *Introduction to the Devout Life* (New York: Harper and Brothers, 1952), p. 128. See chapters 17–22 for his complete treatment of friendship.

33. See John Cassian, *Institutes* (The Nicene and Post-Nicene Fathers), Book II, Chapter XV. For Cassian's conference on friendship, see *Conferences* (Nicene and Post-Nicene Fathers), Conference XVI, pp. 450–460. Also see the article by A. Fiske, "Cassian and Monastic Friendship," *American Benedictine Review* 12 (1961), pp. 190–205.

34. Louis Bouyer, *The Cistercian Heritage*, esp. p. 37.

35. See William Hinnebusch, *The History of the Dominican Order*, vol. II, (New York: Alba House, 1973), pp. 284–288. Also see Gerald Vann's introduction to his translation of the letters, *To Heaven with Diana* (Chicago: Henry Regnery Co., 1965). I quote from his translation in the following references.

36. *To Heaven with Diana*, letter 25.

37. *Ibid.*, letter 50.

38. *Ibid.*, letter 28.

39. *Ibid.*, letter 35.

40. *Ibid.*, letter 48.

41. *Ibid.*, letter 50.

42. Quentin Hakenewerth, *For the Sake of the Kingdom* (Collegeville; The Liturgical Press, 1971), pp. 30–37.

43. *Ibid.*, pp. 36–37.

44. *To Heaven with Diana,* pp. 51–52.

45. See Robert Murray, "Spiritual Friendship," *The Way,* Supplement 10 (1970), pp. 61–73.

46. *The Rule of Taize,* pp. 81–89.

47. Bouyer, *The Cistercian Heritage,* pp. 159–160.

48. Erich Lindemann, "Symtomatology and Management of Acute Grief," *Pastoral Psychology,* 14 (1963), pp. 17–18.

49. John Bowlby, "Grief and Mourning in Infancy and Early Childhood," *The Psychoanalytic Study of the Child,* 15 (1960), pp. 9–52.

50. Augustine, *Confessions,* Book 4, Chapters 4–6.

CHAPTER 7

1. Albert Plé, "Celibacy and the Emotional Life," *Clergy Review,* 55 (1970), p. 27.

2. See Don Goergen, *Personality-in-Process and Teilhard de Chardin* (Dubuque, Iowa: Aquinas Institute Library, 1971), unpublished doctoral dissertation.

3. Ethel Nash, "Sexuality: Rewards and Responsibilities," in Otto, ed., *The New Sexuality,* pp. 228–229.

4. For a study of the reactions to the first experience among adolescents, see Michael Schofield, "Normal Sexuality in Adolescence," *Modern Perspectives in Adolescent Psychiatry,* ed. by John Howells (New York: Brunner/Mazel Publishers, 1971), pp. 45–65.

5. Branden, *op. cit.,* p. 86.

6. The anxiety reactions can be found in any text on psychiatry or psychopathology. For reference, see Norman Cameron, *Personality Development and Psychopathology* (Boston: Houghton Mifflin Co., 1963), pp. 246–275. Oliver S. English and Stuart M. Finch, *Introduction to Psychiatry* (New York: W. W. Norton & Co., 1964), pp. 139–157.

7. Branden, *op. cit.,* p. 87.

8. Bouyer, *The Spirituality of the New Testament and the Fathers,* p. 308.

9. "The Sayings of the Fathers," translated by Helen Waddell, *The Desert Fathers* (Ann Arbor: University of Michigan Press, 1966), pp. 78–79. Also see pages 74–83, 96–99.

10. *Ibid.,* p. 97.

11. Among others, see Lionel Ovesey, *Homosexuality and Pseudohomosexuality* (New York: Science House, Inc., 1969).

12. Geoffrey Moorhouse, *Against All Reason* (Middlesex, England: Penguin Books, 1972), pp. 220–221.

13. W. Norman Pittenger, *Making Sexuality Human* (Philadelphia: Pilgrim Press, 1972), p. 67.

14. E. F. O'Doherty, *Vocation, Formation, Consecration and Vows*, pp. 162–166. For the chum and crush stages, also see Sullivan, *Interpersonal Theory of Psychiatry.*

15. Josselyn, *op. cit*, p. 30.

16. Freud, *Three Essays on a Theory of Sexuality*, p. 27.

17. Arnold Buss, *Psychopathology* (New York: John Wiley and Sons, 1966), pp. 455–456. Also Hooker, *op. cit.*, p. 171.

18. Ellis, *op. cit.*, p. 49.

19. Nowen, *op. cit.*, p. 51.

20. Buss, *op. cit.*, p. 455.

21. *Ibid.*

22. Henri Nouwen, "The Self-availability of the Homosexual," in W. Dwight Oberholtzer, ed., *Is Gay Good?* (Philadelphia: Westminister Press, 1971), p. 207.

23. *Ibid.*, pp. 208–209.

24. *Ibid.*, p. 209.

25. For recent material on theology and homosexuality, see: Derrick Bailey, *Homosexuality and the Western Christian Tradition* (New York: Longmans, Green and Co., 1955); Gregory Baum, "Catholic Homosexuals," *Commonweal*, 99 (1974), pp. 479–482; John C. Bennett, "Toward a Fresh Discussion of Sex Ethics," *Christianity and Crisis* 23 (1963) p. 173; John A. Coleman, "The Churches and the Homosexual," *America* 124 (1971), pp. 113–117; Charles E. Curran, "Homosexuality and Moral Theology: Methodological and Substantive Considerations," *Thomist* 35 (1971), pp. 447–481; Richard Devor, "Homosexuality and St. Paul," *Pastoral Psychology* 23 (1972) pp. 50–58; *Is Gay Good?*; H. Kimball Jones, *Toward a Christian Understanding of the Homosexual* (New York: Association Press, 1966); Joseph A. McCaffrey, "Homosexuality in the Seventies," *Catholic World* 213 (1971), pp. 121–125; Joseph A. McCaffrey, "Homosexuality, Aquinas and the Church," *ibid.*, pp. 183–186; Richard A. McCormick, "Notes on Moral Theology," *Theological Studies* 33 (1972), pp. 112–117; Norman Pittenger, *Making Sexuality Human* (Philadelphia: Pilgrim Press, 1972); *Towards a Quaker View of Sex* (London: Friends House, 1963); Robert Treese, "Homosexuality: A Contemporary View of the Biblical Perspective," prepared for the Consultation on Theology and the Homosexual, 1966, available from the Glide Urban Center, San Francisco; Daniel Day Williams, "Three Studies of Homosexuality in Relation to the Christian Faith," *Social Action* 34 (1967), pp. 30–37; Robert Wood, *Christ and the Homosexual* (New York: Vantage Press, 1960); Elliott Wright, "The Church and the Gay Liberation," *Christian Century* 88 (1971), pp. 281–285; Michael Valente, *Sex—The Radical View of a Catholic Theologian* (New York: Bruce Publishing Co., 1970).

26. Josselyn, *op. cit.*, p. 73.

27. Freud, *Three Essays on a Theory of Sexuality*, pp. 80–90.

28. McCary, *Human Sexuality*, pp. 293–294. Also see Sullivan, *op. cit.*, pp. 270–271. Also Jerrold Greenberg and Francis Archambault, "Masturbation, Self-esteem and Other Variables," *Journal of Sex Research* 9 (1973), pp. 41–51.

29. McCary, *Human Sexuality*, p. 291. James McCary, *Sexual Myths and Fallacies*, p. 110. Otto, *The New Sexuality*, pp. 57–58.

30. Josselyn, *op. cit.*, pp. 55–57, 72–74.

31. Brockman, "Contemporary Attitudes on the Morality of Masturbation," *The American Ecclesiastical Review*, 166 (1972), pp. 597–614.

32. McCary, *Sexual Myths and Fallacies*, p. 113.

33. G. Lombard Kelly, *A Doctor Discusses Menopause* (Chicago: Budlong Press, 1959), available through your doctor. McCary, *Human Sexuality*, pp. 77–79.

34. LeMon Clark, "Emotions and Sexuality in the Man," in Otto, ed., *The New Sexuality*, pp. 47–59. McCary, *Human Sexuality*, pp. 77–79.

35. Madow, *op. cit.*, p. 89. McCary, *Sexual Myths and Fallacies*, pp. 52–57.

36. Simone de Beauvoir, "Joie de Vivre: On Sexuality and Old Age," *Harper's Magazine* (1972), pp. 33–40.

CHAPTER 8

1. Teilhard de Chardin, *The Divine Milieu*, pp. 81–86.

2. May, *Love and Will*, p. 267.

3. *Ibid.*, pp. 262–272.

4. *Ibid.*, p. 268.

5. Teilhard de Chardin, "The Grand Option," in *The Future of Man* (New York: Harper and Row, 1964), p. 47.

6. Soren Kierkegaard, *Purity of Heart is to Will One Thing* (New York: Harper and Row, 1956).

7. Teilhard de Chardin, *The Divine Milieu*, pp. 112–114.

8. Bonhoeffer, *The Cost of Discipleship*, esp. 43–114.

9. Augustine, *Confessions*, Book I, Chapter 1.

10. John Cobb, *God and the World*, (Philadelphia: Westminster Press, 1969), speaks of God as the One who calls.

11. Thomas Merton, "Renewal and Discipline," in *Contemplation in a World of Action* (Garden City: Doubleday Image, 1973), p. 131.

12. Branden, *The Psychology of Self-Esteem*, p. 151.

13. Karl Menninger, *Man Against Himself* (New York: Harcourt, Brace and World, 1938), pp. 77–125.

14. Goble, *op. cit.*, p. 61.

15. Merton, "Renewal and Discipline," p. 123.

16. Gandhi, *Autobiography*, p. 326.

17. Merton, *The Ascent to Truth* (New York: Harcourt, Brace and Co., 1951), p. 158. He speaks of the ascetical life as active purification and the mystical life as passive purification, which is a traditional distinction in spiritual theology.

18. Dan McGuire, *Thomas Merton on the Future of Monasticism* (Dubuque: Aquinas Institute of Theology Library, 1973, unpublished thesis), p. 10.

19. Merton, "Notes for a Philosophy of Solitude," *Disputed Questions* (New York: Farrar, Straus and Cudahy, 1953), pp. 177–207. Also see his "Christian Solitude," in *Contemplation in a World of Action*, pp. 251–264, and *Thoughts in Solitude* (Garden City: Doubleday Image, 1968).

20. "Notes for a Philosophy of Solitude," pp. 177–178.

21. *Ibid.*, pp. 179–180.

22. Matt Fox, in *The Musical Mystical Bear or Spirituality American Style* (New York: Harper and Row, 1972), speaks of faith as a response to life and prayer as a radical response.

23. "Notes for a Philosophy of Solitude," p. 188.

24. *Thomas Merton on Peace* (New York: McCall's Publishing Co., 1971), p. 63.

25. "Notes for a Philosophy of Solitude," p. 199.

26. *Ibid.*, p. 187.

27. *Ibid.*, p. 200.

28. *Ibid.*, p. 206.

29. Bouyer, *The Spirituality of the New Testament and the Fathers*, p. 313.

30. "Notes for a Philosophy of Solitude," p. 205.

31. Clark E. Moustakas, in his classical work, *Loneliness* (Englewood Cliffs, New Jersey: Prentice-Hall, 1961), discusses existential loneliness and loneliness anxiety, the first of which can be constructive and the second of which is destructive. The book is well worth reading, especially for celibate people who find loneliness a particular problem. I prefer to distinguish between loneliness and aloneness. Only the first of these two is an intimacy problem. Also see Moustakas, *Loneliness and Love* (Englewood Cliffs, New Jersey: Prentice-Hall, 1972).

32. An excellent essay on silence, the basis for some of my own thoughts, is "The Eloquence of Silence," in Ivan Illich's *Celebration of Awareness: A Call for Institutional Revolution* (Garden City: Doubleday and Co., 1970), pp. 41–51.

33. Aquinas, *ST*, II-II, q. 28. a. 1.

34. *Ibid.*, a. 4.

Bibliography

This is a bibliography of some of the works to which I have referred in this book and which I consider valuable in the area of celibacy and sexuality. I am not saying that each individual work in itself is pertinent. This depends upon one's own area of interest.

Abraham, Karl. "Manic-Depressive States and the Pre-Genital Levels of the Libido," *Selected Papers*. London: The Hogarth Press, 1949.

Adler, Alfred. *The Practice and Theory of Individual Psychology*. London: Kegan Paul, Trench, Trubner, & Co., 1924.

————. *Superiority and Social Interest*. Evanston: Northwestern Univ. Press, 1964.

Aelred of Rievaulx. *Of Spiritual Friendship*. Paterson, N.J.: St. Anthony's Guild Press, 1948.

Ansbacher, Heinz. "The Structure of Individual Psychology," *Scientific Psychology: Principles and Approaches*. Ed. by Benjamin Wolman. New York: Basic Books, 1965.

Arintero, John G. *The Mystical Evolution in the Development and Vitality of the Church I & II*. St. Louis: B. Herder Book Co., 1950.

Arnold, Vernon. *Roman Stoicism*. New York: Humanities Press, 1958.

Audet, J. P. *Structures of Christian Priesthood. Home, Marriage and Celibacy in the Pastoral Service of the Church*. New York: Macmillan, 1968.

Auer, Alphons. "The Meaning of Celibacy," *The Furrow*. 18 (1967):299–321.

Augustine. *Against Julian*, vol. 35 The Fathers of the Church. New York: Fathers of the Church, Inc., 1957.

———. *City of God*, vol. 2 of Nicene and Post-Nicene Fathers. Grand Rapids: Wm. B. Eerdmans Publishing Co., 1956.

———. *Confessions*. Garden City: Doubleday, 1960.

———. *The Good of Marriage*, vol 27 The Fathers of the Church. New York: Fathers of the Church, Inc., 1957.

Bach, George R. and Peter Wyden. *The Intimate Enemy*. New York: Wm. Morrow & Co., 1969.

Bailey, Derrick. *Homosexuality and the Western Christian Tradition*. New York: Longmans, Green & Co., 1955.

———. *Sexual Relation in Christian Thought*. New York: Harper & Bros., 1959.

Baldwin, John. "A Campaign to Reduce Clerical Celibacy at the Turn of the Twelfth and Thirteenth Centuries," *Etudes d'histoire du droit canonique*, ed. by G. Bras. Paris:1965.

Barclay, Andres. "Sexual Fantasies in Men and Women," *Medical Aspects of Human Sexuality*. 7 (1973):204–216.

Bardwick, Judith M. *Psychology of Women*. New York: Harper and Row, 1971.

Barth, Karl. *Church Dogmatics*, III, 4. Edinburgh: T & T. Clark, 1961.

Baum, Gregory. "Catholic Homosexuals," *Commonweal*. 99 (1974):479–482.

Beach, Frank A. "Characteristics of Masculine 'Sex Drive'," *Nebraska Symposium on Motivation*, ed. M. R. Jones, vol. 4. Lincoln: Univ. of Nebraska Press, 1956.

Beecher, Marguerite and Beecher, Willard. *The Mark of Cain*. New York: Harper & Row, 1971.

Bellah, Robert. "Civil Religion in America," *The Religious Situation: 1968*. Ed. by Donald Cutler. Boston: Beacon Press, 1968.

Bennett, John C. "Toward a Fresh Discussion of Sex Ethics," *Christianity and Crisis*. 23 (1963): 173.

Benoit, Pierre. "Qumran and the New Testament," in *Paul and Qumran*, ed. by Jerome Murphy-O'Connor. Chicago: The Priory Press, 1968.

Berne, Eric. *Games People Play*. New York: Grove Press, 1967.

———. *Principles of Group Treatment*. New York: Oxford Univ. Press, 1966.

———. *Sex and Human Loving*. New York: Simon and Schuster, 1970.

———. *The Structure and Dynamics of Organizations and Groups*. New York: Grove Press, 1966.

Bertrams, Wilhelm. *The Celibacy of the Priest: Meaning and Basis*. Tr. P. Byrne. Westminster: Newman Press, 1963.

Beyer, Jean. "The Call to Perfect Charity," *The Way*. Supplement 10 (1970):33–48.

Blenkinsopp, Joseph. *Celibacy, Ministry, Church*. New York: Herder and Herder, 1968.

———. *Sexuality and the Christian Tradition*. Dayton: Pflaum Press, 1969.

Block, Jeanne Humphrey. "Conceptions of Sex Role: Some Cross Cultural and Longitudinal Perspectives," *American Psychologist*. 28 (1973):512–526.

Bloesch, Donald. *Centers of Christian Renewal*. Philadelphia: United Church Press, 1964.

Bonhoeffer, Dietrich. *The Cost of Discipleship*. New York: Macmillan, 1972.

———. *Creation and Fall*. New York: Macmillan Company, 1969.

———. *Life Together*. New York: Harper and Row, 1954.

Bouyer, Louis. *The Cistercian Heritage*. Westminster: Newman Press, 1958.

———. *A History of Christian Spirituality*. New York: Desclee Company, 1960.

Bowlby, John. *Attachment*. New York: Basic Books, Inc., 1969.

———. "Grief and Mourning in Early Infancy and Childhood," *The Psychoanalytic Study of the Child*. 15 (1960):9–52.

———. *Separation: Anxiety and Anger*. New York: Basic Books, Inc., 1973.

Branden, Nathaniel, *The Disowned Self*. New York: Bantam Books, 1973.

———. *The Psychology of Self-Esteem*. New York: Bantam Books, Inc., 1971.

Brockman, Norbert. "Contemporary Attitudes on the Morality of Masturbation," *The American Ecclesiastical Review*. 166 (1972):597–614.

Brown, Peter. *Augustine of Hippo*. Berkeley: Univ. of California Press, 1969.

Brown, Raymond. "The Problem of the Virginal Conception of Jesus," *Theological Studies*. vol. 33 (1972):3–25.

———. *The Virginal Conception and Bodily Resurrection of Jesus*. New York: Paulist Press, 1973.

Bunnik, Rudd J. *Priests for Tomorrow*. New York: Holt, Rinehart, Winston, 1969.

———. "The Question of Married Priests," and "The Question of Married Priests—II," *Cross Currents*. XV (1965):407–431; XVI (1966):81–112.

Burtt, *The Teachings of the Compassionate Buddha*. New York: Mentor Books, 1963.

Buss, Arnold, *Psychopathology*. New York: John Wiley and Sons, 1966.

Callahan, Sidney. *Beyond Birth Control*. New York: Sheed and Ward, 1968.

Cameron, Norman. *Personality Development and Psychopathology*. Boston: Houghton Mifflin Co., 1963.

Cassian, John. *Conferences*. The Nicene and Post-Nicene Fathers, Conference XVI. Philadelphia: Westminster Press, 1958.

———. *Institutes*. The Nicene and Post-Nicene Fathers, Book II, Chapter XV. Philadelphia: Westminster Press, 1958.

Caudill, W. and Plath, D. W. "Who Sleeps by Whom? Parent-Child Involvement in Urban Japanese Families," *Psychiatry*. 29 (1966):344–366.

Célibat et Sexualité. Paris: Editions du Seuil, 1970.

Clarke, Thomas E. "Celibacy: Challenge to Tribalism," *America*. (1969):464–467.

———. *New Passion or New Pentecost*. New York: Paulist Press, 1973.

Clayton, Paula, Lynn and George. "A Study of Normal Bereavement," *American Journal of Psychiatry*. 125 (1968):168–178.

Cobb, John. *God and the World*. Philadelphia: Westminster, 1969.

Cofer, Charles N. *Motivation and Emotion*. Glenview: Scott, Foresman & Co., 1972.

Cofer, Charles N. and M. H. Appley. *Motivation: Theory and Research*. New York: John Wiley and Sons, 1965.

Cole, William Graham. *Sex in Christianity and Psychoanalysis*. New York: Oxford Univ. Press, 1955.

Coleman, John A. "The Churches and the Homosexual," *America*. 124 (1971):113–117.

Conze, E. *Buddhism: Its Essence and Development*. New York: Harper and Row, 1959.

Craghan, John. "The Gospel Witness to Mary's Ante Partum Virginity," *Marian Studies*. 21 (1970):28–68.

———. "Mary's Ante Partum Virginity: The Biblical View," *American Ecclesiastical Review*. 162 (1970):361–372.

Croft, George. "Affective Maturity," *The Way*. Supplement 10 (1970):84–91.

Crouzel, Henri. "Marriage and Virginity," *The Way*. Supplement 10 (1970):3–23.

Curran, Charles E. "Homosexuality and Moral Theology: Methodological and Substantive Considerations," *Thomist*. 35 (1971):447–481.

Dank, Barry. "Why Homosexuals Marry Women," *Medical Aspects of Human Sexuality*. 6 (1972):14–23.

De Beauvoir, Simone. "Joie de Vivre: On Sexuality and Old Age," *Harper's Magazine*. 244 (1972):33–40.

Dedek, John F. "Celibacy," *Chicago Studies*. IX (1970):3–17.

Delhaye, Philippe. "History of Celibacy," *The Catholic Encyclopedia*. III. New York: McGraw-Hill, 1967.

De Lubac, Henri. *The Eternal Feminine*. New York: Harper and Row, 1971.

Deutsch, Helen. "Absence of Grief," *The Psychoanalytic Quarterly*. 6 (1937):12–22.

Devor, Richard. "Homosexuality and St. Paul," *Pastoral Psychology*. 23 (1972):50–58.

Driver, Tom. "Sexuality and Jesus," *New Theology No. 3*, ed. Marty and Peerman. New York: Macmillan, 1966.

Drummond, Richard. *Gautama the Buddha: An Essay in Religious Understanding*. Grand Rapids: Wm. B. Eerdmans, 1974.

Dupont, Jacques. *Marriage et divorce dans l'Evangile*. Belgium: Abbaye de Saint-André, 1959.

Dutt, S. *Buddhist Monks and Monasteries of India*. New York: Fernhill House, 1962.

Eliot, Thomas D. "The Bereaved Family," *The Annals of the American Academy of Political and Social Science*. 160 (1932):184–190.

Elisofon, Eliot and Alan Watts. *Erotic Spirituality*. New York: Macmillan Co., 1971.

Ellis, Albert. *Homosexuality: Its Causes and Cure*. New York: Lyle Stuart, Inc., 1965.

———. *Sex Without Guilt*. New York: Lyle Stuart, 1973.

Ellis, Peter. *The Yahwist*. Notre Dame: Fides Publishers, Inc., 1968.

Embree, Ainslie, ed. *The Hindu Tradition*. New York: Vintage Books, 1972.

English, Oliver S. and Stuart M. Finch. *Introduction to Psychiatry*. New York: W. W. Norton & Co., 1964.

Enroth, Ronald and Gerald Jamison. *The Gay Church*. Grand Rapids: Wm. B. Erdmans, 1974.

Erikson, Erik. *Childhood and Society*. New York: W. W. Norton & Co., Inc., 1963.

Festinger, Leon. "The Motivating Effect of Cognitive Dissonance," *Assessment of Human Motives*. Ed. G. Lindzey. New York: Rinehart & Co., 1958.

Fine, Reuben. *The Development of Freud's Thought*. New York: Jason Aronson, Inc., 1973.

Fischer, Louis. *Ghandhi, His Life and Message for the World*. New York: Mentor Books, 1954.

Fischer, Louis. *The Life of Mahatma Gandhi.* New York: Collier Books, 1966.

Fiske, A. "Aelred's of Rievaulx Idea of Friendship and Love," *Citeaux.* 13 (1962):5–17; 97–132.

———. "Cassian and Monastic Friendship," *American Benedictine Review.* 12 (1961):190–205.

———. "Saint Anselm and Friendship," *Studia Monastica.* 3 (1961):260–290.

———. "William of St. Thierry and Friendship," *Citeaux.* 12 (1961):5–27.

Fleming, Thomas. "Christ and Divorce," *Theological Studies* 24 (1963):106–120.

Ford, J. Massingberd. "The Meaning of Virgin," *New Testament Studies* 12 (1966):293–299.

———. *A Trilogy on Wisdom and Celibacy.* Notre Dame: Univ. of Notre Dame Press, 1967.

Fox, Matthew. *The Musical Mystical Bear or Spirituality American Style.* New York: Harper & Row, 1972.

Francis de Sales. *Introduction to the Devout Life.* New York: Harper & Brothers, 1952.

Francoeur, Robert. *Eve's New Rib.* New York: Harcourt, Brace, Javanovich, 1972.

———. *Utopian Motherhood.* Garden City: Doubleday & Co., 1970.

Frankl, Viktor. *The Doctor and the Soul.* New York: Stanton Books, 1967.

———. *Man's Search for Meaning.* New York: Washington Square Press, 1965.

Freible, Charles. "Teilhard, Sexual Love, and Celibacy," *Review for Religious.* 26 (1967):282–294.

Frein, George H., ed. *Celibacy, The Necessary Option.* Symposium on Clerical Celibacy, Univ. of Notre Dame, 1967. New York: Herder and Herder, 1968.

Freud, Anna. *Normality and Pathology in Childhood.* New York: International Universities Press, 1965.

Freud, Sigmund. *Beyond the Pleasure Principle.* New York: Bantom Books, 1967.

———. *The Complete Introductory Lectures on Psychoanalysis.* New York: W. W. Norton & Co., 1966.

———. "Instincts and Their Vicissitudes," *The Complete Psychological Works of Sigmund Freud* 14. London: Hogarth Press, 1964.

———. "The Libido Theory," *Collected Papers* 5. New York: Basic Books, Inc., 1959.

———. *Three Contributions to a Theory of Sexuality.* New York: Avon Books, 1971.

Fromm, Erich. *The Art of Loving.* New York: Harper & Row, 1956.

Fulcomer, David. *The Adjustive Behavior of Some Recently Bereaved Spouses: A Psychosociological Study.* Chicago: Northwestern Univ., 1942. Unpublished.

Gandhi, Mohandas. *Autobiography of the Story of My Experiments with Truth.* Boston: Beacon Press, 1968.

Gandhi. *The Love of Continence: Brahmacharya.* Bombay, India: Bharatiya Vidya Bhavan, 1964.

Ganz, Madelaine. *The Psychology of Alfred Adler and the Development of the Child.* London: Routledge and Kegan Paul, 1953.

Goble, Frank. *The Third Force: The Psychology of Abraham Maslow.* New York: Grossman Publishers, 1970.

Goergen, Donald. *Personality-in-Process and Teilhard de Chardin.* Dubuque: Aquinas Institute Library, 1970. Unpublished.

Golden, Joshua. "Sexual Frustration," *Medical Aspects of Human Sexuality.* 7 (1973):30–39.

Gordis, Robert. *The Song of Songs.* New York: Jewish Theological Seminary of America, 1961.

Gordon, David Cole. *Self Love.* Baltimore: Penguin, 1972.

Greeley, Andrew. *The Catholic Priest in the United States—Sociological Investigations.* Washington, D.C.: United States Catholic Conference, 1972.

————. *The Friendship Game.* New York: Doubleday, 1970.

Greenberg, Jerrold and Francis Archambault. "Masturbation, Self-esteem and Other Variables," *Journal of Sex Research.* 9 (1973):41–51.

Greene, Richard. *Sexual Identity Conflict in Children and Adults.* New York: Basic Books, 1974.

Grelot, Pierre. *Man and Wife in Scripture.* New York: Herder and Herder, 1964.

Gryson, Roger. *Les origines du célibat ecclésiastique.* Gembloux: J. Duculot, 1970.

Hakenewerth, Quentin. *For the Sake of the Kingdom.* Collegeville: The Liturgical Press, 1971.

Hall, Calvin. *A Primer of Freudian Psychology.* New York: Mentor Books, 1954.

Hall, Calvin S. and Gardner Lindzey. *Theories of Personality.* New York: John Wiley & Sons, 1957.

Hallier, Amedee. *The Monastic Theology of Aelred of Rievaulx.* Spencer, Mass: Cistercian Publications, 1969.

Harkx, Peter. *The Fathers on Celibacy.* DePere, Wis.: St. Norbert Abbey Press, 1968.

Harrington, Wilfred. "The New Testament and Divorce," *Irish Theological Quarterly.* 39 (1972):178–193.

Harris, Thomas A. *I'm O.K., You're O.K.: A Practical Guide to Transactional Analysis*. New York: Harper and Row, 1969.

Hatch, Edwin. *The Influence of Greek Ideas on Christianity*. New York: Harper & Row, 1957.

Heidegger, Martin. *Being and Time*. New York: Harper and Row, 1962.

Heijke, John. *An Ecumenical Light on the Renewal of Religious Community Life–Taizé*. Pittsburgh: Duquesne University Press, 1967.

Henry, Jules. *Culture Against Man*. New York: Vantage Books, 1963.

Herbert, Albert. *Priestly Celibacy—Recurrent Battle and Lasting Values*. Houston: Lumen Christi Press, 1971.

Hermand, P. *The Priest, Celibate or Married*. Baltimore: Helicon, 1966.

Hinnebusch, Paul. *Friendship in the Lord*. Notre Dame: Ave Maria Press, 1974.

Hinnebusch, William. *The History of the Dominican Order* I & II. New York: Alba House, 1973.

Hoffman, Martin. "Homosexuals," *Psychology Today*. (1969):43–45, 70.
———. *The Gay World*. New York: Bantam Books, 1969.

Homans, Peter. *Theology After Freud*. New York: Bobbs-Merrill Co., 1970.

Hooker, Evelyn. "The Adjustment of the Overt Male Homosexual," *Journal of Projective Techniques*. XXI (1957):1–31.
———. "Homosexuality—Summary of Studies," *Sex Ways—In Fact and Fate*. Ed. E. Duvall and S. Duvall. New York: Association Press, 1961.

Hopkins, Thomas. *The Hindu Religious Tradition*. Encino, California: Dickenson Publishing Co., Inc., 1971.

Houghton, Rosemary. *The Theology of Experience*. New York: Newman Press, 1972.

Hunt, Morton. *Sexual Behavior in the 1970's*. Chicago: Playboy Press Book, 1974.

Illich, Ivan. *Celebration of Awareness: A Call for Institutional Revolution*. Garden City: Doubleday & Co., 1970.

Jeanniere, Abel. *The Anthropology of Sex*. New York: Harper & Row, 1967.

Jelly, Frederick. "Mary's Virginity in the Symbols and Councils," *Marian Studies*. 21 (1970):69–93.

Johann, Robert. *The Meaning of Love*. Westminster: Newman, 1959.

Jones, H. Kimball. *Toward A Christian Understanding of the Homosexual*. New York: Association Press, 1966.

Josselyn, Irene. *Adolescence*. New York: Harper & Row, 1971.

Joyce, Mary Rosera, "Celibacy and Sexual Freedom," *America*. 120 (1969):468–470.

Karley, Arno. *Sexuality and Hmosexuality.* New York: W. W. Norton & Co., Inc., 1971.

Kazantzakis, Nikos. *The Last Temptation of Christ.* New York: Simon and Schuster, 1966.

Kelly, G. Lombard. *A Doctor Discusses Menopause.* Chicago: Budlong Press, 1959.

Kennedy, Eugene. *The New Sexuality: Myths, Fables, and Hang-Ups.* Garden City: Doubleday, 1972.

Kennedy, Eugene and Victor Heckler. *The Catholic Priest in the United States—Psychological Investigations.* Washington, D.C.: United States Catholic Conference, 1971.

Kierkegaard, Soren. *Purity of Heart is to Will One Thing.* New York: Harper and Row, 1956.

Kiesling, Christopher. "Celibacy, Friendship and Prayer," *Review for Religious.* 30 (1971):595–617.

Kinsey, Alfred. *Sexual Behavior in the Human Female.* Philadelphia: W. B. Saunders, 1953.

────── *Sexual Behavior in the Human Male.* Philadelphia: W. B. Saunders Co., 1948.

La Sor, William S. *The Dead Sea Scrolls and the New Testament.* Grand Rapids, Michigan: Wm. B. Eerdmans Pub. Co., 1972.

Lea, Henry C. *History of Sacerdotal Celibacy in the Christian Church.* London: Watts & Co., 1932.

Leaney, A. R. C. *The Rule of Qumran and Its Meaning.* Philadelphia: Westminster Press, 1966.

Lederer, William and Don Jackson. *The Mirages of Marriage.* New York: W. W. Norton & Co., 1968.

Legrand, L. *The Biblical Doctrine of Virginity.* New York: Sheed and Ward, 1963.

Lepp, Ignace. *The Psychology of Loving.* Baltimore: Helicon, 1963.

────── *The Ways of Friendship.* New York: Macmillan, 1968.

Levinson, Harry, *et alii. Men, Management and Mental Health.* Cambridge: Harvard Univ. Press, 1962.

Lewis, C. S. *The Four Loves.* London: Collins, 1960.

Lindemann, Eric. "Symtomatology and Management of Acute Grief," *Pastoral Psychology.* 14 (1963):8–18.

Madow, Leo. *Anger.* New York: Charles Scribner's Sons, 1972.

Maly, Eugene H. "Celibacy," *The Bible Today.* (1968):2392–2400.

Marcuse, Herbert. *Eros and Civilization.* New York: Vantage Books, 1962.

Maslow, Abraham. *The Farther Reaches of Human Nature.* New York: The Viking Press, 1972.

────── *Motivation and Personality.* New York: Harper & Row, 1970.

Maslow, Abraham. "Neurosis as a Failure of Personal Growth," *Humanitas*. III (1963):153–169.

———. *Religion, Values and Peak Experiences*. New York: Viking Press, 1970.

———. *Toward a Psychology of Being*. New York: Van Nostrand, Reinhold, & Co., 1968.

Matura, Thaddee. *Celibacy and Community*. Chicago: Franciscan Herald Press, 1968.

May, Rollo. *Love and Will*. New York: W. W. Norton & Co., 1969.

———. *Power and Innocence*. New York: W. W. Norton & Co., 1972.

Mc Caffrey, Joseph A. "Homosexuality in the Seventies," *Catholic World*. 213 (1971):121–125.

McCary, James. *Human Sexuality*. New York: Van Nostrand, Reinhold Co., 1967.

———. *Sexual Myths and Fallacies*. New York: Van Nostrand, Reinhold Co., 1971.

McCormick, Richard A. "Notes on Moral Theology," *Theological Studies*. 33 (1972):68–119.

McGonigle, Thomas. "Sex in the Scriptures," *Listening*. 2 (1967):113–120.

McGuire, Dan. *Thomas Merton on the Future of Monasticism*. Dubuque: Aquinas Institute Library, 1973. Unpublished.

McKenzie, John. *The Power and the Wisdom*. Milwaukee: Bruce Publishing Co., 1965.

Mead, Margaret and Frances Cooke. *Growth and Culture: A Photographic Study of Balinese Childhood*. New York: G. P. Putnam's Sons, 1951.

Meany, John O. "The Psychology of Celibacy: An In-Depth View," *Catholic Mind*. 69 (1971):11–20.

Meissner, W. W. "Affective Response to Psychoanalytic Death Symbols," *Journal of Abonormal and Social Psychology*. 56 (1958):295–299.

Menninger, Karl. *Love Against Hate*. New York: Harcourt, Brace & World, 1942.

———. *Man Against Himself*. New York: Harcourt, Brace & World, 1938.

———. *The Vital Balance: The Life Process in Mental Health and Illness*. New York: Viking Press, 1963.

Merton, Thomas. *The Ascent to Truth*. New York: Harcourt, Brace and Co., 1951.

———. *Contemplation in a World of Action*. Garden City: Doubleday-Image, 1973.

———. "Notes for a Philosophy of Solitude," *Disputed Questions*. New York: Farrar, Strauss & Cudahy, 1953.

———. *Peace*. New York: McCall's Publishing Co., 1971.

———. *Thoughts in Solitude*. Garden City: Doubleday-Image, 1968.

Mitchell, Kenneth. "The Secret Contracts of Marriage," *The Mennninger Quarterly*. 23 (1969):13–22.

Mohler, James. *The Heresy of Monasticism*. Staten Island: Alba House, 1971.

———. *The Origin and Evolution of the Priesthood*. New York: Alba House, 1969.

Montagu, Ashley. *Touching: The Human Significance of the Skin*. New York: Harper & Row, 1972.

Moorhouse, Geoffrey. *Against All Reason*. Harmondsworth, England: Penguin Books, 1972.

Moreno, J. L. "The Social Atom and Death," *Sociometry: A Journal of Interpersonal Relations*. 10 (1947):80–84.

Moustakas, Clark. *Loneliness*. Englewood Cliffs: Prentice-Hall, 1961.

———. *Loneliness and Love*. Englewood Cliffs: Prentice-Hall, 1972.

Murphy, Roland. *Seven Books of Wisdom*. Milwaukee: Bruce Publishing Co., 1960.

Murphy-O'Connor, Jerome. "What is the Religious Life?" *Doctrine and Life*. 11 (1974):3–69.

Murray, Robert. "Spiritual Friendship." *The Way*. 10 (1970):61–73.

Noonan, John T. *Contraception*. Cambridge: Harvard Univ. Press, 1965.

Nouwen, Henri. *Intimacy*. Notre Dame: Fides Press, 1969.

———. "The Self-availability of the Homosexual," *Is Gay Good?*. Philadelphia: Westminster Press, 1971.

Oates, Wayne. *Anxiety in Christian Experience*. Philadelphia: Westminister Press, 1955.

O'Doherty, E. F. *Vocation, Formation, Consecration and Vows*. Staten Island: Alba House, 1971.

O'Meara, Thomas F. *Holiness and Radicalism in Religious Life*. New York: Herder & Herder, 1970.

O'Neill, David P. *Priestly Celibacy and Maturity*. New York: Sheed and Ward, 1965.

O'Neill, Nena and George. *Open Marriage*. New York: Avon Books, 1972.

Oraison, Marc. *Being Together: Our Relationships With Other People*. New York: Doubleday, 1971.

———. *The Celibate Condition and Sex*. New York: Sheed and Ward, 1967.

———. *The Human Mystery of Sexuality*. New York: Sheed and Ward, 1967.

Ortega y Gasset, Jose. *Man and People*. New York: W. W. Norton and Co., 1957.

Otto, Herbert. Ed. *The New Sexuality*. Palo Alto: Science and Behavior Books, Inc., 1971.

Ovesey, Lionel. *Homosexuality and Pseudo-Homosexuality*. New York: Science House, Inc. 1969.

Palmer, Paul. "A Case for Priestly Celibacy," *Thought*. 43 (1968):348–364.

Payne, Robert. *The Life and Death of Mahatma Gandhi*. New York: E. P. Dutton and Co., 1969.

Penrose, Sr. M. Romanus. "Virginity and the Cosmic Christ," *Review for Religious*. 31 (1972):187–194.

Perls, Frederick. *Gestalt Therapy Verbatim*. Moab, Utah: Real People Press, 1969.

Piegler, M. *Celibacy*. London: Sheed and Ward, 1967.

Phipps, William E. *The Sexuality of Jesus*. New York: Harper & Row, 1973.

Piper, Otto. *The Christian Interpretation of Sex*. New York: Charles Scribner's Sons, 1941.

Pittenger, Norman. *Love and Control in Sexuality*. Philadelphia: United Church Press, 1974.

———. *Making Sexuality Human*. Philadelphia: Pilgrim Press, 1972.

Plé, Albert. "Celibacy and the Emotional Life," *Clergy Review*. 55 (1970):27–43.

———. *Chastity and the Affective Life*. New York: Herder and Herder, 1966.

Quesnell, Quentin. "Made Themselves Eunuchs for the Kingdom of Heaven," *Catholic Biblical Quarterly*. 30 (1968):335–358.

Quinn, Jerome. "Celibacy and the Ministry in Scripture," *The Bible Today*. (1970):3163–3175.

Rahner, Karl. "The Celibacy of the Secular Priest Today: An Open Letter," *Servants of the Lord*. New York: Herder and Herder, 1968.

Richardson, Herbert. *Nun, Witch, Playmate*. New York: Harper and Row, 1971.

———. "The Symbol of Virginity," *The Religious Situation: 1969*, ed. Donald Cutler. Boston: Beacon Press, 1969.

Robinson, Richard. *The Buddhist Religion*. Belmont: Dickenson Publishing Co., 1970.

Rowley, H. H. "The Interpretation of the Song of Songs," *The Journal of Theological Studies*. 38 (1937):337–363.

Roy, Della and Rustum. *Honest Sex*. New York: New American Library, 1969.

Royce, Mary Rosera. "Celibacy and Sexual Freedom," *America*. 120 (1969):468–470.

Sabourin, Leopold. "The Positive Values of Consecrated Celibacy," *The Way.* 10 (1970):49–60.

Schillebeeckx, E. *Celibacy.* New York: Sheed and Ward, 1968.

Schofield, Michael. "Normal Sexuality in Adolescence," *Modern Perspectives in Adolescent Psychiatry.* Ed. John Howells. New York: Brunner/Mazel Publishers, 1971.

Schoonenberg, Piet. "The Dutch Catechism Controversy," *Herder Correspondence.* 4 (1967):156–159.

———. "The Dutch Catechism Defended," *Herder Correspondence.* 4 (1967):94–95.

Schutz, Roger. *The Rule of Taizé.* New York: The Seabury Press, 1974.

Schwarz, Gerhart. "Devices to Prevent Masturbation," *Medical Aspects of Human Sexuality.* 7 (1973):140–153.

Sen, K. M. *Hinduism.* Baltimore: Penguin Books, Inc., 1970.

Sheets, John. "For the Sake of the Kingdom," *The Way.* 10 (1970):74–83.

———. "Priestly Celibacy," *Worship.* 45 (1971):465–479.

Shemaryahu, Talmon. "The New Covenanters of Qumran," *Scientific American.* 225 (1974):73–81.

Shields, Mary Lou. "Celibacy—the New Frontier," *The Village Voice.* (July 18, 1974):17–18.

Siecus, ed. *Sexuality and Man.* New York: Charles Scribner's Sons, 1970.

Stoller, Robert. *Sex and Gender.* New York: Science House, 1968.

Sullivan, Harry Stack. *The Interpersonal Theory of Psychiatry.* New York: W. W. Norton & Co., 1953.

Switzer, David. *The Dynamics of Grief.* New York: Abingdon Press, 1970.

Taylor, Michael. Ed. *Sex: Thoughts for Contemporary Christians.* Garden City: Doubleday and Co., 1972.

Taylor, Vincent. *The Historical Evidence of the Virginal Birth.* Oxford: Clarendon Press, 1920.

Teilhard de Chardin, Pierre. *The Divine Milieu.* New York: Harper and Row, 1960.

———. *The Future of Man.* New York: Harper and Row, 1964.

———. *Human Energy.* New York: Harcourt, Brace, Jovanovich, 1970.

———. *Letters to Leontine Zanta.* New York: Harper and Row, 1969.

———. *Writings in Time of War.* New York: Harper and Row, 1968.

Thomas Aquinas. "On Chastity and Virginity," *Summa Theologiae,* II–II, questions 151 and 152.

Thurian, Max. *Marriage and Celibacy.* London: SCM Press, 1969.

Towards a Quaker View of Sex. London: Friends House, 1963.

Trautman, Donald. *The Eunuch Logion of Matthew 19:12 Historical and Exegetical Dimensions as Related to Celibacy.* Rome: Catholic Book Agency, 1966.

Treese, Robert. "Homosexuality: A Contemporary View of the Biblical Perspective," prepared for the Consultation on Theology and the Homosexual, 1966, available from the Glide Urban Center, San Francisco.

Valente, Michael. *Sex—The Radical View of a Catholic Theologian.* New York: Bruce Publishing Co., 1970.

Vann, Gerald. *To Heaven with Diana.* Chicago: Henry Regnery Co., 1965.

Van Kaam, Adrian. *The Vowed Life.* Denville: Dimension Books, 1968.

Vaughan, Austin. "Interpreting the Ordinary Magisterium on Mary's Virginity," *Marian Studies.* 22 (1971):75–90.

"Viewpoints: Is Homosexuality Pathologic or a Normal Variant of Sexuality?" *Medical Aspects of Human Sexuality.* 7 (1973):10–26.

Von Campenhausen, Hans. *The Virgin Birth in the Theology of the Ancient Church.* Naperville: A. R. Allenson, 1964.

Von Rad, Gerhard. *Genesis.* Philadelphia: Westminster Press, 1961.

Waddell, Helen. tr. "The Sayings of the Fathers," in *The Desert Fathers.* Ann Arbor: Univ. of Michigan Press, 1966.

Wade, Joseph. *Chastity, Sexuality and Personal Hangups.* Staten Island: Alba House, 1971.

Weinberg, George. *Society and the Healthy Homosexual.* New York: St. Martin's Press, 1972.

Weinberg, Martin and Colin Williams. *Male Homosexuals.* New York: Oxford Univ. Press, 1974.

Wessels, Cletus. "Our Lady and the Incarnation," *Marian Studies.* 17 (1966):46–64.

White, Robert W. "Competence and the Psycho-Sexual Stages of Development," *Nebraska Symposium on Motivation*, vol. 8. Lincoln: Univ. of Nebraska Press, 1960:97–141.

Williams, Daniel Day. "Three Studies of Homosexuality in Relation to the Christian Faith," *Social Action.* 34 (1967):30–39.

Wills, Garry. *Bare Ruined Choirs: Doubt, Prophecy and Radical Religion.* Garden City: Doubleday & Co., 1971.

Wilson, George. "Christian Commitment," *The Way.* 10 (1970):24–32.

Wood, Robert. *Christ and the Homososexual.* New York: Vintage Press, 1960.

Wright, Elliott. "The Church and Gay Liberation," *Chiristian Century.* 88 (1971):281–285.

Zubin, Joseph and John Money. ed. *Contemporary Sexual Behavior: Critical Issues in the 1970's.* Baltimore: Johns Hopkins Univ. Press, 1973.

Index

225; psychology of, 46–87; theology of, 2, 13–45, 129, 224–225. *See also* Abstinence; Affective sexuality; Genital sexuality; Heterosexual sexuality; Homosexual sexuality; Human sexuality; Intercourse; Procreative sexuality
Solitude, 59, 108, 158, 217–220
Song of Songs, 13, 16–22, 23, 29, 30, 35, 36, 37, 41, 42, 43, 76, 140, 220
Spiritual awakening, 210, 211
Spiritual identity, 210–211, 218
Spirituality, 2, 36, 95, 96, 97, 100, 101, 110, 111, 122, 123, 124, 129, 130, 133, 138, 139, 166–174, 177, 178, 179, 201, 203, 207, 209–223, 224, 226
Stoicism, 35, 38, 40, 42
Sublimation, 52
Sullivan, Harry Stack, 55, 58, 63, 83, 159, 160, 193

Tactility, 89–95, 98, 99, 102, 103, 159
Taize, 7–8, 174
Teilhard de Chardin, 57, 68, 110, 139, 179, 211, 212, 214
Theodore of Mopsuestia, 17
Third Force, 59, 60
Touch. *See* Tactility

Vocation, 104–108, 115
Vow, 2, 5, 96, 100, 105, 115, 146, 148, 187
Virginity, 7, 30, 35, 36, 96, 120, 121, 125–141; of Mary, 7, 126–131
Virtue, 96, 97, 113, 226

Woman, 3, 15, 64, 65, 68, 69, 78, 85, 94, 204–205. *See also* Female; Femininity

Yahwist, 13, 14–16, 18, 21, 23, 24, 28, 29, 36, 42, 43, 163, 182, 225